BOOKS BY RALPH ELLISON

Invisible Man

Shadow and Act

Going to the Territory

GOING TO THE TERRITORY

GOING TO THE TERRITORY

Ralph Ellison

RANDOM HOUSE
NEW YORK

 Published in the United States by Random House, Inc., New York, and simultaneously in Canada by Random House of Canada Limited, Toronto.

The author wishes to thank the following for permission to reprint material:

"The Little Man at Chehaw Station." Originally published in *The American Scholar,* December 13, 1977. Copyright © 1977 by Ralph Ellison.

"On Initiation Rites and Power." Originally published in *Contemporary Literature,* Spring 1974. Copyright © 1974 by Ralph Ellison.

"What These Children Are Like." Originally published in *Education of the Deprived and Segregated:* Report of a Seminar conducted by Bank Street College of Education, September 13–15, 1963. Copyright © 1963 by Ralph Ellison.

"The Myth of the Flawed White Southerner." Originally published in *To Heal and To Build,* edited by James McGregor Burns, by McGraw-Hill, Inc., 1968. Copyright © 1968 by Ralph Ellison.

"If the Twain Shall Meet." Originally published in *Book Week,* Sunday *New York Herald Tribune,* November 8, 1964. Copyright © 1964 by Ralph Ellison.

"What America Would Be Like Without Blacks." Originally published in *Time,* April 6, 1970. Copyright © 1970 by Ralph Ellison.

"Portrait of Inman Page" and "Going to the Territory." Originally published in *The Carleton Miscellany,* vol. XVIII, no. 3, Winter 1980. Copyright © 1981 by Ralph Ellison.

"Homage to Duke Ellington on His Birthday." Originally published in *The Sunday Star,* April 27, 1969. Copyright © 1969 by Ralph Ellison.

"The Art of Romare Bearden." Originally published as an Introduction to "Romare Bearden: Paintings and Projections," 1968, by the Art Gallery: State University of New York at Albany. Copyright © 1968 by Ralph Ellison.

"Society, Morality, and the Novel." Reprinted with permission of Macmillan Publishing Company from *The Living Novel,* edited by Granville Hicks. Copyright © 1957 by Macmillan Publishing Company.

"A Very Stern Discipline." Reprinted from the March 1967 issue of *Harper's Magazine* by special permission. Copyright © 1967 by *Harper's Magazine.* All rights reserved.

"The Novel as a Function of American Democracy." Originally published in *Wilson Library Bulletin,* June 1967. Copyright © 1967 by Ralph Ellison.

"Perspective of Literature." Originally published in *American Law: The Third Century,* The Law Bicentennial Volume. Published by Fred B. Rothman & Co., 1967. Reprinted by permission of New York University.

Library of Congress Cataloging-in-Publication Data
Ellison, Ralph.
Going to the territory.
I. Title.
PS3555.L625G6 1986 818'.5409 85-28117
ISBN 0-394-54050-6

Manufactured in the United States of America

24689753
First Edition

To my wife,
Fanny

Contents

GOING TO THE TERRITORY

The Little Man at Chehaw Station

The American Artist and His Audience

It was at Tuskegee Institute during the mid-1930s that I was made aware of the little man behind the stove. At the time I was a trumpeter majoring in music and had aspirations of becoming a classical composer. As such, shortly before the little man came to my attention, I had outraged the faculty members who judged my monthly student's recital by substituting a certain skill of lips and fingers for the intelligent and artistic structuring of emotion that was demanded in performing the music assigned to me. Afterward, still dressed in my hired tuxedo, my ears burning from the harsh negatives of their criticism, I had sought solace in the basement studio of Hazel Harrison, a highly respected concert pianist and teacher. Miss Harrison had been one of Ferruccio Busoni's prize pupils, had lived (until the rise of Hitler had driven her back to a U.S.A. that was not yet ready to recognize her talents) in Busoni's home in Berlin, and was a friend of such masters as Egon Petri, Percy Grainger, and Sergei Prokofiev. It was not the first time that I had appealed to Miss Harrison's generosity of spirit, but today her reaction to my rather adolescent complaint was less than sympathetic.

"But, baby," she said, "in this country you must always prepare yourself to play your very best wherever you are, and on all occasions."

"But everybody tells you that," I said.

"Yes," she said, "but there's more to it than you're usually told. Of course you've always been taught to *do* your best, *look* your best, *be* your best. You've been told such things all your life. But now you're becoming a musician, an artist, and when it comes to performing the classics in this country, there's something more involved."

Watching me closely, she paused. "Are you ready to listen?"

"Yes, ma'am."

"All right," she said, "you must *always* play your best, even if it's only in the waiting room at Chehaw Station, because in this country there'll always be a little man hidden behind the stove."

"A *what?*"

She nodded. "That's right," she said. "There'll always be the little man whom you don't expect, and he'll know the *music,* and the *tradition,* and the standards of *musicianship* required for whatever you set out to perform!"

Speechless, I stared at her. After the working-over I'd just received from the faculty, I was in no mood for joking. But no, Miss Harrison's face was quite serious. So what did she mean? Chehaw Station was a lonely whistle-stop where swift north- or southbound trains paused with haughty impatience to drop off or take on passengers; the point where, on homecoming weekends, special coaches crowded with festive visitors were cut loose, coupled to a waiting switch engine, and hauled to Tuskegee's railroad siding. I knew it well, and as I stood beside Miss Harrison's piano, visualizing the station, I told myself, *She has GOT to be kidding!*

For, in my view, the atmosphere of Chehaw's claustrophobic little waiting room was enough to discourage even a blind street musician from picking out blues on his guitar, no matter how tedious his wait for a train. Biased toward disaster by bruised feelings, my imagination pictured the vibrations set in motion by the winding of a trumpet within that drab, utilitarian structure: first shattering, then bringing its walls "a-tumbling down"—like Jericho's at the sounding of Joshua's priest-blown ram horns.

True, Tuskegee possessed a rich musical tradition, both classical and folk, and many music lovers and musicians lived or moved through its environs, but—and my regard for Miss Harrison notwithstanding—Chehaw Station was the last place in the area where I would expect to encounter a connoisseur lying in wait to pounce upon some rash, unsuspecting musician. Sure, a connoisseur might hear the haunting, blues-echoing, train-whistle rhapsodies blared by fast express trains as they thundered past—but the classics? Not a chance!

So as Miss Harrison watched to see the effect of her words, I said with a shrug, "Yes, ma'am."

She smiled, her prominent eyes a-twinkle. "I hope so," she said. "But if you don't just now, you will by the time you become an artist. So remember the little man behind the stove."

With that, seating herself at her piano, she began thumbing through a sheaf of scores—a signal that our discussion was ended.

So, I thought, *you ask for sympathy and you get a riddle.* I would have felt better if she had said, "Sorry, baby, I know how you feel, but after all, I was *there*, I *heard* you; and you treated your audience as though you were some kind of confidence man with a horn. So forget it, because I will not violate my own standards by condoning sterile musicianship." Some such reply, by reaffirming the "sacred principles" of art to which we were both committed, would have done much to supply the emotional catharsis for which I was appealing. By refusing, she forced me to accept full responsibility and thus learn from my offense. The condition of artistic communication is, as the saying goes, hard but fair.

But although disappointed and puzzled by Miss Harrison's sibylline response, I respected her artistry and experience too highly to dismiss it. Besides, something about her warning of a cultivated taste that asserted its authority out of obscurity sounded faintly familiar. Hadn't I once worked for an eccentric millionaire who prowled the halls and ballrooms of his fine hotel looking like a derelict who had wandered in off the street? Yes! And woe unto the busboy or waiter, hallman or maid—or anyone else—caught debasing the standards of that old man's house. For then, lashing out with the abruptness of reality shattering the contrived façade of a practical joke, the apparent beggar revealed himself as an extremely irate, and exacting, host of taste.

Thus, as I leaned into the curve of Miss Harrison's Steinway and listened to an interpretation of a Liszt rhapsody (during which she carried on an enthusiastic, stylistic analysis of passages that Busoni himself had marked for expressional subtlety), the little man of Chehaw Station fixed himself in my memory. And so vividly that today he not only continues to engage my mind, but often materializes when I least expect him.

As, for instance, when I'm brooding over some problem of literary criticism—like, say, the rhetoric of American fiction. Indeed, the little stove warmer has come to symbolize nothing less than the enigma of aesthetic communication in American democracy. I especially associate him with the metamorphic character of the general American audience, and with the unrecognized and unassimilated elements of its taste. For me he represents that unknown quality which renders the American audience far more than a receptive instrument that may be dominated through a skillful exercise of the sheerly "rhetorical" elements—the flash and filigree—of the artist's craft. While that audience is eager to be transported, astounded, thrilled, it counters the artist's manipulation of forms with an attitude of antagonistic cooperation; acting, for better or worse, as both collaborator and judge. Like a strange orchestra upon which a guest conductor would impose his artistic vision, it must be exhorted, persuaded—even wooed—as the price of its applause. It must be appealed to on the basis of what it assumes to be truth as a means of inducting it into new dimensions of artistic truth. By playing artfully upon the audience's sense of experience and form, the artist seeks to shape its emotions and perceptions to his vision; while it, in turn, simultaneously cooperates and resists, says yes and says no in an it-takes-two-to-tango binary response to his effort. As representative of the American audience writ small, the little man draws upon the uncodified *Americanness* of his experience—whether of life or of art—as he engages in a silent dialogue with the artist's exposition of forms, offering or rejecting the work of art on the basis of what he feels to be its affirmation or distortion of American experience.

Perhaps if they were fully aware of his incongruous existence, the little man's neighbors would reject him as a source of confusion, a threat to social order, and a reminder of the unfinished details of this powerful nation. But out of a stubborn individualism born of his democratic origins, he insists upon the cultural necessity of his role, and argues that if he didn't exist, he would have to be invented. If he were not already manifest in the flesh, he would still exist and function as an idea and ideal because —like such character traits as individualism, restlessness, self-reliance, love of the new, and so on—he is a linguistic product of the American scene and language, and a manifestation of the idealistic action of the American Word as it goads its users toward a perfection of our revolutionary ideals.

For the artist, a lightning rod attracting unexpected insights and a warning against stale preconceptions, the man behind Chehaw's stove also serves as a metaphor for those individuals we sometimes meet whose refinement of sensibility is inadequately explained by family background, formal education, or social status. These individuals seem to have been sensitized by some obscure force that issues undetected from the chromatic scale of American social hierarchy: a force that throws off strange, ultrasonic ultrasemi-semitones that create within those attuned to its vibrations a mysterious enrichment of personality. In this, heredity doubtless plays an important role, but whatever that role may be, it would appear that culturally and environmentally, such individuals are products of errant but sympathetic vibrations set up by the tension between America's social mobility, its universal education, and its relative freedom of cultural information. Characterized by a much broader "random accessibility" than class and economic restrictions would appear to allow, this cultural information includes many of the finest products of the arts and intellect—products that are so abundantly available in the form of books, graphics, recordings, and pictorial reproductions as to escape sustained attempts at critical evaluation. Just how these characteristics operate in concert involves the mysterious interaction between environment and personality, instinct and culture. But the frequency and wide dispersal of individuals who reveal the effects of this mysterious configuration of forces endows each American audience, whether of musician, poet, or plastic artist, with a special mystery of its own.

I say "mystery," but perhaps the phenomenon is simply

a product of our neglect of serious cultural introspection, our failure to conceive of our fractured, vernacular-weighted culture as an intricate whole. And since there is no reliable sociology of the dispersal of ideas, styles, or tastes in this turbulent American society, it is possible that, personal origins aside, the cultural circumstances here described offer the intellectually adventurous individual what might be termed a broad "social mobility of intellect and taste"—plus an incalculable scale of possibilities for self-creation. While the force that seems to have sensitized those who share the little man of Chehaw Station's unaccountable knowingness—call it a climate of free-floating sensibility—appears to be a random effect generated by a society in which certain assertions of personality, formerly the prerogative of high social rank, have become the privilege of the anonymous and the lowly.

If this be true, the matter of the artist's ability to identify the mixed background and general character of his audience can be more problematical than might be assumed. In the field of literature it presents a problem of rhetoric, a question of how to fashion strategies of communication that will bridge the many divisions of background and taste which any representative American audience embodies. To the extent that American literature is both an art of discovery and an artistic agency for creating a consciousness of cultural identity, it is of such crucial importance as to demand of the artist not only an eclectic resourcefulness of skill, but an act of democratic faith. In this light, the American artist will do his best not only because of his dedication to his form, his craft, but because he realizes that despite an inevitable unevenness of composition, the chances are that any American audience will conceal at least *one* individual whose knowledge and taste will complement, or surpass, his own. This (to paraphrase Miss Harrison) is because even the most homogeneous audiences are culturally mixed and embody, in their relative anonymity, the mystery of American cultural identity.

That identity—tentative, controversial, constantly changing—is confusing to artist and audience alike. To the audience, because it is itself of mixed background, and seldom fully conscious of the cultural (or even political) implications of its own wide democratic range. To the artist, because in the broadest thrust of his effort he directs his finest effects to an abstract (and thus ideal) refinement of sensibility which, because it is not the exclusive property of a highly visible elite, is difficult to pinpoint. As one who operates within the historical frame of his given art, the artist may direct himself to those who are conscious of the most advanced state of his art: his artistic peers. But if his work has social impact, which is one gauge of its success as symbolic communication, it will reach into unpredictable areas. Many of us, by the way, read our first Hemingway, Fitzgerald, Mann in barbershops, heard our first opera on phonographs. Thus, the ideal level of sensibility to which the American artist would address himself tends to transcend the lines of class, religion, region, and race—floating, as it were, free in the crowd. There, like the memory registers of certain computer systems, it is simultaneously accessible at any point in American society. Such are the circumstances that render the little man at Chehaw Station not only possible but inevitable.

But who, then, *is* this little man of Miss Harrison's riddle? From behind what unlikely mask does he render his judgments? And by what magic of art can his most receptive attention, his grudging admiration, be excited? No idle questions these; like Shakespeare's Hamlet, the little man has his pride and complexity. He values his personal uniqueness, cherishes his privacy, and clings to that tricky democratic anonymity which makes locating him an unending challenge. Hamlet masked himself with madness; the little man plays mute. Drawn to the brightness of bright lights, he cloaks himself in invisibility—perhaps because in the shadow of his anonymity he can be both the vernacular cat who looks at (and listens to) the tradition-bound or fad-struck king *and* the little boy who sees clearly the artist-emperor's pretentious nakedness. García Lorca writes of a singer who presented an audience of *cante hondo* lovers with a voice and restraint of passion better suited to a recital of *bel canto.* "Hurray," responded a deadpan Spanish cousin of the ghost of Chehaw Station, "for the school of Paris!"

Which is to say that, having been randomly exposed to diverse artistic conventions, the little man has learned to detect the true transcendent ambience created by successful art from chic shinola. "Form should fit function," says he, "and style theme. Just as punishment should fit crime—which it seldom does nowadays—or as a well-made shoe the foot." Something of an autodidact, he has his own hierarchal ranking of human values, both native American and universal. And along with these, his own range of pieties—filial, sacred, racial—which constitute, in effect, the rhetorical "stops" through which his sensibilities are made responsive to artistic structurings of symbolic form.

Connoisseur, critic, trickster, the little man is also a day-coach, cabin-class traveler—but the timing of his arrivals and departures is uncertain. Sometimes he's there, sometimes he's here. Being quintessentially American, he enjoys the joke, the confounding of hierarchal expectations, fostered by his mask: that cultural incongruity through which he, like Brer Rabbit, is able to convert even the most decorous of audiences into his own brier patch and temper the chilliest of classics to his own vernacular taste. Hence, as a practitioner of art, a form of symbolic communication that depends upon a calculated refinement of statement and affect, the American artist must also know the special qualities of that second instrument: his native audience; an audience upon which—arousing, frustrating, and fulfilling its expectations to the conventionalized contours of symbolic action—he is called upon to play as a pianist upon a piano. But here a special, most American problem arises. Thanks to the presence of the little man, this second instrument can be most unstable in its tuning, and downright ornery in its responses. In approaching it, the artist may, if he will, play fast and loose with modes and traditions, techniques and styles; but only at his peril does he treat an American audience as though it were as easily manipulated as a jukebox.

Reject the little man in the name of purity or as one who aspires beyond his social station or cultural capacity—fine! But it is worth remembering that one of the implicitly creative functions of art in the U.S.A. (and certainly of narrative art) is the defining and correlating of diverse American experiences by bringing previously unknown patterns, details, and emotions into view along with those that are generally recognized. Here one of the highest awards of art is the achievement of that electrifying and creative collaboration between the work of art and its audience that occurs when, through the unifying force of its vision and its power to give meaningful focus to apparently unrelated emotions and experiences, art becomes simultaneously definitive of specific and universal truths.

In this country, the artist is free to choose, but cannot limit, his audience. He may ignore the unknown or unplaced sector of the public, but the mystifications of snobbery are of no avail against the little man's art hunger. Having arrived at his interest in art through familiar but uncharted channels, he disdains its use either as a form of social climbing or of social exclusion. Democratically innocent of hierarchal striving, he takes his classics as he takes his tall tales or jazz—without frills. But while self-effacing, he is nevertheless given to a democratic touchiness, and is suspicious of all easy assumptions of superiority based upon appearances. When fretted by an obtuse artistic hand, he can be quite irritable, and what frets him utterly is any attitude that offends his quite human pieties by ignorance or disregard for his existence.

And yet the little man feels no urge to impose censorship upon the artist. Possessing an American-vernacular receptivity to change, a healthy delight in creative attempts at formalizing irreverence, and a Yankee trader's respect for the experimental, he is repelled by works of art that would strip human experience—especially American experience—of its wonder and stubborn complexity. Not that he demands that his own shadowy image be dragged into each and every artistic effort; that would make a shambles of art's necessary illusion by violating the social reality in which he finds his being. It is enough that the artist (above all, the novelist, dramatist, poet) forge images of American experience that resonate symbolically with his own ubiquitous presence. In *The Great Gatsby,* Nick Carraway tells us, by way of outlining his background's influence upon his moral judgments, that his family fortune was started by an Irish uncle who immigrated during the Civil War, paid a substitute to fight in his stead, and went on to become wealthy from war profiteering. Enough said! This takes hardly a paragraph, but the themes of history, wealth, immigration are struck like so many notes on a chime. Assuming his Afro-American identity, costume, and mask, the little man behind the stove would make the subtle symbolic connections among Gatsby's ill-fated social climbing, the wealthy wastrels whose manners and morals are the focus of the action, the tragic ironies echoing so faintly from the Civil War (that seedbed of so many Northern fortunes), and his own social condition; among the principles of democracy that form the ground upon which the novel's drama of manners and social hierarchy is enacted, and the cost to Gatsby of confusing the promises of democracy with the terms governing their attainment. In so doing, the little underground-outsider would incorporate the inside-outsider Gatz-Gatsby's experience into his own, and his own into Gatsby's: a transposition that Gatsby would probably have abhorred but one that might have saved his life.

Or again, the little man, by imposing collaboratively his own vision of American experience upon that of the author, would extend the novel's truth to levels below the threshold of that frustrating and illusory social mobility which forms the core of Gatsby's anguish. Responding out of a knowledge of the manner in which the mystique of wealth is intertwined with the American mysteries of class and color, he would aid the author in achieving the more complex vision of American experience that was implicit in his material. As a citizen, the little man endures with a certain grace the social restrictions that limit his own social mobility; but *as a reader,* he demands that the relationship between his own condition and that of those more highly placed be recognized. He senses that American experience is of a whole, and he wants the interconnections revealed. And not out of a penchant for protest, nor out of petulant vanity, but because he sees his own condition as an inseparable part of a larger truth in which the high and the lowly, the known and the unrecognized, the comic and the tragic are woven into the American skein. Having been attuned at Chehaw Station to the clangor of diverse bell sounds, he asks not for *whom* the bell tolls, only that it be struck artfully and with that fullness of resonance which warns all men of man's fate. At his best he does not ask for scapegoats, but for the hero as witness. How ironic it was that in the world of *The Great Gatsby* the witness who could have identified the driver of the death car that led to Gatsby's murder was a black man whose ability to communicate (and communication implies moral judgment) was of no more consequence to the action than that of an ox that might have observed Icarus's sad plunge into the sea. (This, by the way, is not intended as a criticism of Fitzgerald, only to suggest some of the problems and possibilities of artistic communication in the U.S.A.) In this light, the little man is a cautionary figure who challenges the artist to reach out for new heights of expressiveness. If we ignore his possible presence, violence might well be done to that ideal of cultivated democratic sensibility which was the goal of the likes of Emerson and Whitman, and for which the man at Chehaw Station is a metaphor. Respect his presence and even the most avant-garde art may become an agency for raising the general level of artistic taste. The work of art is, after all, an act of faith in our ability to communicate symbolically.

But why would Hazel Harrison associate her humble metaphor for the diffusion of democratic sensibility with a mere whistle-stop? Today I would guess that it was because Chehaw Station functioned as a point of arrival and departure for people representing a wide diversity of tastes and styles of living. Philanthropists, businessmen, sharecroppers, students, artistic types passed through its doors. But the same, in a more exalted fashion, is true of Carnegie Hall and the Metropolitan Museum; all three structures are meeting places for motley mixtures of people. So while it might require a Melvillean imagination to reduce American society to the dimensions of either concert hall or railroad station, their common feature as gathering places, as juncture points for random assemblies of sensibilities, reminds us again that in this particular country even the most homogeneous gatherings of people are mixed and pluralistic. Perhaps the mystery of American cultural identity contained in such motley mixtures arises out of our persistent attempts to reduce our cultural diversity to an easily recognizable unity.

On the other hand, Americans tend to focus on the diverse parts of their culture (with which they can more easily identify) rather than on its complex and pluralistic wholeness. But perhaps they identify with the parts because the whole is greater, if not of a different quality, than its parts. That difference, that new and problematic quality—call it our "Americanness"—creates out of its incongruity an uneasiness within us, because it is a constant reminder that American democracy is not only a political collectivity of individuals but, culturally, a collectivity of styles, tastes, and traditions.

In this lies the source of many of our problems, especially those centering upon American identity. In relationship to the cultural whole, we are, all of us—white or black, native-born or immigrant—members of minority groups. Beset by feelings of isolation because of the fluid, pluralistic turbulence of the democratic process, we cling desperately to our own familiar fragment of the democratic rock, and from such fragments we confront our fellow Americans in that combat of civility, piety, and tradition which is the drama of American social hierarchy. Holding desperately to our familiar turf, we engage in that ceaseless contention whose uneasily accepted but unrejectable purpose is the projection of an ever more encompassing and acceptable definition of our corporate identity as Americans. Usually this contest (our improvised moral equivalent for armed warfare) proceeds as a war of words, a clash of styles—or as rites of symbolic sacrifice in which cabalistic code words are used to designate victims consumed with an Aztec voracity for scapegoats. Indeed, so frequently does this conflict erupt into physical violence that one sometimes wonders if there is any other viable possibility for co-existing in so abstract and futuristic a nation as this.

The rock, the terrain upon which we struggle, is itself abstract, a terrain of ideas that, although man-made, exert the compelling force of the ideal, of the sublime; ideas that draw their power from the Declaration of Independence, the Constitution, and the Bill of Rights. We stand, as we say, united in the name of these sacred principles. But, indeed, it is in the name of these same principles that we ceaselessly contend, affirming our ideals even as we do them violence.

For while we are but human and thus given to the fears and temptations of the flesh, we are dedicated to principles that are abstract, ideal, spiritual: principles that were conceived linguistically and committed to paper during that contention over political ideals and economic interests which was released and given focus during the period of our revolutionary break with traditional forms of society; principles that were enshrined—again linguistically—in the documents of state upon which this nation was founded. Actuated by passionate feats of revolutionary will which released that dynamic power for moralizing both man and nature, instinct and society, which is a property of linguistic forms of symbolic action, these principles—democracy, equality, individual freedom, and universal justice—now move us as articles of faith. Holding them sacred, we act (or *fail* to act) in their names. And in the freewheeling fashion of words that are summoned up to name the ideal, they prod us ceaselessly toward the refinement and perfection of those formulations of policy and configurations of social forms of which they are the signs and symbols. As we strive to conduct social action in accordance with the ideals they evoke, they in turn insist upon being made flesh. Inspiriting our minds and bodies, they dance around in our bones, spurring us to make them ever more manifest in the structures and processes of ourselves and of our society. As a nation, we exist in the communication of our principles, and we argue over their application and interpretation as over the rights of property or the exercise and sharing of authority. As elsewhere, they influence our expositions in the area of artistic form and are involved in our search for a system of aesthetics capable of projecting our corporate, pluralistic identity. They interrogate us endlessly as to who and what we are; they demand that we keep the democratic faith.

Words that evoke our principles are, according to Kenneth Burke, charismatic terms for transcendent order, for perfection. Being forms of symbolic action, they tend, through their nature as language, to sweep us in tow as they move by a process of linguistic negation toward the ideal. As a form of *symbolic* action, they operate by negating nature as a given and amoral condition, creating endless series of man-made or man-imagined positives. By so doing, they nudge us toward that state of human rectitude for which, ideally, we strive. In this way, Burke contends, man uses language to moralize both nature and himself. Thus, in this nation the word democracy possesses the aura of what Burke calls a "god-term," and all that we are, and do, exists in the magnitude of its intricate symbolism. It is the rock upon which we toil, and we thrive or wane in the communication of those symbols and processes set in motion in its name.

In our national beginnings, all redolent with Edenic promises, was the word *democratic,* and since we vowed in a war rite of blood and sacrifice to keep its commandments, we act in the name of a word made sacred. Yes, but since we are, as Burke holds, language-using, language-misusing animals—beings who are by nature vulnerable to both the negative *and* the positive promptings of language as symbolic action—we Americans are given to eating, regurgitating, and, alas, re-eating even our most sacred words. It is as though they contain a substance that is crucial to our national existence but that, except in minute and infrequently ingested doses, we find extremely indigestible. Some would call this national habit of word-eating an exercise in the art of the impossible; others attribute it to the limitations imposed by the human condition. Still others would describe it as springing from the pathology of social hierarchy, a reaction to certain built-in conditions of our democracy that are capable of amelioration but impossible to cure. Whatever the case may be, it would seem that for many our cultural diversity is as indigestible as the concept of democracy in which it is grounded. For one thing, principles in action are enactments of ideals grounded in a vision of perfection that transcends the limitations of death and dying. By arousing in the believer a sense of the disrelation between the ideal and the actual, between the perfect word and the errant flesh, they partake of mystery. Here the most agonizing mystery sponsored by the democratic ideal is that of our unity-in-diversity, our oneness-in-manyness. Pragmatically, we cooperate and communicate across this mystery, but the problem of identity that it poses often goads us to symbolic acts of disaffiliation. So we seek psychic security from within our inherited divisions of the corporate American culture while gazing out upon our fellows with a mixed attitude of fear, suspicion, and yearning. We repress an underlying anxiety aroused by the awareness that we are representative not only of one but of several overlapping and constantly shifting social categories; and we stress our affiliation with that segment of the corporate culture which has emerged out of our parents' past—racial, cultural, religious—and which we assume, on the basis of such magical talismans as our mother's milk or father's beard, that we "know." Grounding our sense of identity in such primary and affect-charged symbols, we seek to avoid the mysteries and pathologies of the democratic process. But that process was designed to overcome the dominance of tradition by promoting an open society in which the individual could achieve his potential unhindered by his ties to the past. Here, theoretically, social categories are open, and the individual is not only considered capable of transforming himself, but is encouraged to do so. However, in undertaking such transformations he opts for that psychic uncertainty which is a condition of his achieving his potential—a state he yearns to avoid. So despite any self-assurance he might achieve in dealing with his familiars, he is nevertheless (and by the nature of his indefinite relationship to the fluid social hierarchy) a lonely individual who must find his own way within a crowd of other lonely individuals. Here the security offered by his familiar symbols of identity is equivocal. And an overdependence upon them as points of orientation leads him to become bemused, gazing backward at a swiftly receding—if not quasi-mythical—past, while stumbling headlong into a predescribed but unknown future.

So perhaps we shy from confronting our cultural wholeness because it offers no easily recognizable points of rest, no facile certainties as to who, what, or where (culturally or historically) we are. Instead, the whole is always in cacophonic motion. Constantly changing its mode, it appears as a vortex of discordant ways of living and tastes, values and traditions; a whirlpool of odds and ends in which the past courses in uneasy juxtaposition with those bright, futuristic principles and promises to which we, as a nation, are politically committed. In our vaguely perceived here and now, even the sounds and symbols spun off by the clashing of group against group appear not only alarmingly off-key, but threatening to our inherited eyes, ears, and appetites. Thus, in our intergroup familiarity there is a brooding strangeness, and in our underlying sense of alienation a poignant—although distrusted—sense of fraternity. Deep down, the American condition is a state of unease.

During the nineteenth century an attempt was made to impose a loose conceptual order upon the chaos of American society by viewing it as a melting pot. Today that metaphor is noisily rejected, vehemently disavowed. In fact, it has come under attack in the name of the newly fashionable code word "ethnicity," reminding us that in this country code words are linguistic agencies for the designation of sacrificial victims, and are circulated to sanction the abandonment of policies and the degrading of ideals. So today, before the glaring inequities, unfulfilled promises, and rich possibilities of democracy, we hear heady evocations of European, African, and Asian backgrounds accompanied by chants proclaiming the inviolability of ancestral blood. Today blood magic and blood thinking, never really dormant in American society, are rampant among us, often leading to brutal racial assaults in areas where these seldom occurred before. And while this goes on, the challenge of arriving at an adequate definition of American cultural identity goes unanswered. (What, by the way, is one to make of a white youngster who, with a transistor radio, screaming a Stevie Wonder tune, glued to his ear, shouts racial epithets at black youngsters trying to swim at a public beach—and this in the name of the ethnic sanctity of what has been declared a neighborhood turf?)

The proponents of ethnicity—ill concealing an underlying anxiety, and given a bizarre bebopish stridency by the obviously American vernacular inspiration of the costumes and rituals ragged out to dramatize their claims to ethnic (and genetic) insularity—have helped give our streets and campuses a rowdy, All Fool's Day, carnival atmosphere. In many ways, then, the call for a new social order based upon the glorification of ancestral blood and ethnic background acts as a call to cultural and aesthetic chaos. Yet while this latest farcical phase in the drama of American social hierarchy unfolds, the irrepressible movement of American culture toward the integration of its diverse elements continues, confounding the circumlocutions of its staunchest opponents.

In this regard I am reminded of a light-skinned, blue-eyed, Afro-American-featured individual who could have been taken for anything from a sun-tinged white Anglo-Saxon, an Egyptian, or a mixed-breed American Indian to a strayed member of certain tribes of Jews. This young man appeared one sunny Sunday afternoon on New York's Riverside Drive near 151st Street, where he disrupted the visual peace of the promenading throng by racing up in a shiny new blue Volkswagen Beetle decked out with a gleaming Rolls-Royce radiator. As the flow of strollers came to an abrupt halt, this man of parts emerged from his carriage with something of that magical cornucopian combustion by which a dozen circus clowns are exploded from an even more miniaturized automobile. Looming as tall as a professional basketball center, he unfolded himself and stretched to his full imposing height.

Clad in handsome black riding boots and fawn-colored riding breeches of English tailoring, he took the curb wielding—with an ultra-pukka-sahib haughtiness—a leather riding crop. A dashy dashiki (as bright and as many-colored as the coat that initiated poor Joseph's troubles in biblical times) flowed from his broad shoulders down to the arrogant, military flare of his breeches-tops, while six feet six inches or so above his heels, a black Homburg hat, tilted at a jaunty angle, floated majestically on the crest of his huge Afro-coiffed head.

As though all this were not enough to amaze, delight, or discombobulate his observers—or precipitate an international incident involving charges of a crass invasion of stylistic boundaries—he proceeded to unlimber an expensive Japanese single-lens reflex camera, position it atop the ornamental masonry balustrade which girds Riverside Park in that area, and activate its self-timer. Then, with a ballet leap across the walk, he assumed a position beside his car. There he rested his elbow upon its top, smiled, and gave himself sharp movie director's commands as to desired poses, then began taking a series of self-portraits. This done, he placed the camera upon the hood of his Volkswagen and took another series of self-shots in which, manipulating a lengthy ebony cigarette holder, he posed himself in various fanciful attitudes against the not-too-distant background of the George Washington Bridge. All in all, he made a scene to haunt one's midnight dreams and one's noon repose.

Now, I can only speculate as to what was going on in the elegant gentleman's mind, who he was, or what visual statement he intended to communicate. I only know that his carefully stylized movements (especially his "pimp-limp" walk) marked him as a native of the U.S.A., a home-boy bent upon projecting and recording with native verve something of his complex sense of cultural identity. Clearly he had his own style; but if—as has been repeatedly argued —the style is the man, who on earth was this fellow? Viewed from a rigid ethno-cultural perspective, neither his features, nor his car, nor his dress was of a whole. Yet he conducted himself with an obvious pride of person and of property, inviting all and sundry to admire and wonder in response to himself as his own sign and symbol, his own work of art. He had gotten himself, as the Harlem saying goes, "together," and whatever sheerly ethnic identity was communicated by his costume depended upon the observer's ability to see order in an apparent cultural chaos. The man himself was hidden somewhere within, his complex identity concealed by his aesthetic gesturing. And his essence lay, not in the somewhat comic clashing of styles, but in the mixture, the improvised form, the willful juxtaposition of modes.

Perhaps to the jaundiced eyes of an adversary of the melting-pot concept, the man would have appeared to be a militant black nationalist bent upon dramatizing his feelings of alienation—and he might have been. But most surely he was not an African or an Englishman. His Volks–Rolls-Royce might well have been loaded with Marxist tracts and Molotov cocktails, but his clashing of styles nevertheless sounded an integrative, vernacular note—an American compulsion to improvise upon the given. His garments were, literally and figuratively, of many colors and cultures, his racial identity interwoven of many strands. Whatever his politics, sources of income, hierarchal status, and such, he revealed his essential "Americanness" in his freewheeling assault upon traditional forms of the Western aesthetic. Whatever the identity he presumed to project, he was exercising an American freedom and was a product of the melting pot and the conscious or unconscious comedy it brews. Culturally, he was an American joker. If his Afro and dashiki symbolized protest, his boots, camera, Volkswagen, and Homburg imposed certain qualifications upon that protest. In doing so, they played irreverently upon the symbolism of status, property, and authority, and suggested new possibilities of perfection. More than expressing protest, these symbols ask the old, abiding American questions: Who am I? What about me?

Still, ignoring such questions (as they would ignore the little man of Chehaw Station), the opponents of the melting-pot concept utter their disavowals with an old-fashioned, camp-meeting fervor—solemnly, and with an air of divine revelation. Most amazingly, these attacks upon the melting pot are led by the descendants of peasants, or slaves, or inhabitants of European ghettos—people whose status as spokesmen is a product of that very melting of hierarchal barriers they now deny. With such an attitude, it is fortunate that they, too, are caught up in the society's built-in, democracy-prodded movement toward a perfection of self-definition. Hence, such disavowals, despite their negative posture, have their positive content. And to the extent that they are negatives uttered in an attempt to create certain attitudes and conditions that their exponents conceive as positives, these disavowals are, in part, affirmations of the diverse and unique pasts out of which have emerged the many groups that this nation comprises. As such they might well contribute to a clarification of our pluralistic cultural identity, and are thus a step in the direction of creating a much-needed cultural introspection.

As of now, however, I see the denial of that goal of cultural integration for which the melting pot was an accented metaphor as the current form of an abiding American self-distrust. I see it as an effort to dismiss the mystery of American identity (our unity-within-diversity) with a gesture of democracy-weary resignation, as an attempt to dispel by sociological word-magic the turbulence of the present, and as a self-satisfied vote against that hope which is so crucial to our cultural and political fulfillment. For if such disavowals be viable, what about the little man behind the stove?

Ironically, the attacks on the melting-pot idea issue from those who have "made it." Having been reborn into a higher hierarchal status, they now view those who have not made it as threats to their newly achieved status, and therefore would change both the rules and the game plan. Thus they demonstrate anew the built-in opportunism of their characteristically American shortness of memory. But lest we ourselves forget, the melting-pot concept was never so simplistic or abstract as current arguments would have it. Americans of an earlier day, despite their booster extravagances, recognized the difference between the ideal and the practical—even as they clung desperately to, and sought to default upon, the responsibilities that went with achieving their democratic ideal. Their outlook was pragmatic, their way with culture vernacular, an eclectic mixing of modes. Having rejected the hierarchal ordering of traditional societies, they improvised their culture as they did their politics and institutions: touch and go, by ear and by eye; fitting new form to new function, new function to old form. Deep down they sensed that in the process of nation-building their *culture,* like their institutions, was always more "American" (that futuristic concept) than they could perceive—or even fully accept—it to be. Even the slaves, although thrust below the threshold of social hierarchy, were given a prominent place in our national iconography; their music, poetic imagery, and choreography were grudgingly recognized as seminal sources of American art. In the process of creating (and re-creating or diverting) themselves, the melting-pot Americans brazenly violated their ideals. They kept slaves or battened on the products of slave labor. They exploited and abused those who arrived later than themselves—kinsmen and aliens alike. While paying lip service to their vaunted forms of justice, they betrayed, brutalized, and scapegoated one another in the name of the Constitution, the Bill of Rights, and the Ten Commandments. But because of their fidelity to their parents' customs and their respect for the pieties of their traditions—if not for those of their fellows—none of the groups that made up the total culture ever really desired to lose its sense of its unique past, not even when that past lay clouded in slavery.

Instead, they wished to use the techniques, ways of life, and values developed within their respective backgrounds as sources of morale in that continuing process of antagonistic cooperation, of adjusting the past to the present in the interest of the future, which was so necessary in building what they imagined as a more humane society. Indeed, during their most candid, self-accepting moments they saw themselves as living embodiments of the ancestral past, people who had seized the democracy-sponsored opportunity to have a second chance. As such, they saw themselves as the best guarantee that whatever was most desirable and salvageable from that past would be retained and brought to flower, free of hierarchal hindrances. The little man behind the stove would know from his own condition that the melting-pot concept was a conceit, but his forced awareness of American cultural pluralism would assure him that it was by no means the product of a con game contrived by the powerful. Here not even the powerful were so perceptive.

So our current disavowals are not only misdirected; they are productive of more social disorder, more crises of cultural and personal identity than they could possibly resolve. It is here, on the level of culture, that the diverse elements of our various backgrounds, our heterogeneous pasts, have indeed come together, "melted," and undergone metamorphosis. It is here, if we would but recognize it, that elements of the many available tastes, traditions, ways of life, and values that make up the total culture have been ceaselessly appropriated and made their own—consciously, unselfconsciously, or imperialistically—by groups and individuals to whose own backgrounds and traditions they are historically alien. Indeed, it was through this process of cultural appropriation (and misappropriation) that Englishmen, Europeans, Africans, and Asians *became* Americans.

The Pilgrims began by appropriating the agricultural, military, and meteorological lore of the Indians—including much of their terminology. The Africans, thrown together from numerous ravaged tribes, took up the English language and the biblical legends of the ancient Hebrews and were "Americanizing" themselves long before the American Revolution. They also had imposed upon them a goodly portion of European chromosomes, and thereby "inherited" both an immunity to certain European diseases and a complexity of bloodlines and physical characteristics that have much to do with the white American's reluctance to differentiate between race and culture, African and American, and are a major source of our general confusion over American identity. One of the many questions posed by the man on Riverside Drive is how one so "white" could be simply "black" without being impossibly simple-minded. Especially when his skin and facial bone structure ask, "Where went the blood of yesteryear?" And there is no point in answering the question as did Villon, because the man's face was as Anglo and his hairstyle as Afro as his car's radiator and body were English and German.

Everyone played the appropriation game. The whites took over any elements of Afro-American culture that seemed useful: the imagery of folklore, ways of speaking, endurance of what appeared to be hopeless hardship, and singing and dancing—including the combination of Afro-American art forms that produced the first musical theater of national appeal—the minstrel show. And in improvising their rather tawdry and opportunistic version of a national mythology, the moviemakers—Christian and Jewish, Northerners and Southerners—ransacked and distorted to their own purposes the backgrounds and images of everyone, including the American Indians.

So, melting-pot disclaimers notwithstanding, Americans seem to have sensed intuitively that the possibility of enriching the individual self by such pragmatic and opportunistic appropriations has constituted one of the most precious of their many freedoms. Having opted for the new, and being unable to create it out of thin air or from words inscribed on documents of state, they did what came naturally: they pressured the elements of the past and present into new amalgams. In lieu of a usable cultural tradition, there were always the cultural improvisations of the Afro-Americans, the immigrants, or design-gifted religious groups like the Shakers—all so close to eye and ear, hand and imagination. Considering that the newness achieved by Americans has often been a matter of adapting to function and a matter of naming—of designation—we are reminded of how greatly the "Americanness" of American culture has been a matter of Adamic wordplay—of trying, in the interest of a futuristic dream, to impose unity upon an experience that changes too rapidly for linguistic or political exactitude. In this effort we are often less interested in what we are than in projecting what we will be. But in our freewheeling appropriations of culture we appear to act on the assumption that as members of a "nation of nations," we are, by definition and by the processes of democratic cultural integration, the inheritors, creators, and creations of a culture of cultures.

So perhaps the complex actuality of our cultural pluralism is perplexing because the diverse interacting elements that surround us, traditional and vernacular, not only elude accepted formulations, but take on a character that is something other than their various parts. Our old familiar pasts become, in juxtaposition with elements appropriated from other backgrounds, incongruously transformed, exerting an energy (or synergy) of a different order than that generated by their separate parts. And this with incalculable results. Nor should we forget the role played by objects and technology in the integration of our cultural styles and in the regional and political unification of the nation. If we put the blues, bluegrass music, English folk songs, et cetera, together with Afro-American rhythms and gospel shouts, we have—God help us—first rock and now "funk," that most odoriferous of musical(?) styles. Still, such mixtures of cultural elements are capable of igniting exciting transformations of culture. Even more mysteriously (and here, perhaps, we have a further source of the little man of Chehaw Station's rich sensibility), they provide for exciting and most unexpected metamorphoses within the self-creating personality.

Frankly, many of the foregoing speculations have been arrived at over the years since I left Tuskegee. If I had been more mature or perceptive back when I first heard of the little man behind the stove, an object that lay atop Miss Harrison's piano would have been most enlightening. It was a signed Prokofiev manuscript that had been presented to her by the composer. Except for the signature, it looked like countless other manuscripts. Yet I suspect that to anyone who possessed a conventional notion of cultural and hierarchal order, its presence in such a setting would have been as incongruous as a Gutenberg Bible on the altar of a black sharecropper's church or a dashiki worn with a Homburg hat. Still, there it was: an artifact of contemporary music, a folio whose signs and symbols resonated in that setting with the intricate harmonies of friendship, admiration, and shared ideals through which it had found its way from Berlin to Tuskegee. Once there, and the arrangement of society beyond the campus notwithstanding, it spoke eloquently of the unstructured possibilities of culture in this pluralistic democracy. Yet despite its meticulous artistic form, in certain conventional minds its presence could arouse intimations of the irrational—of cultural, if not social, chaos.

Given the logic of a society ordered along racial lines, Miss Harrison's studio (or even the library) was simply off limits for such an artifact, certainly in its original form. But there it was, lying in wait to play havoc with conventional ideas of order, lending a wry reality to Malraux's observation that art is an assault upon logic. Through its presence, the manuscript had become an agency of cultural transformation and synthesis. By charging Miss Harrison's basement studio with the spirit of living personages, ideals, and purposes from afar, it had transformed that modest room from a mere spot on a segregated Negro campus into an advanced outpost on the frontiers of contemporary music, thus adding an unexpected (if undetected) dimension to Alabama's cultural atmosphere. In my innocence I viewed the manuscript as a property of Miss Harrison's, a sign of her connection with gifted artists across the ocean. It spoke to me of possibility. But that it also endowed the scene—place, studio, campus—with a complex cultural ambiguity escaped my conscious mind. Though aware of certain details of the total scene, I was unattuned to the context in which they sounded, the cultural unity-within-diversity that the combination of details made manifest. Perhaps we are able to see only that which we are prepared to see, and in our culture the cost of insight is an uncertainty that threatens our already unstable sense of order and requires a constant questioning of accepted assumptions.

Had I questioned Miss Harrison as to how the racial identity of her little Chehaw man squared with the culture she credited to him, she might well have replied:

"Look, baby, the society beyond this campus is constantly trying to confuse you as to the relationship between culture and race. Well, if you ask me, artistic talent might have something to do with race, but you do *not* inherit culture and artistic skill through your genes. No, sir. These come as a result of personal conquest, of the individual's applying himself to that art, that music—whether jazz, classical, or folk—which helps him to realize and complete himself. And that's true *wherever* the music or art of his choice originates."

Or, in the words of André Malraux (whom I was to discover a year or two later), she might have told me that music is important as an artistic form of symbolic action "because its function is to let men escape from their human condition, not by means of an evasion, but through a possession, [for] art is a way of possessing destiny." And that therefore, even at racially segregated Tuskegee (as witnessed by, among countless other details, the library and her Prokofiev manuscript), one's "cultural heritage is the totality, not of works that men must respect [or that are used to enhance the mystifications that support an elite], but those that can help them live." Entering into a dialogue with Malraux, she might have added on a more specifically American note: "Yes, and most important, you must remember that in this country things are always all-shook-up, so that people are constantly moving around and, culturally, rubbing off on one another. Nor should you forget that here all things—institutions, individuals, and roles—offer more than the function assigned them—because beyond their intended function they provide forms of education and criticism. They challenge, they ask questions, they offer suggestive answers to those who would pause and probe their mystery. Most of all, remember that it is not only the images of art or the sound of music that pass through walls to give pleasure and inspiration—it is in the very *spirit* of art to be defiant of categories and obstacles. They are, as transcendent forms of symbolic expression, agencies of human freedom."

Three years later, after having abandoned my hope of becoming a musician, I had just about forgotten Miss Harrison's mythical little man behind the stove. Then, in faraway New York, concrete evidence of his actual existence arose and blasted me like the heat from an internally combusted ton of coal.

As a member of the Federal Writers' Project, I was

spending a clammy late-fall afternoon of freedom circulating a petition in support of some now long-forgotten social issue that I regarded as indispensable to the public good. I found myself inside a tenement building in San Juan Hill, a Negro district that disappeared with the coming of Lincoln Center. Starting on the top floor of the building, I had collected an acceptable number of signatures, and having descended from the ground floor to the basement level, was moving along the dimly lit hallway toward a door through which I could hear loud voices. They were male Afro-American voices, raised in violent argument. The language was profane, the style of speech a Southern idiomatic vernacular such as was spoken by formally uneducated Afro-American workingmen. Reaching the door, I paused, sounding out the lay of the land before knocking to present my petition.

But my delay led to indecision. Not, however, because of the loud, unmistakable anger sounding within; being myself a slum dweller, I knew that voices in slums are often raised in anger, but that the *rhetoric* of anger, being in itself cathartic, is not necessarily a prelude to physical violence. Rather, it is frequently a form of symbolic action, a verbal equivalent of fisticuffs. No, I hesitated because I realized that behind the door a mystery was unfolding. A mystery so incongruous, outrageous, and surreal that it struck me as a threat to my sense of rational order. It was as though a bizarre practical joke had been staged and its perpetrators were waiting for me, its designated but unknowing scapegoat, to arrive; a joke designed to assault my knowledge of American culture and its hierarchal dispersal. At the very least, it appeared that my pride in my knowledge of my own people was under attack.

For the angry voices behind the door were proclaiming an intimate familiarity with a subject of which, by all the logic of their linguistically projected social status, they should have been oblivious. The subject of their contention confounded all my assumptions regarding the correlation between educational levels, class, race, and the possession of conscious culture. Impossible as it seemed, these foul-mouthed black workingmen were locked in verbal combat over which of two celebrated Metropolitan Opera divas was the superior soprano!

I myself attended the opera only when I could raise the funds, and I knew full well that opera-going was far from the usual cultural pursuit of men identified with the linguistic style of such voices. And yet, confounding such facile logic, they were voicing (and loudly) a familiarity with the Met far greater than my own. In their graphic, irreverent, and vehement criticism they were describing not only the sopranos' acting abilities but were ridiculing the gestures with which each gave animation to her roles, and they shouted strong opinions as to the ranges of the divas' vocal equipment. Thus, with such a distortion of perspective being imposed upon me, I was challenged either to solve the mystery of their knowledge by entering into their midst or to leave the building with my sense of logic reduced forever to a level of college-trained absurdity.

So challenged, I knocked. I knocked out of curiosity, I knocked out of outrage. I knocked in fear and trembling. I knocked in anticipation of whatever insights—malicious or transcendent, I no longer cared which—I would discover beyond the door.

For a moment there was an abrupt and portentous silence; then came the sound of chair legs thumping dully upon the floor, followed by further silence. I knocked again, loudly, with an authority fired by an impatient and anxious urgency.

Again silence—until a gravel voice boomed an annoyed "Come in!"

Opening the door with an unsteady hand, I looked inside, and was even less prepared for the scene that met my eyes than for the content of their loudmouthed contention.

In a small, rank-smelling, lamplit room, four huge black men sat sprawled around a circular dining-room table, looking toward me with undisguised hostility. The sooty-chimneyed lamp glowed in the center of the bare oak table, casting its yellow light upon four water tumblers and a half-empty pint of whiskey. As the men straightened in their chairs I became aware of a fireplace with a coal fire glowing in its grate, and leaning against the ornate marble facing of its mantelpiece, I saw four enormous coal scoops.

"All right," one of the men said, rising to his feet. "What the hell can we do for *you?*"

"And we ain't buying nothing, buddy," one of the seated men added, his palm slapping the table.

Closing the door, I moved forward, holding my petition like a flag of truce before me, noting that the men wore faded blue overalls and jumper jackets, and becoming aware that while all were of dark complexion, their blackness was accentuated in the dim lamplight by the dust and grime of their profession.

"Come on, man, speak up," the man who had arisen said. "We ain't got all day."

"I'm sorry to interrupt," I said, "but I thought you might be interested in supporting my petition," and began hurriedly to explain.

"Say," one of the men said, "you look like one of them relief investigators. You're not out to jive us, are you?"

"Oh, no, sir," I said. "I happen to work on the Writers' Project . . ."

The standing man leaned toward me. "You on the Writers' Project?" he said, looking me up and down.

"That's right," I said. "I'm a writer."

"Now is that right?" he said. "How long you been writing?"

I hesitated. "About a year," I said.

He grinned, looking at the others. "Y'all hear that? Ol' Home-boy here has done up and jumped on the *gravy* train! Now that's pretty good. Pretty damn good! So what did you do before that?" he said.

"I studied music," I said, "at Tuskegee."

"Hey, now!" the standing man said. "They got a damn good choir down there. Y'all remember back when they opened Radio City? They had that fellow William L. Dawson for a director. Son, let's see that paper."

Relieved, I handed him the petition, watching him stretch it between his hardened hands. After a moment of soundlessly mouthing the words of its appeal, he gave me a skeptical look and turned to the others.

"What the hell," he said, "signing this piece of paper won't do no good, but since Home here's a musician, it won't do us no harm to help him out. Let's go along with him."

Fishing a blunt-pointed pencil from the bib of his overalls, he wrote his name and passed the petition to his friends, who followed suit.

This took some time, and as I watched the petition move from hand to hand, I could barely contain myself or control my need to unravel the mystery that had now become far more important than just getting their signatures on my petition.

"There you go," the last one said, extending the petition toward me. "Having our names on there don't mean a thing, but you got 'em."

"Thank you," I said. "Thank you very much."

They watched me with amused eyes, expecting me to leave, but, clearing my throat nervously, I stood in my tracks, too intrigued to leave and suddenly too embarrassed to ask my question.

"So what'er you waiting for?" one of them said. "You got what you came for. What else do you want?"

And then I blurted it out. "I'd like to ask you just one question," I said.

"Like what?" the standing one said.

"Like where on earth did you gentlemen learn so much about grand opera?"

For a moment he stared at me with parted lips; then, pounding the mantelpiece with his palm, he collapsed with a roar of laughter. As the laughter of the others erupted like a string of giant firecrackers I looked on with growing feelings of embarrassment and insult, trying to grasp the handle to what appeared to be an unfriendly joke. Finally, wiping coal-dust-stained tears from his cheeks, he interrupted his laughter long enough to initiate me into the mystery.

"Hell, son," he laughed, "we learn it down at the Met, that's where . . ."

"You learned it *where?*"

"At the Metropolitan Opera, just like I told you. Strip us fellows down and give us some costumes and we make about the finest damn bunch of Egyptians you ever seen. Hell, we been down there wearing leopard skins and carrying spears or waving things like palm leafs and ostrich-tail fans for *years!*"

Now, purged by the revelation, and with Hazel Harrison's voice echoing in my ears, it was my turn to roar with laughter. With a shock of recognition I joined them in appreciation of the hilarious American joke that centered on the incongruities of race, economic status, and culture. My sense of order restored, my appreciation of the arcane ways of American cultural possibility was vastly extended. The men were products of both past *and* present; were both coal heavers *and* Met extras; were both workingmen *and* opera buffs. Seen in the clear, pluralistic, melting-pot light of American cultural possibility there was no contradiction. The joke, the apparent contradiction, sprang from my attempting to see them by the light of social concepts that cast less illumination than an inert lump of coal. I was delighted, because during a moment when I least expected to encounter the little man behind the stove (Miss Harrison's vernacular music critic, as it were), I had stumbled upon four such men. Not behind the stove, it is true, but even more wondrously, they had materialized at an even more unexpected location: at the depth of the American social hierarchy and, of all possible hiding places, behind a coal pile. Where there's a melting pot there's smoke, and where there's smoke it is not simply optimistic to expect fire, it's imperative to watch for the phoenix's vernacular, but transcendent, rising.

—From *The American Scholar,* Winter 1977/78

On Initiation Rites and Power: Ralph Ellison Speaks at West Point

I hardly know where to start. It should be with an apology, I suppose, because as I recall how annoyed I was that I had been assigned certain novels as a student, I find it extremely ironic that now . . . my own is being passed along to you, and that I'm responsible.

I suppose the best way to get into this is to just be autobiographical, since you are concerned with my novel, because the novel isn't autobiographical in an immediate sense; and it'll be necessary to enlarge upon what Colonel Capps had to say about my background in order to spell out to you just why, and in what way, it is *not* autobiographical. I was, as he said, a music major at Tuskegee; but I was also one who read a lot, who lived in books as well as in the sound of music. At Tuskegee, I found myself reading *The Waste Land,* and for the first time I was caught up in a piece of poetry which moved me but which I couldn't reduce to a logical system. I didn't know quite why it was working on me, but being close to the jazz experience—that is, the culture of jazz—I had a sense that some of the same sensibility was being expressed in poetry.

Now, the jazz musician, the jazz soloist, is anything if not eclectic. He knows his rhythms; he knows the tradition of his form, so to speak; and he can draw upon an endless pattern of sounds which he recombines on the spur of the moment into a meaningful musical experience, if he's successful. And I had a sense that all of these references of Eliot's, all of this snatching of phrases from the German, from the French, from the Sanskrit, and so on, were attuned to that type of American cultural expressiveness which one got in jazz and which one still gets in good jazz. Well, between feeling intuitively that that was what was going on and being able to confirm it, there was quite a gap. Fortunately, Mr. Eliot appended to the original edition of *The Waste Land* a long body of footnotes, and I began to get the books out of the library and read these books. That really was a beginning of my literary education and, actually, it was the beginning of my transformation (or shall we say, metamorphosis) from a would-be composer into some sort of novelist.

The thing about the reading of these footnotes, and about reading criticism generally, is that they made me as conscious of the elements, the traditions, which went into the creation of literature as I had long been taught to be conscious of the various elements which went into musical styles and traditions. One had to be conscious; there was no question about this. And for me there was another powerful motive for being conscious, and that was because I came out of my particular Southwestern background (as an Oklahoma native), with parents who were from Georgia and South Carolina, and my racial background, which naturally at that moment seemed to separate me from the conscious intentions of American literature. Because in far too many instances, I seemed to appear, or my *people* seemed to appear, only in the less meaningful writing. I felt that I would have to make some sort of closer identification with the tradition of American literature, if only by way of finding out why I was *not* there—or better, by way of finding how I could use that very powerful literary tradition by way of making literature my own, and by way of using literature as a means of clarifying the peculiar and particular experience out of which I came.

Well, to jump ahead. During the war, I was a sea cook in the Merchant Marine. During the winter of 1944, I had received a fellowship from the Rosenwald Foundation in order to write a novel. It was about $1,500 as I recall, and I had a very interesting story to tell. Some of my friends were in the Air Force. That is, friends from college, friends from Tuskegee, had become pilots, combat pilots, and so on; and during that moment of the war, they were very active. But preceding that activity, there had been a lot of political agitation on the part of Negro Americans because we were not being allowed to fight; and those young men, those friends of mine, those pilots, were being withheld from duty, and that concerned me very much. So I thought that my first novel would have such a plot as this (you can see that I was very naïve at the time) and I set my story in Nazi Germany in a prisoner-of-war camp. (And this is where it becomes complicated.) The ranking officer of the camp was to have been a black pilot who had beneath him in rank a whole slew of white pilots. The devil of the piece was to have been a Machiavellian Nazi prison-camp official who spent his time pitting the black American against the white Americans. I was trying to write this, by the way, as our ship traveled in convoys of some eighty ships and flat-tops, and so on, taking supplies over during what was actually the Battle of the Bulge. Well, we got into Le Havre during the night, and it was so "hot" around there that that novel went up in sweat, and it's very good that it did.

However, one good effect of that experience was that I not only forgot the novel, but I experienced such tension under these conditions of combat that when I got back to stateside the physicians told me that I should take a rest. I took that rest by going up to Waitsfield, Vermont, where a friend had an old farmhouse on which a few years before I'd helped make some repairs. While there, I tried to write, not knowing quite what I would write but quite aware that my original idea would not work. One afternoon I wrote some words while sitting in an old barn looking out on the mountain; and these words were "I'm an invisible man." I didn't know quite what they meant, and I didn't know where the idea came from; but the moment I started to abandon them, I thought: "Well, maybe I should try to discover exactly what it was that lay behind the statement. What type of man would make that type of statement, would conceive of himself in such terms? What lay behind him?" And then after that, it was a process of trying to make a meaningful story out of what seemed to be a rather wild notion.

Now, having said that, let me say something else. By this time I was very much aware of the elements which went into fiction. I wanted to tell a story. I felt that there was a great deal about the nature of American experience which was not understood by most Americans. I felt also that the diversity of the total experience rendered much of it mysterious. And I felt that because so much of it which appeared unrelated was actually most intimately intertwined, it needed exploring. In fact, I believed that unless we continually explored the network of complex relationships which bind us together, we would continue being the victims of various inadequate conceptions of ourselves, both as individuals and as citizens of a nation of diverse peoples.

For after all, American diversity is not simply a matter of race, region, or religion. It is a product of the complex of intermixing of all these categories. For even our racial experience is diverse within itself and rendered more complex by the special relationships existing between my own group and the various regions in which Negro Americans find their existence—and by reason of the varied relationships shared by blacks and whites of various social backgrounds. These, in turn, are shaped by the politics, the social history, and the climatic conditions existing within the country's various political and geographical regions. Nor is this all, for there is also the abiding condition of mystery generated by the diversity of cultural and political experience within the Negro American group itself. For despite the overall unity of black experience in the United States, the experience of Southern blacks differs in certain important aspects, both cultural and political, from that of Northern blacks; that of Southwestern blacks differs from that of *Southeastern* blacks, while the experience of those who grew up in Nevada, California, and Washington State differs in many ways from all of these—if only for having developed during a later period of historical time. Such factors make for important variations in experience and make necessary the exercise of conscious thought even on the part of those black Americans who would "know the Negro." So that was one part of it.

The other part of it was the fact that I was reading certain books. I was reading Lord Raglan's *The Hero,* which has to do with tradition, myth, and drama. As you will recall, Lord Raglan was concerned with the manner in which myth became involved with the histories of living persons, became incorporated into their personal legends. I seem to recall that he noted about twenty-two aspects of character and experience that were attributed to most heroes, and he discovered that historical figures—figures from religion, military heroes, and so on—all tended to embody clusterings of these same mythological aspects; and this whether they were figures of fact or fantasy. Thus it would seem that the human imagination finds it necessary to take exemplary people—charismatic personalities, cultural heroes—and enlarge upon them. The mythmaking tendency of the human imagination enlarges such figures by adding to their specific histories and characters accomplishments and characteristics attributed to heroes in the past. So that it isn't unusual in the mythology of mankind to find figures said to have been conceived (that's the proper term, anyway you see it) through virgins. Nor is it unusual to find leaders who were exposed to death as infants only to have their lives saved by humble people, and who then through various accidents attending the mysterious process of life, and through their own heroic assertions in the drama of social intercourse, became great leaders. According to various accounts, a number of them married their mothers and killed their fathers, but if that still happens today, we no longer talk about it.

Anyway, I was much concerned with such findings of Lord Raglan's as a literary matter; but at the same time I was concerned with the nature of leadership, and thus with the nature of the hero, precisely because during the historical moment when I was working out the concept of *Invisible Man* my people were involved in a terrific quarrel with the federal government over our not being allowed to participate in the war as combat personnel in the armed forces on an equal basis, and because we were not even being allowed to work in the war industries on an equal basis with other Americans. This quarrel led to my concern with the nature of leadership, to the nature of Negro leadership, from a different and nonliterary direction. I was very much involved with the question of just why our Negro leadership was never able to enforce its will. Just what was there about the structure of American society that prevented Negroes from throwing up effective leaders? Thus it was no accident that the young man in my book turned out to be hungry and thirsty to prove to himself that he could be an effective leader.

On the other hand, as I began working seriously on the novel, I had to become aware of something else. I had to learn that in such a large and diverse country, with such a complex social structure, a writer was called upon to conceive some sort of model which would represent that great diversity—account for all these people and for the various types of social manners found within various levels of the social hierarchy, a structure of symbolic actions which could depict the various relationships between groups and classes of people. He was called upon to conceive some way of getting that complexity into his work in the form of symbolic action and metaphor. In other words, I discovered, for myself at least, that it was necessary to work out some imaginative integration of the total American experience and discover through the work of the imagination some way of moving a young black boy from a particular area and level of the society as close as he could be "realistically" moved to sources of political power. This was not only necessary in order to structure a meaningful story, but also necessary if I were to relate myself to certain important and abiding themes which were present—or which I *thought* were present—in the best of American literature.

So now I was working in the exalted form of the novel, or trying to work in that literary form, and as I read back in American literature and tried very seriously to identify myself with the concerns of the classical American novelists, it began to seem to me that American fiction had played a special role in the development of the American nation. It had had to play that role, had had to concern itself with certain uniquely American tasks even in those instances in which it was not read (or not widely read, and I think here of *Moby-Dick*). And this for a number of reasons. One, as a literary form the novel has been primarily concerned with charting changes within society and with changes in personality as affected by society. Two, the novel developed during a period which marked the breakup of traditional societies, of kingship, and so on; and by the 1850s, the great masters of the nineteenth century had fashioned it into a most sensitive and brilliant form for revealing new possibilities of human freedom, for depicting the effects of new technologies upon personality, and for charting the effects wrought by new horizons of expectation upon the total society.

And of course this type of change (and its consequences) has been an enduring part of the American experience, and it has ever concerned our great American novelists. But even if we concern ourselves with those American writers who were *not* novelists, we see that the makers of American literature had been also concerned with spelling out that which was peculiarly *American* about the American experience—this, because we did not start here. We started in Europe. We made a formulation here of what we were and who we were, and what we expected to be; and we wrote it down in the documents of the Bill of Rights, the Constitution, the Declaration of Independence. I mean that we put ourselves on the books as to what we were and would become, and we were stuck with it. And we were stuck with it partially through a process of deification which came through the spilling of blood and through the sacrifices which were endured by those people who set up this great institution here on this particular point of the Hudson River.

By the 1830s, or the late 1820s, several things were being demanded. One, that we have a literature which would be specifically American, which would tell us who we are and how we varied, and how we had grown, and where we are going—and most importantly, how the ideals for which we had sacrificed so many young men were being made manifest within the society. There's no point in spelling this out too much. I think the very walls around here speak to you about such matters. But for novelists, for poets, for men of literature, something else obtains. You find that American artists are stuck with two major problems which come upon them through the very tradition itself, through the very history of this society. One is the necessity of being conscious of how one section of the country differs from the others, of how one section of the society differs from the others. And, two, we have upon our shoulders the burden of conscientiousness. I think in your motto you say "duty," a sense of duty, a sense of responsibility, for the health of the society. You might not like the society; invariably we Americans (as Henry James pointed out, and as others have pointed out) have a quarrel, we have an on-going quarrel, with our lives, with the condition that we live in. At our best moments we have a quarrel with how we treat or fail to treat and extend the better part, the better aspects, the better values, the good things of the society, to all levels of the society.

So I found, as I worked with my little book—trying to build my fiction, trying to structure my "lie" in such a way as would reveal a certain amount of truth—that I, too, had to be aware of how we were faring and where we were going. I realized, fighting for a certain orientation (as a Negro writer who was taking on the burden of the American literary tradition), that I would have to master, or at least make myself familiar with, the major motives of American literature—*even when written by people who philosophically would reject me as a member of the American community.* How would I do that without being, in my own eyes, something of a slave, something less than a man?

It occurred to me that what some of my "teachers" were calling "white literature" was not really *white* at all. Because as I began to grasp the background of the American experience in literature, I began to realize that even before we were a nation, people of African background had been influencing the nature of the American language, that amalgam of English English, of French and German and Dutch and American Indian dialects, and so on. All of this, long before we were a nation, had already begun to form; American culture began to evolve before we were a nation. And some of the people contributing to it were my own people. This was very necessary for my sense of morale and for my sense of the complexity of the society, or at least of the *culture* of the society, because there's no doubt that we were slaves; both of my grandparents on both sides were slaves. (It hasn't been that long ago.) But, nevertheless, part of the music of the language, part of the folklore which informed our conscious American literature came through the interaction of the slave and the white man, and particularly so in the South. Mr. Faulkner, who has lectured here, had no doubt about that, and some of our most meaningful insights into the experience of the South have come through his understanding of that complex relationship. And because he did [understand], he has been responsible for some of the real glories of our literature.

But here again, I had to find out where *I* stood. In reading, I came across Whitman, who was writing very early (I think 1848 or so), as finding in the American Negro dialect—the dialect of the slaves, as he put it—the possibility of an American grand opera, the possibility of a new music in the speech. Of course this possibility was there. And as I looked around the South, and as I looked around New York, and as I noticed the white crewmen on my ships at sea, I began to say, "Well now, something here that you are saying, a certain rhythm in your speech, I first heard in my particular community. A certain way that you swing your shoulders, or your legs when you walk (especially Southern boys), you have gotten a lot of that from us." Maybe we got it from them, too. The point, of course, was to be relieved of the burden of interpreting all of life and its works in racial terms. Therefore, for me personally, it was a matter of saying, "I am going to learn how to write a novel; I will not ignore the racial dimensions at all, but I will try to put them into a human perspective."

And so my little book starts out by taking a young man who has an infinite capacity for making mistakes (and being a fool, I think), and who—in his *passion* for leadership, in his *passion* to prove himself within the limitations of a segregated society—blunders from one point to another until he finally realizes that American society cannot define the role of the individual, or at least not that of the *responsible* individual. For it is our fate as Americans to achieve that sense of self-consciousness through our own efforts.

The story itself, after all this pretentious-sounding talk, was a rather simple story: about how a young man grew up and about the conditions which it was necessary for him to confront as he grew up. Because our society was divided, at that time, into one region which was primarily agricultural, and another which was primarily industrial (or more dominated by technological considerations than by the seasons), the narrator of the story goes through a number of rites of passage, rites of initiation. And as I tried to tell my story, I began looking at the meaning of certain rituals. No one had ever told me that the "battle royal" was a rite, but I came to see that it was. It was a rite which could be used to project certain racial divisions into the society and reinforce the idea of white racial superiority. On the other hand, as a literary person trying to make up stories out of recognizable experience, and as one who was reading a lot about myth and the function of myth and ritual in literature, it was necessary that I see the "battle royal" situation as something more than a group of white men having sadistic fun with a group of Negro boys. Indeed, I would have to see it for what it was beyond the question of the racial identities of the actors involved: a ritual through which important social values were projected and reinforced.

To use it artistically, I would have to step away from it a bit so that I could see it even more objectively and identify it as one of those rites of initiation called "fool's errands." When I played hooky for the first time and went to water the elephants of the Ringling Brothers Circus in Oklahoma City, I was sent on such an errand. The circus workers told me to go to a certain man and bring back the "tent wrench." Well, after I had exhausted myself traveling around the circus grounds I learned that there was no such thing as a "tent wrench." But I also discovered that this practical joke was not necessarily a racial device, because I observed it being used on other people as well. In hotels new workers ("squares") are also sent on such errands. In fact, many of the rites of passage, those rituals of growing up, found in our society are in the form of such comic, practical-joking affairs—which we ignore in the belief that they possess no deeper significance. Yet it is precisely in their being regarded as unimportant that they take on importance. For in them we ritualize and dramatize attitudes which contradict and often embarrass the sacred values which we proclaim through our solemn ceremonies and rituals of nationhood.

Because while great institutions glamorize themselves through rituals, Americans tend to require supplementary rites that are more modest, more down-to-earth, and often it is these which serve to give dramatic form to our warmest emotions.

But in our democratic society, which is relatively unstructured as societies go (and unstructured precisely because we had to play it by ear as we got it going), such patterns are not widely recognized for what they are, or at least they are not codified and, thus, they are not institutionalized. Primitive societies are much more efficient and consistent; they are much more concerned with guiding the young through each stage of their social development, while we leave much of this to chance, perhaps as part of the responsibility of freedom. Today we are having great trouble with young people of educated, sheltered, and financially well-heeled backgrounds who despite their social advantages have not been taught that they shouldn't play with heroin. I suppose that in a tightly structured and well-run society we would develop a special rite of initiation for dealing with the availability of drugs. Or at least we would teach such individuals how to take heroin without destroying themselves. Now that, of course, is a joke, meant to demonstrate that it is indeed possible to make comedy of such serious matters.

But not only have we failed to provide rites of passage adequate to the wide variety and broad freedom of experience available to the young, we also have failed to find ways of keeping up with much of what happens in our society. Therefore, one of the things I wanted to do was to provide the reader with—or discover for myself—some sense of how *ideas* moved from one level of society to another. This was important for me to understand, because, after all, when I was at Tuskegee, where I couldn't go to a theater without being discriminated against, and in Birmingham, where I couldn't move around the streets without worrying about Bull Conner (oh yes, Bull Conner was there even then), yet under such conditions of social deprivation, I was reading T. S. Eliot; I was concerned with the nature of power; I was trying to find a way of relating myself to the major concerns of our society.

So I felt that if we had a real sociology of ideas in this country, we would have a means of judging the impact of ideas as they came to rest within the diverse groups which make up American society. We would have a way of predicting, of saying, "Well now, out there in such and such a section there are persons whose background, experience, and temperament have made them receptive to certain notions, to certain concepts, certain ideas. Therefore, we can expect some one or two such people to go about making something out of them, or at least making a try." But our failure to deal with the mystery of our diversity makes such generalized predictions impossible. Relying upon race, class, and religion as guides, we underestimate the impact of ideas and the power of life-styles and fashion to upset custom and tradition. Some of our intellectuals even forget that Negroes are not just influenced by ideas that are within the public domain, and that such is the nature of freedom in our democracy that even shoeshine boys may criticize the life-styles and tastes of great entrepreneurs—which shoeshine boys are given to doing—and that they can also go to the library and read books which entrepreneurs *should* be reading but usually don't. So that our failure to grasp the mysterious possibilities generated by our unity within diversity and our freedom within unfreedom can lead to great confusion. It also leads to the loss of potential talent, just as our failure to recognize the social implications of cultural developments taking place on the lower levels of the social hierarchy can lead to social confrontations which can rock society to its very summit.

But however we choose to look at it, there exist pressures which compel the individual American (and the individual black American) to respond to the intellectual, the emotional, the political currents and pressures which affect the entire society—just as the stock market or fads in clothing or automobiles affect the lives of sharecroppers, whether or not the sharecropper knows that the stock market exists. And thus I tried as best I could to weave a tale which would at least be cognizant of these many, many interconnecting possibilities of relationships.

About the story, there is little I can say, unless you ask me questions. Because I haven't read it in a good while and I don't think I'll ever read it again in its entirety. It was too difficult for me to get rid of, and not because I didn't write fast and wasn't inventive. But there was something else. There was a sense of isolation, a feeling that for all my concern to make it so, it couldn't possibly have much value to others. I thought that I would be lucky if I sold between five hundred and a thousand copies. I was very, very much concerned with the link between the scenes and the actions —that is, the problem of continuity—because I realized even then that it was not enough for me simply to be angry, or simply to present horrendous events or ironic events. I would have to do what every novelist does—tell my tale and make it believable, at least for as long as it engaged the attention of the reader. I could not violate the reader's sense of reality, his sense of the way things were done, at least on the surface. My task would be to give him the surface and then try to take him into the internalities, take him below the level of racial structuring and down into those areas where we are simply men and women, human beings living on this blue orb, and not always living so well. This is what I tried to do.

The rest became a confrontation with technical problems: How do you "tell" it, how do you put it together? How do you foreshadow events, how do you handle irony? How do you fabricate that artifact which we call a novel? How, in other words, do you tell a story that will not embarrass the great literature which has gone before you? How do you join the club? How do you justify the assertion of arrogance that is necessary to a man who would take a society which everyone "knows" and abstract certain of its elements in an effort to reduce it to a symbolic form which will simultaneously involve the reader's sense of life while giving expression to his, the writer's, own most deeply held values? I refer to the arrogance of the artist, and a very necessary arrogance it is. For I think it is one reason why the novel is important. I think its presence aids the novelist in attacking the enormity of his task, which is that of reducing a society—and through the agency of mere words—to manageable proportions; to proportions which will reflect *one* man's vision, *one* man's sense of the human condition, and in such volatile and eloquent ways that each rhythm, each nuance of character and mood, indeed each punctuation mark, becomes expressive of *his* sense of life and, by extension, that of the reader.

Related to this is a discovery which I think most American writers must make before they are through: it is that each writer has a triple responsibility—to himself, to his immediate group, and to his region. He must convey each of these aspects of his own experience as he knows them. And he must convey them not only in such a manner that members of his own particular group can become aware of what has been happening in the flux and flow, the thunder and lightning of daily living, but in such a way that individuals belonging to groups and regions of the society other than his own can have his report on what was happening—in his particular area of the society, to his particular type of people, and at that particular point in time. All this, so that readers may become more conscious of themselves and more aware of the complex unity and diversity not only of Americans but of all human life. Here the movement is from the specifically imagined individuals to the group, to the nation, and, it is hoped, to the universal.

This becomes a function of creating and broadening our consciousness of American character, of creating and re-creating the American experience. And it is a serious function because it is our good-and-bad fortune that we Americans exist at our best only when we are conscious of who we are and where we are going. In this process our traditions and national ideals move and function like a firm ground bass, like the deep tones of your marvelous organ there in the chapel, repeating themselves continually while new melodies and obbligatos sound high above. In literature this is the process by which the values, ideals, assumptions, and memories of unique individuals and groups reach out across the divisions wrought by our national diversity and touch us all. It is one of the important social functions of literature because our traditions and values must be constantly revivified; again and again they must be given further extension.

Having said all that, I'll now say this, and then I'm finished. My first principal in grade school was a Professor Whittaker. He was a man of erect military bearing although he must have been fairly old when I knew him. He had white hair, clear, piercing blue eyes, and a goatee. Professor Whittaker was a West Point man. Somehow he did not graduate; he must have been here during the Reconstruction. Nevertheless, he was a marvelous man who managed to get something of West Point into those little Negro grade and high schools in which he taught when I was growing up. I suppose I mention him because I never thought I would ever come to West Point. But I also mention him by way of suggesting that even here, there are extensions and dimensions of which we are not aware and of which we *should* be aware. Because in these United States the crucial question is not one of having a perfect society, or even of having at any given moment a viable—as they say—society. Rather, it is to keep struggling, to keep trying to reduce to consciousness all of the complex experience which ceaselessly unfolds within this great nation. Certainly, that was all I was trying to do with my book. And if

I managed even a little of that, then I think the effort worthwhile.

I'm pleased to have been here, and if you have questions, I would be very pleased to answer them, or to try.

Q. Mr. Ellison, I have a question about the whole point of the novel, the purpose of the novel, whether you considered it to be just about the Negro relationship with the white man, or, as your last statement indicates, perhaps to everyone. Part of the class thought it was just the Negro-white man relationship, and then that perhaps toward the end as an afterthought you sort of put in the everyone idea, because it didn't seem to tie in. And the other part of the class thought you tried to show the relationship between all minority groups and majority groups.

A. Yes, thank you. Well, I conceived of the novel as an account, on the specific level, of a young Negro American's experience. But I hoped at the same time to write so well that anyone who shared everything except his racial identity could identify with it, because there was never any question in my mind that Negroes were human, and thus being human, their experience became metaphors for the experiences of other people. I thought, further, that if literature has any general function within any society and throughout the world, it must serve at its best as a study in comparative humanity. And the role of the writer, from that point of view, is to structure fiction which will allow a universal identification, while at the same time not violating the specificity of the particular experience and the particular character.

Q. Mr. Ellison, concerning your novel, I'd like to know exactly to what extent some of the scenes in it happened to you.

A. Well, let's put it this way, they all happened to me—in my head. All right, now, remember you're dealing with the imagination and not with sociology. For instance, one summer when I was still in high school, I was looking for a job (and it gets to be 105 to 110 in the shade in Oklahoma City; it used to, anyway). I met a friend and he said, "If you go up to Broadway between Ninth and Tenth, there is a car lot there and the man wants someone to help him around the car lot." He said, "I couldn't take it because I got another job, but you better hurry up there." So I turned on the fan, as they say, and by the time I arrived, I was pretty moist. There was this white man sitting out under a tree; and I said, "Sir, I understand you need someone to work here"; and he said, "Yes, sit over here on this box." (He had a crate with a cushion on it.) He said, "Sit over here and tell me about yourself." He began to ask me about my grades, about my parents, and so on; and I began to feel that I was getting the job. And then, at the moment when I was most certain that the job was mine, I felt a charge of electricity in my tail, and I went up into the air and I came down.

The whole thing, again, was a ritual of initiation—a practical joke—wherein a Ford coil, a coil from the old Model T Ford, had been hooked up to a battery. That was the whole point. Of course, there was no job. But what my imagination has made of that is the scene in the battle royal where the boys struggle for money on the rug. Am I giving away secrets, do you believe that? But that's how the imagination worked and conjured up the scene.

Q. Sir, your novel has been called "episodic," with the theme of white domination over the Negro with the express purpose of keeping the Negro in his primitive state; however, in your lecture here I've gotten a different idea, that it was merely a thematic representation of the American

Negro and his drive to excel. The question I have—was it your purpose to show this white domination over the Negro and of keeping the Negro in his primitive state; or was it merely to show in an episodic manner this drive to excel?

A. Certainly I didn't start— Do you want to repeat that? The answer is *No.*

Q. Mr. Ellison, would you consider yourself a pioneer in writing about the Negro relationship to white groups; and if not, who else besides Eliot influenced your writing?

A. Well, in the first place, I don't think that it's a function of writing to tell the reader what it feels like to be a Negro, as critics say over and over again about plays and novels and poems by black writers. I think the function of literature, all literature that's worthy of the name, is to remind us of our common humanity and the cost of that humanity. This is the abiding theme of great literature, and all serious writers find themselves drawn to spelling it out in all of its detail and multiplicity. As for people who influenced me, the first two novels that I read when I arrived in New York were given to me by Langston Hughes (whom I had just met), who wanted me to deliver them to a friend of his; but he told me that I could keep them long enough to read them. Those two novels were André Malraux's *Man's Fate* and *The Days of Wrath.* I have certainly been influenced by Dostoevsky. The first words of *Invisible Man,* the rhythm of the Prologue, go right back to *Notes from the Underground.* I have been influenced by Malraux, by Melville, by Faulkner, by almost all of the good ones.

Q. Sir, in your story it seems as if the narrator was struggling with disillusionment; and then toward the end of the story, when you cut it off, you didn't explain simply whether he found himself or not. Was it your intention to start the narrator off being disillusioned and follow him throughout this complete cycle to where he did find himself, or were we just supposed to draw our own conclusion?

A. Well, as I recall the book . . . the narrator managed to avoid a basic confrontation through most of the story; and when he finally makes that confrontation, he's freed. Part of his problem was not that of being dominated by white society. Part of his problem was a refusal to demand that people see him for what he wanted to be. Always, he was accommodating. If you notice, he was being told who he was, he was given several names throughout the novel; and, always, he accepted them till the very last. As to the last part of your question, I would say that, yes, he comes out of the ground; and this can be seen when you realize that although *Invisible Man* is *my* novel, it is really *his* memoir. I'm a little prejudiced here, because I do feel that books represent socially useful acts—so we can say that. I left it at this point because I assumed that by finally taking the initial step of trying to sum up the meaning of his experience, he had moved to another stage of his development.

Q. Mr. Ellison, the brotherhood has the characteristics of a socialistic society; I was wondering what this had to do with the Communist tradition that in such an organization, the depressed can find a way out of their condition.

A. Here again is a fabrication, just as the machines in the paint factory are fabrications. They never existed. They're images there for certain literary reasons. I did not want to describe an existing Socialist or Communist or Marxist political group . . . primarily because it would have allowed the reader to escape confronting certain political patterns, patterns which still exist and of which our two major political parties are guilty in their relationships to Negro Americans.

But what I wanted to do at the same time was to touch upon certain techniques of struggle, of political struggle, certain concepts of equality and political possibility which were very, very much present in our society. I think we have absorbed them into the larger parties in many ways.

I also wanted to draw upon the tinge of subversion which some of these parties tend to represent. So the brotherhood was this; but at the same time, in the life of the narrator, it was one more obstacle that he had to confront in order to arrive at some viable assessment of his own possibilities as a political leader. Remember, Tod Clifton is killed, and there's a funeral, an improvisation, an improvised funeral, that he (the narrator) leads which sort of polarizes feelings around what the narrator thought would have been to the brotherhood's best interest. But they were no longer interested because they were not concerned basically with Negro freedom but with effecting their own ends. It was very important for this young man, this would-be leader, to understand that political parties, all political parties, are basically concerned with power and with maintaining power, not with humanitarian issues in the raw and abstract state.

Q. Mr. Ellison, could you tell us the significance of the scene near the end of *Invisible Man* when the narrator fell down the open manhole? Two white men had been chasing him, and after he falls in the manhole he tells them, "I still have you in this brief case."

A. Well, I'll try. What I wanted him to be saying was that these men who were hurling racial epithets down at him were not aware that *their* fate was in this bag that he carried—this bag that he had hauled around with his various identifications, his diploma, with Clifton's doll, with Tarp's slavery chainlink, and so on; that this contained a very important part of their history and of their lives. And I was trying to say, also, that you will have to become aware of the connection between what is in this bag (which is his fate, that is, the fate of the narrator, of the Negro narrator) and the racist whites who looked upon him mainly as a buffoon and a victim.

Q. Sir, there seem to be a few comparisons between your novel and *Native Son* in that both protagonists seem to be fighting a losing cause through the entire novel and the fact that they both have ties with the Communist party and confront white women. Was this by coincidence or were you influenced by Mr. Wright as you wrote the novel?

A. I knew Mr. Wright from about the second day he arrived in New York in 1937; I guess it was June. I wrote my first book review for him, a published book review; and I wrote my first short story for a magazine which he was in New York to edit. It was a Harlem-based magazine, a literary magazine, and not a Communist organ. But he accepted my story, and then the magazine failed. By 1940, I was not showing Mr. Wright any of my writing, because by that time I understood that our sensibilities were quite different, and what I was hoping to achieve in fiction was something quite different from what he wanted to achieve.

As to what you call communism and the white women, I would say that anyone writing from the Negro American point of view with any sort of thoroughness would certainly have had to write about the potential meaning and the effects of the relationship between black women and white men and black men and white women, because this became an essence; and a great part of the society was controlled by the taboos built around the fear of the white woman and the black man getting together. Great political power and, to some extent, great military ardor were brewed from this socio-sexual polarization. And so, any novelist who is going to write from the Negro background would certainly have to deal with these particular aspects of our society. They're unpleasant; and yet, it is in the unpleasant, in that which is charged with emotion, with fears, with irrationality, that we find great potential for transforming attitudes. So I tried to face them with a certain forthrightness, to treat them ironically, because they are really destructive in a kind of comic and absurd way—except when we consider the old rite of lynching. And you'll notice that I did not drag in that particular aspect of the sociology of interracial relationships.

Q. Sir, was it your intention to include any protest in the novel?

A. Protest in the novel?

Q. Yes, sir, would you call it a protest novel?

A. I would think that implicitly the novel protests. It protests the agonies of growing up. It protests the problem of trying to find a way into a complex, intricately structured society in a way which would allow this particular man to behave in a manly way and which would allow him to seize some instrumentalities of political power. That is where the protest is on one level. On another level, the protest lies in my trying to make a story out of these elements without falling into the clichés which have marked and marred most fiction about American Negroes, that is, to write literature instead of political protest. Beyond this, I would say very simply that in the very act of trying to create something, there is implicit a protest against the way things are—a protest against man's vulnerability before the larger forces of society and the universe. We make fiction out of that kind of protest which is similar to the kind of protest that is involved in your mastering your bodies; your mastering the disciplines—the physical and intellectual disciplines, the military disciplines, the legal disciplines—which you are here for. All of this is a protest, a human protest against that which *is,* against the raw and unformed way that we come into the world. I don't think you have to demand any more protest than that. I think, on the other hand, if the novelist tells the truth, if he writes eloquently and depicts believable human beings and believable human situations, then he has done more than simply protest. I think that his task is to present the human, to make it eloquent, and to provide some sense of transcendence over the given, that is, to make his protest meaningful, significant, and eloquent of human value.

—From *Contemporary Literature,* Spring 1974;
transcript of address given on March 26, 1969

What These Children Are Like

I assume you all know that I really have no business attending this sort of conference. I have no technical terminology and no knowledge of an academic discipline—which isn't boasting, nor is it really an apology. It is just a means of reminding myself of what my reality has been and of what I am. At this point it might be useful for us to ask ourselves a few questions: what is this act, what is this scene in which the action is taking place, what is this agency and what is its purpose?

The act is to discuss the difficult thirty percent. We know this very well; it has been hammered out again and again. But the matter of *scene* seems to get us into trouble.

The American scene is a diversified one, and the society which gives it its character is a pluralistic society—or at least it is supposed to be. Ideally it is. But we seem to insist, on the other hand, that this society is *not* pluralistic. We have been speaking as though it were *not* made up of diversified cultures but were in fact one monolithic culture. And one which is perfect, the best of all possible cultures, with the best of all people affirming its perfection.

Well, if this were true, there would be no point in our being here. But we are here, and since we are, let us try to see American society in all of its diversity. One of the things that has been left out in our discussion is imagination. But imagination exists even in the backwoods of Alabama, and here too is to be found a forthright attitude toward what it is possible to achieve and to become in this country.

The education which goes on outside the classrooms, which goes on as they walk within the mixed environment of Alabama, teaches children that they should not reach out for certain things. Much of the education that I received at Tuskegee (now, this isn't quite true of Oklahoma City) was an education away from the uses of the imagination, away from the attitudes of aggression and courage. This is not an attack. This is descriptive, this is autobiographic. You did not do certain things because you might be destroyed. You didn't do certain things because you were going to be frustrated. I mean that there were things you didn't do because the world outside was not about to accommodate you.

But we're still talking about scene, and thus we're talking about environment. A discussion of scene in terms of culture and diversity serves to remind us that there is no absolutely segregated part of this country. There is no such thing as a culturally deprived kid. That kid down in Alabama, whose parents have no food, where the mill owner has dismantled the mills and moved out west and left them to forage in the garbage cans of Tuskegee, has, nevertheless, some awareness that he is part of a larger American scene. And he is being influenced by this scene. But how *does* the fluctuation of the stock market get down there, get to him? How does the electronic manipulation of music get into his musical language? How do the literary theories of the "Fugitives," which have so much prestige in the North, influence his destiny? How is his badly trained teacher going to view him and his possibilities as a future American adult? What I'm trying to say is that the problem seems to me to be one of really scrutinizing the goals of American education.

It does me no good to be told that I'm down on the bottom of the pile and that I have nothing with which to get out. I know better. It does me no good to be told that I have no heroes, that I have no respect for the father principle because my father is a drunk. I would just say to you that there are good drunks and bad drunks. The Eskimos have sixteen or more words to describe snow because they live with snow. I have about twenty-five different words to describe Negroes because I live principally with Negroes. "Language is equipment for living," to quote Kenneth Burke. One uses the language which helps to preserve one's life, which helps to make one feel at peace in the world, and which screens out the greatest amount of chaos. *All* human beings do this.

When you have one body of people who have been sewn together by a common experience—I won't even talk about the cultural heritage from Africa—and when you plant this people in a highly pressurized situation and they survive, they're surviving with all of those motivations and with all of the basic ingenuity which any group develops in order to remain alive. Let's not play these kids cheap; let's find out what they have. What do they have that is a strength? What do they have that you can approach and build a bridge upon? Education is all a matter of building bridges, it seems to me. Environment is bouncing everything off everybody in this country. It is wide open; television is around—you see antennas on shacks; electric iceboxes on back porches, with the electricity brought in from a neighbor's pole; the cars are flying around; the jazz musicians are invading the backwoods with modifications of language, verbal as well as musical; new styles of dress are being introduced. The things which come at you in a Negro grade school are just as diverse as those which will come at you in an upper-class white school. The question is how can you relate the environment to yourself? How can one discover, for instance, that well-cooked chitterlings are part of a cuisine? It took me a lot of living and going to France to realize this obvious fact. I said to myself, "What on earth are these Frenchmen doing? This is peasant food—chitterlings are peasant food. There are some great masters of Negro cooking. Chitterlings must be part of a high low-class cuisine!"

There it is—I only had to recognize it to see the wonder and the glamour in it. Some of us look at the Negro community in the South and say that these kids have no capacity to manipulate the language. Well, these are not the Negroes I know. Because I know that the word play of Negro kids in the South would make the experimental poets, the modern poets, green with envy. I don't mean that these kids possess broad dictionary knowledge, but within the bounds of their familiar environment and within the bounds of their rich oral culture, they possess a great virtuosity with the music, the poetry, of words. The question is how can you get this skill into the mainstream of the language, because it is, without doubt, there. And much of it finds its way into the broader language. Now *I* know this just as William Faulkner knew it. This does not require a lot of testing; all you have to do is to walk into a Negro church.

What filters out this richness when the children come North? It is, in part, a reflection of their sense of being dispossessed of the reality to which their vocabulary referred. Where they once possessed the keys to a traditional environment—the South—they now confront an environment that appears strange and hostile. An environment cluttered with objects and processes for which they have no words and which too often they are prevented from approaching by poverty, custom, and race. They are being educated in the streets.

Sanity suggests that the street child learns that which prepares him to live in a world that is immediate, that is real. To fail to recognize this is to expect far too much of a human being while crediting him with far too little humanity.

Thus we must recognize that the children in question are not so much "culturally deprived" as products of a different cultural complex. I'm talking about how people deal with their environment, about what they make of what is abiding in it, about what helps them to find their way, and about that which helps them to be at home in the world. All this seems to me to constitute a culture. If you can abstract their manners, their codes, their customs and attitudes into forms of expression, if you can convert them into forms of art, if you can stylize them and give them many and subtle ranges of reference, then you are dealing with a culture. People have learned this culture; it has been transferred to them from generation to generation, and in its forms they have projected their most transcendent images of themselves and of the world.

Therefore, one of the problems is to get the so-called "culturally deprived" to realize that if they take what we would give them, they don't have to give up all of that which gives them their own sense of identity. Indeed, the nation needs some of the very traits which they bring with them: the group discipline, the patience, the ability to withstand ceaseless provocation without breaking down or losing sight of their ultimate objective. We need aggressiveness. We need daring. We even need the little guy who, in order to prove himself, goes out to conquer the world. Psychologically, Napoleon was not different from the slum kid who tries to take over the block; he just had big armies through which to amplify his aggression.

But how can we keep the daring, the resourcefulness, which we often find among the dropouts? I ask this as one whose work depends upon the freshness of language. How can we keep the discord flowing into the mainstream of the language without destroying it? One of the characteristics of a healthy society is its ability to rationalize and contain social chaos. It is the steady filtering of diverse types and diverse cultural influences that keeps us a healthy and growing nation. The American language is a great instrument for poets and novelists precisely because it could absorb the contributions of those Negroes back there saying "dese" and "dose" and forcing the language to sound and bend under the pressure of their need to express their sense of the real. The damage done to formal grammar is frightful, but it isn't absolutely bad, for here is one of the streams of verbal richness.

As we approach the dropouts, let us identify who *we* are and where we are. And let us have a little bit of respect for what we were and from whence we came. There is a bit of the phony built into every American. This is inevitable in a conscious society that has developed as swiftly as ours has done. We are faced with endless possibilities for change, for metamorphosis. We change our environment, our speech, our styles of living, our dress, and often our values. And so, in effect, we become somebody else—or so we are tempted to believe. And often we act as though we have no connection with our past. We are all tempted to become actors, and when we forget who we are and where we are from, our phony selves take command.

Well, when the phony me appears, there is a favor I would ask of anyone: nudge me and say, "Look, you, you're really just *you!*" Because the great mystery of identity in this country—really on the level of a religious mystery—and one of our greatest challenges, is that everybody here is an American and yet he is a member of some unique minority.

Everyone knows this when he starts out into the world, but often we forget it. The best teacher, it seems to me, for those Negro youngsters who have been so harmed, so maimed by the sudden confrontation of a world that is more complex than any that they are prepared to deal with, is the teacher who can convey to them an awareness that they do indeed come from somewhere, some place of human value, and that what they've learned there does count in the larger society.

Let us remind ourselves that it is not merely the lower-class Negro child who has difficulties in dealing with our society. For after teaching three years in a progressive school where I had only two or three Negro students, I am aware that we here should also be concerned with people who come from sections of the society lying far distant from the Negro slums. Therefore, I do not believe that the basic problem is a Negro problem, no matter what the statistics tell us. I do believe that there has to be some effort made to bring our system of education into line with what we say we are and into line with those ideals which we celebrate in ritual and ceremony on patriotic occasions. If you have a society in which all men are declared equal (I am not speaking racially now), then it seems to me that you must act out of an assumption that any people which has not been destroyed after three hundred years of our history and which is still here among us is a people possessing great human potentialities and strengths which its members have derived from their background. And it follows that those potentialities are to be respected.

One of the worst things for a teacher to do to a Negro child is to treat him as though he were completely emasculated of potentiality. And this, I'm sorry to say, is also true of some Negro teachers. Not all, fortunately, but far too many. At Tuskegee during the thirties, most of the teachers would not speak to a student outside the classroom. The students resented it, *I* resented it—I'll speak personally—I could never take them very seriously as teachers. Something was in the way. A fatal noise had been introduced into the communication.

As you can see, I am not making this a racial matter. I insist, in fact, that the harm can be done by anyone from any background. To speak topically, there are a lot of distortions getting into the picture of the Negro situation now as we Negroes become more publicly agitated over our condition. Our enemies are being sharply designated, and this is a good thing. Nevertheless, the first people to do Negroes damage are usually other Negroes. If it were otherwise, we wouldn't be human; we'd be somehow immune to the shaping force of our parents and relatives and to the presence of our immediate community. Much of the damage sustained by Negroes begins in the Negro family, and much of it occurs in the Negro nursery school, the kindergarten, and the first few grades. Worse, the people who do the harm are not always vicious. But very often they dislike themselves, and very often they have utter contempt for us little "burr-heads."

And consider this: one of the most influential musicians to come out of Oklahoma was a gifted boy who never took part in school musical activities (and ours was a musically oriented Negro community) because he was considered "lower class" in his attitudes. I refer to Charlie Christian, the jazz guitarist, who accomplished that rare feat of discovering the jazz idiom, the jazz voice, of a classical instrument. And yet, here was a child who lived in a hotbed of everything that middle-class people fear—the tuberculosis rate was sky-high, crime, prostitution, bootlegging, illness. There was all of the disintegration which you find among rural Negroes who are pounding themselves to death against the sharp edges of an urban environment. Yet this was one of the most wonderful places I've ever known.

Here imagination was freely exercised by the kids. They made toys. They made and taught themselves to play musical instruments. They lived near the city dump, and they converted the treasures they found there to their own uses. This was an alive community in which the harshness of slum life was inescapable, but in which the strength, the imagination of the people, was much in evidence. And yet you would have to say that it was indeed lower class, and lower-lower class, and according to the sociologists, utterly hopeless. Certainly it was no place to search for good minds or fine talent.

But how many geniuses do you get *anywhere*? And where *do* you find a first-class imagination? Who really knows? Imagination is where you find it; thus we must search the whole scene. Oh, but how many pretentious little kids have we been able to develop through progressive education! We can turn out a hell of a lot of these. I once taught at Bard College, where the students were highly articulate, some of them highly imaginative and creative. But many were utterly unprepared by their education to live in this world without extensive aid. What I'm trying to say is that it is *not* that we are all estranged from our backgrounds and given skills that don't apply to the real world, but that something basically wrong is happening to our educational system. We are missing the target, and all of our children are suffering as a result. To be ill-clothed, ill-housed, and ill-fed is not the only way to suffer deprivation. Frank Reissman, who taught at Bard, has much to say about the "culturally deprived child," but does he recognize that many there were also culturally deprived kids? When a child has no sense of how he should fit into the society around him, he is culturally deprived—no matter how high his parents' income. When a child has no fruitful way of relating the cultural traditions and values of his parents to the diversity of cultural forces with which he must live in a pluralistic society, he is culturally deprived. When he has to spend a great part of his time in the care of a psychoanalyst, he is, again, culturally deprived. Thus I would broaden the definition.

Now, what is the source of this trouble? Obviously, this is not a Negro problem. Obviously, it is not only the result of great cultural deprivation or family dislocation, because the students there were for the most part middle class, and in fact eighty percent were Jewish. When compared with the Negro slum family, their backgrounds were quite stable indeed. Therefore, it seems to me that there has been some more basic dislocation between that which an education is supposed to guarantee the child and the nature of the world in which he has to live. For one thing, many American children have not been trained to reject enough of the negative values which our society presses upon them. Nor have they been trained sufficiently to preserve those values which sustained their forefathers and which constitute an important part of their heritage. Frequently they are not trained to identify those aspects of the environment to which it is to their best interest—and to the best interest of the nation—to say "No." Too often they have not been taught that there are situations, processes, experiences that are not only to be avoided, but feared. Think of how many of our youth from the best middle-class families have taken to drugs.

Which brings me back to the education the child gets in the street. There is a conflict between the child's own knowledge, his own intuitive feeling, and the sense of security he gets through the gang that leads him to *reject* many of the values which are offered him by the schools. He has found a counter-scheme for living. Museums are rejected because they make him think of going places and doing things that are ultimately frustrating. The New York theaters have been open to Negroes for years and years. How many attend them? How many of us do you see in downtown audiences? More than ever before, true, but certainly not in proportion to the Negro population. Let us not discuss the irrelevance of the plays presented there. The point is that this represents a world beyond reach. Indeed, do I dare turn my imagination, even as a writer, upon the possibility of living in that world from which I'm partially barred? I could do so only as an act of faith or recklessness. The schools weren't the least bit encouraging. But I was always interested in writing, and finally I became interested in how writing was written. And then I realized that I couldn't afford *not* to become a writer; I had to become a writer because I had gotten the spirit of literature and had become aware of the possibilities offered by literature—not to make money, but to feel at home in the world, to feel that I could come into the possession of a certain part of reality.

I'm fascinated by this whole question of language, because when you get people who come from a Southern background where language is manipulated with great skill and verve, and who upon coming north become inarticulate, then you *know* that the proper function of language is being frustrated.

The great body of Negro slang—that unorthodox language—exists precisely because Negroes need words which will communicate, which will designate the objects, the processes, the manners and subtleties of their urban experience with the least amount of distortion from the outside. So the problem is, once again, what do we choose and what do we reject of what the greater society makes available? These kids with whom we're concerned, these dropouts, are living critics of their environment, of our society, and of our educational system. And they are quite savage critics of some of their teachers.

Now, I don't know what intelligence is. But this I do know, both from life and from literature: whenever you reduce human life to two plus two equals four, the human element within the human animal says, "I don't give a damn." You can work on that basis, but the kids cannot. If you can show me how I can cling to that which is real to me, while teaching me a way into the larger society, then I will not only drop my defenses and my hostility, but I will sing your praises and I will help you to make the desert bear fruit.

—Lecture given at seminar on "Education for Culturally Different Youth," conducted by Bank Street College of Education at Dedham, Mass., September 3–15, 1963

The Myth of the Flawed White Southerner

The question of how I regarded the President's statement that "Art is not a political weapon" was put to me by a group of young Negro writers during 1965, following President Johnson's sponsoring of a National Festival for the Arts at the White House. The Festival had been attacked by certain well-known writers, and these young men were seriously concerned with the proper relationship between the artist and government. I replied to their question by reading aloud from the President's address to the artists attending the Festival:

> "Your art is not a political weapon, yet much of what you do is profoundly political, for you seek out the common pleasures and visions, the terrors and cruelties of man's day on this planet. And I would hope you would help dissolve the barriers of hatred and ignorance which are the source of so much of our pain and danger . . ."

a statement to which I was sympathetic, both as a foreshortened description and as the expression of a hope.

The young men then asked my opinion of the President's grasp of political reality, and I replied that I thought him far ahead of most of the intellectuals who were critical of him, "especially those Northern liberals who have become, in the name of the highest motives, the new apologists for segregation," and I went on to say that "President Johnson's speech at Howard University spelled out the meaning of full integration for Negroes in a way that no one, no President, not Abraham Lincoln nor Franklin Roosevelt, no matter how much we loved and respected them, has ever done before. There was no hedging in it, no escape clauses."

My reference to the segregationist tendencies of certain intellectuals and Northern liberals caused a few of my white colleagues to charge that I had "changed" or sold out to the "establishment," and I lost a few friends. The incident forced me to realize once again that for all the values that I shared, and still share, with my fellow intellectuals, there are nevertheless certain basic perspectives and attitudes toward art and politics, cultural affairs and politicians, which we are far from sharing, and I had to accept the fact that if I tried to adapt to their point of view, I would not only be dishonest but would violate disastrously that sense of complexity, historical and cultural, political and personal, out of which it is my fate and privilege to write. My colleagues spoke out of their own interests, and properly so, but I found it irritating that they seemed to assume that *their* interests were automatically mine, and that, supposedly, I and those of my background possess no interest that they, my friends and colleagues, had any need to understand or respect.

Later, in thinking of this disagreement, I found myself recalling that during 1963, I was among those present at the White House for a celebration of the First Centennial of the Emancipation Proclamation given by President John

F. Kennedy, an occasion of special significance for me, both as the grandson of slaves and as a writer and former student of Tuskegee Institute. For I was aware of the fact that in 1901, during the first month of his administration, Theodore Roosevelt had provoked a national scandal by inviting Booker T. Washington, Tuskegee's founder, to a White House dinner—a gesture taken by some as more menacing to the national security than an armed attack from a foreign nation. The invitation changed political alignments in the South, upset the structure of the Republican party, and caused President Roosevelt to advise Negro Americans to avoid careers in the professions and to subjugate their own political and social interests to those of antagonistic white Southerners.

As a novelist interested in that area of the national life where political power is institutionalized and translated into democratic ritual and national style, I was impressed by the vividness with which a White House invitation had illuminated the emotional complexities and political dynamite underlying American social manners, and I welcomed the opportunity for closer observation that the occasion afforded. It seemed to me that one of the advantages that a novelist such as Henry James had over those of my generation was his familiarity with the movers and shakers of the nation, an advantage springing from his upper-class background and the easy availability of those who exercised political and social power. Artists who came later were likely to view such figures from a distance, and thus have little opportunity to know at firsthand the personalities who shaped the nation's affairs. It is fortunate that with the Kennedy and Johnson administrations, this was no longer true.

At the celebration of the Emancipation Proclamation, some sixty-two years after the Washington incident, the majority of the four hundred or more White House guests were Negroes, and I was struck by how a cordial gesture once considered threatening to the national stability had with the passing of time become an accepted routine. Where Theodore Roosevelt had been put on the defensive and bowed before anti-Negro taboos, President Kennedy was free to celebrate the freeing of the slaves as an important step toward achieving a truer American democracy. So as I brooded over the Festival controversy I asked myself if my memory of the Booker T. Washington incident had influenced the stand I took, and whether I had been so influenced by historical and racial considerations that I underevaluated the issues which so concerned my fellow intellectuals.

I concluded that perhaps I had. Nor was it simply that as a charter member of the National Council on the Arts, I felt that governmental aid to the American arts and artists was of a more abiding importance than my hopes that the Vietnam war would be brought to a swift conclusion. My response to the President's critics was shaped, in fact, by that personal and group history which had shaped my background and guided my consciousness, a history and background that marked a basic divergence between my own experience and that of the dissenting intellectuals. So for me the Festival was charged with meanings that went deeper than the issue of the government's role in the arts or the issue of Vietnam; it had also to do with the President's own background, his accent of speech, and his values. And when I put the two social occasions into juxtaposition, the Emancipation celebration and the Festival for the Arts, I found it symbolic that my disagreement with my fellow intellectuals had been brought into focus around the figure of a President of Southern origin.

I say symbolic because, historically speaking, my presence at the Festival for the Arts was the long-range result of an act, in 1863, of an even more controversial holder of the presidency, Abraham Lincoln. For it was Lincoln who, after a struggle involving much vacillation, procrastination, and rescissions, finally issued the Proclamation that allowed me to be born a relatively free American. Obviously, this was not so important a factor in my friends' conception of the nation's history, therefore it has not become a functioning factor in shaping their social and political awareness. Hence, while we may agree as to the importance of art in shaping the values of American society, we are apt to disagree as to the priorities in attacking social and political issues.

Some of the intellectuals in question spring from impoverished backgrounds, but for historical reasons none have ever been poor in the special ways that Negro Americans are poor. Some began to write, as did I, during the 1930s, but here again none came to writing careers from a background so barren of writers as mine. And to these racial and historical differences is added the fact that we spring from different regions of the land. I had come from a different part of the country and had been born of parents who were of this land far longer than many of theirs had been, and I had grown up under conditions far more explicitly difficult than they. Which outlines another important difference: I had come from a region adjacent to that from which the President emerged and where the American language was spoken—by whites at least—with an accent much like that with which he speaks. It is a region that has grown faster and in a more unplanned way than the East has grown, and it is a place where one must listen beneath the surface of what a man has to say, and where rhetorical style is far less important than the relationship between a man's statements and his conduct.

When I was growing up, a Negro Oklahoman always listened for a threat in the accent of a white Texan, but one learned to listen to the individual intonation, to *what* was said as well as to *how* it was said, to content and implication as well as to style. Black provincials cannot afford the luxury of being either snobbish or provincial. Nor can they ignore the evidence of concrete acts.

President Johnson's style and accent are said to be an important factor in his difficulties with many intellectuals, especially those of the literary camp. But perhaps what one listens for in the utterance of any President is very similar to what one listens for in a novel: the degree to which it contains what Henry James termed "felt life," which can here be translated to mean that quality conveyed by the speaker's knowledge and feeling for the regional, racial, religious, and class unities and differences within the land, and his awareness of the hopes and values of a diverse people struggling to achieve the American promise in their own time, in their own place, and with the means at hand.

It would seem that a few literary intellectuals would impose a different style and accent upon the President, but they forget that all individual American styles reflect a regional background, and this holds true for national leaders no less than others. Thus, while a President's style and way with language are of national importance, still he cannot violate the integrity between his inherited idiom and his office without doing violence to his initial source of strength. For in fact his style and idiom form a connective linkage between his identity as representative of a particular group and region of people and his identity as President of *all* the people.

It is possible that much of the intellectuals' distrust of President Johnson springs from a false knowledge drawn from the shabby myths purveyed by Western movies. Perhaps they feel that a Texan intoning the values of humanism in an unreconstructed Texas accent is to be regarded as suspiciously as a Greek bearing gifts; thus they can listen to what he says with provincial ears and can ignore the

President's concrete achievements here at home while staring blindly at the fires of a distant war.

Well, I too am concerned with the war in Vietnam and would like to see it ended, but the fact remains that I am also familiar with other costly wars of much longer duration right here at home, the war against poverty and the war for racial equality, and therefore I cannot so easily ignore the changes that the President has made in the condition of my people and still consider myself a responsible intellectual. My sense of priorities is of necessity different.

One thing is certain. I must look at the figure of the President from a slightly different angle, and although I try to approach people and events with something of that special alertness granted to those who give themselves over to the perceptive powers of the novel, I must dismiss any temptation to see President Johnson, or any living President, strictly in terms of his possibilities as a fictional character—which, I believe, is an impulse of many literary intellectuals when confronting the presidential role.

For example, when the image of President Lincoln is evoked by the resemblance between the 1960s and the 1860s—war, racial unrest, technological change, the inadequacies of established institutions and processes before the demand for broader economic and social freedom—the Lincoln who emerges is that figure released by the bullets fired at Ford's Theatre. It is not the backwoods politician who fought throughout the tragic years of the Civil War to keep the nation whole, not the troubled man who rode the whirlwind of national chaos until released by death while watching the comedy *Our American Cousin.*

Yet it was that unpopular, controversial Lincoln whose deeds, whose manipulation of power—political, rhetorical, and moral—who made possible the figure we create for ourselves whenever we think of the personification of democratic grandeur and political sainthood.

Lyndon B. Johnson is credited even by his enemies as being a political genius, but the phenomenon of a great politician becoming President confronts us with a dual figure, for even while entangled in the difficulties of his office, he is identified by role with the achievements of the proven great who preceded him there. In our minds he is locked in a struggle with the illustrious dead even though he must be a man who manipulates power and involves himself in the muck and mire out of which great political parties are composed. He must be a man who initiates uneasy compromises and deals, who blends ideals and expediencies, who achieves what he can so as to give reality to his vision. He is a figure who knows better than most of us that politics is the art of the possible, but *only* of the possible, and that it is only by fighting against the limits of the politically possible that he can demonstrate his mastery and his worth.

But when such a figure is elevated to the presidency an element of doubt soon enters the picture. Political action, his native mode, is tied to techniques—persuasion, eloquence, social pressure, compromises, and deals—all techniques that during our troubled times are increasingly confounded by the press and by the apparent clairvoyance of electronic data media which, as they seek to convert events into drama, work to undermine the mysteries of presidential power. The question of credibility is raised, and we approach the presidency with demands for a minute-to-minute knowledge of intricate events that is impossible even between the most devoted husband and wife. Little allowance is made for secrecy, for indecision, for interpersonal or international process. He is expected to be master not only of the present but of the future as well, and able to make decisions with the omniscience of a god and, most of all, he is expected to be an incarnation of Justice.

Part of the difficulty springs from the notion that great

personalities are the results not of technical mastery but of some mysterious leap out of the past of race, class, family onto a plateau from which an inherent mastery may be exercised with a superhuman facility. To this view great deeds are assumed to be the attributes of great personality. President Lincoln is taken to be the author of great deeds not because he was a great and persistent politician but because he possessed a great personality, very much as great poets are assumed to be great men because they compose great poems. And in the case of great Presidents now dead, the arrogance, the blind spots, the failures of will and vision are forgotten before the great transforming deeds that their deaths delineated as having marked their administrations.

Literary intellectuals make this mistake because they owe the formation of their functional personalities and their dreams to literature. Thus, for them a great President is first of all a master of "style," a mythical figure born of all the great (and preferably eloquent) Presidents who preceded him. But having attained the presidency, he is paradoxically expected to have no further function as a politician. Indeed, he is expected to be above politics in a way virtually impossible if he is to exercise the powers and responsibilities of office.

But to my mind, in these perpetually troubled United States a great President is one through whom the essential conflicts of democracy—the struggle between past and present, class and class, race and race, region and region—are brought into the most intense and creative focus. He is one who releases chaos as he creates order. He arouses hopes and expectations, even as he strives to modify the structures that have supported an unjust stability, in the interest of securing a broader social freedom. He is not necessarily a man possessing a new style of action or eloquence, but rather one who recognizes that the American is one whose basic problem is that of accepting the difficult demands of his essential newness in a world grown increasingly turbulent. He is one who knows instinctively, in the words of W. H. Auden, that for the American "it is not a question of the Old Man transforming himself into the New, but of the New Man becoming alive to the fact that he is new, that he has been transformed [by the land, by technology, by the break with the past, by the diversity of a pluralistic society] without his having realized it."

The great President is also a man possessed by his role and who becomes, to a painful extent, a prisoner of his role, and there is evidence that President Johnson is aware of this. "Every day," he has said,

> there come to this office new problems and new crises and new difficulties demanding discussion and consultation and decision. I must deal with them, possessing no gift of prophecy, no special insight into history. Instead, I must depend, as my thirty-five predecessors depended, on the best wisdom and judgment that can be summoned to the service of the nation. This counsel must come from people who represent the diversity of America.

Nor is he unaware of the limitations of his power:

> A President must have a vision of the America and the world he wants to see. But the President does not put his purely personal stamp upon the future. His vision is compounded of the hopes and anxieties and values of the people he serves. The President can help guide them toward the highest and most noble of their desires. He cannot take them where they do not want to go. Nor can he hope to move ahead without the help of all those who share a common purpose. I believe the presidency was conceived as an office of persuasion more than of sheer power. That is how I have tried to use the office since it was thrust upon me.

One of the most persistent criticisms of President Johnson is that he is arrogant (few who echo the charge bother to question its source or the sinister irony it expresses). But although it is too early for final judgments, it is possible that what has been called the President's arrogance is actually an expression of a profound and dedicated humility before the demands and responsibilities of his office. Perhaps he is becoming possessed by the office in much the manner that Abraham Lincoln was possessed, and is being consumed before our television-focused eyes by the role that he might well have expected, as politician, to have dominated.

As I see it, there is anguish here: an anguish born of strenuous efforts which turn endlessly into their opposites, of efforts to communicate which fail to get through, an anguish born of measures passed and projects set up, only to be blocked, stalled, deprived of funds, and kept from functioning often by those who should in the nation's broader interest render all assistance. His most successful measures have produced impatience and released forces and energies which obscure the full extent of his accomplishments. And they are great accomplishments. No one has initiated more legislation for education, for health, for racial justice, for the arts, for urban reform than he. Currently it is the fashion of many intellectuals to ignore these accomplishments, these promises of a broader freedom to come, but if those of other backgrounds and interests can afford to be blind to their existence, my own interests and background compel me to bear witness.

For I must be true to the hopes, dreams, and myths of my people. So perhaps I am motivated here by an old slave-born myth of the Negroes—not the myth of the "good white man," nor that of the "great white father," but the myth, secret and questioning, of the flawed white Southerner who while true to his Southern roots has confronted the injustices of the past and been redeemed. Such a man, the myth holds, will do the right thing however great the cost, whether he likes Negroes or not, and will move with tragic vulnerability toward the broader ideals of American democracy. The figure evoked by this myth is one who will grapple with complex situations that have evolved through history, and is a man who has so identified with his task that personal considerations have become secondary. Judge Waties J. Waring of South Carolina was such a man, and so—one hopes, one suspects—is Lyndon Baines Johnson. If this seems optimistic, it is perhaps because I am of a hopeful people. Considering that he has changed inescapably the iconography of federal power, from his military aides to the Cabinet, the Federal Reserve Board to the Supreme Court, there appears to be ample reason for hope.

When all of the returns are in, perhaps President Johnson will have to settle for being recognized as the greatest American President for the poor and for the Negroes, but that, as I see it, is a very great honor indeed.

—From *To Heal and To Build,* McGraw-Hill, Inc., 1968

If the Twain Shall Meet

Howard Zinn's *The Southern Mystique* is yet another reminder that American history is caught again in the excruciating process of executing a spiral—that is, in returning at a later point in time to an earlier point in historical space—and the point of maximum tortuosity is once again the South.

It would seem that the basic themes of our history may be repressed in the public mind, but like corpses in mystery dramas, they always turn up again—and are frequently more troublesome. Yes, and with an added element of mystery. "To hit," as the hunters say, "is history, to miss is mystery." For while our history is characterized by a swift and tightly telescoped continuity, our *consciousness* of history is typically discontinuous. Like quiescent organisms in the blood, our unresolved issues persist, but with our attention turned to other concerns we come to regard the eruption of boils and chancres that mark their presence with our well-known "American innocence." Naturally, this leaves us vulnerable to superstition, rumor, and the manipulation of political medicine men.

Nevertheless, so imperative are our national commitments that while one group in our historical drama inevitably becomes inactive once the issues that aroused it are repressed, a resuscitation of the old themes will find a quite similar group taking its place on the redecorated stage. Frequently unaware of the earlier performers of its roles—because flawed, as are most Americans, by an ignorance of history—the new group dresses in quite different costumes but speaks in its own accents the old vital lines of freedom.

Thus, the First Reconstruction saw a wave of young whites hurrying South to staff the schools the Freedmen's Bureau was establishing for the emancipated slaves. Enthusiastic, energetic, self-sacrificial, these young teachers are long forgotten, yet they were the true predecessors of the young white Northerners now participating in the sit-ins and voter-registration drives that mark the Second—or resumption of—Reconstruction. Today's young crusaders are predominantly students, but here too, acting in the ranks and as advisers, are teachers like the author of *The Southern Mystique.*

Currently an associate professor of government at Boston University, Mr. Zinn has been chairman of the history department at Spelman College, a school for Negro women located in Atlanta, Georgia. His book is an account of his experiences as a member of an integrated faculty, as a resident in a predominantly Negro university community, and as an adviser to the Student Non-Violent Coordinating Committee. It attempts to confront the problems arising from the Negro's quest for civil rights—and the white Southerner's agony in accepting change—not with slogans nor with that smug attitude of moral superiority typical of many Northerners' approach to the South, but with a passion to discover a rationale for hope and a theoretical basis for constructive action. Significantly, Mr. Zinn places the burden of insight and sympathy upon the outsider, and thus upon himself.

With such works as *The Southern Mystique,* Calvin Trillin's *An Education in Georgia,* and Bernard Taper's *Gomillion vs. Lightfoot,* the Second Reconstruction is receiving its on-the-spot documentation, as once again young Northerners are bent upon trying to reduce the chaos and mystery of the South, and our involvement in it, to some semblance of human order. Mr. Zinn would give us a human perspective on the present struggle, and in this sense his book belongs with such works of the First Reconstruction as *The Journal of Charlotte L. Forten* and Thomas Wentworth Higginson's *Army Life in a Black Regiment.* Like these, in reporting a social action it reveals a state of mind.

In achieving change Mr. Zinn would base his actions upon sound thinking. He would not only reexamine our major assumptions concerning man and society; he would also appropriate any new concepts developed by social psychology, Neo-Freudian analysis, and the findings of such specialists in Southern history as C. Vann Woodward. Philosophically, he has tried to forge, for himself at least, a fresh concept of man. In the areas of race relations this is a most necessary endeavor, and while I disagree with some of his procedures and conclusions, I am sympathetic with his attempt to do pragmatically what our best critical minds have failed even to recognize as important.

Mr. Zinn's example reminds us that one of the most exciting intellectual phenomenons of recent years has been the stir created among Northern intellectuals by the French Existentialists' theory of *engagement.* How frequently has the word turned up in their writings! How often have I been asked to sign, and have signed, their petitions decrying injustices in Europe, Asia, and the Middle East! Yes, and how sensitive have they been to those who have struggled in the Soviet Union, in Hungary, in Algeria—and well they might, for injustice wears ever the same harsh face wherever it shows itself. And yet, today, one of the most startling disjunctures in our national life has been the failure of many of these intellectuals to involve themselves either by their writings or their activities (except, perhaps, for wearing CORE's equality buttons in their lapels) in our own great national struggle.

One wouldn't suspect that the South has been the center of our national dilemma, both political and moral, for most intellectuals have never seriously confronted the South or its people, few have visited there, and most have drawn their notions about Southerners from novels or from political theorists and sociologists who themselves have never been there. And while in all probability most of these intellectuals reject the values or debasement of values for which the South has stood (even though they admire and often imitate the poets, novelists, and critics whom the South has produced), few feel any obligation to obtain firsthand knowledge—not even those who write so confidently (and there are Negroes among these) about the "meaning" of Negro experience. The events set in motion by the Supreme Court decision of 1954 and accelerated by the Civil Rights Act of 1964, and which are now transforming not only the South but the entire nation—events that are creating a revolution not only in our race relations but in our political morality—have found them ominously silent.

My complaint isn't simply that they don't know the South or the Negro, but that their failures to learn about the country leave them at the mercy of politicians, unreliable reporters, and rumor-mongers. Nor does it help their posture of intellectual authority. Indeed, many confuse the "Negro revolution" with the so-called "sexual revolution" (really a *homo*-sexual revolution), and this has led them to praise unbelievably bad art in the mistaken notion that they're helping to extend Negro freedom. No wonder that when the civil rights struggle moves into their own neighborhoods, many of them have nothing to fall back upon except the same tired clichés about sexual rivalry, miscegenation, and Negro self-hate that have clouded the human realities of the South.

Well, Howard Zinn is no Zen Buddhist; he is a passionate reformer, and his passion lends his book the overtones of symbolic action. In this sense it involves a dual journey, one leg of which took him and his family to live in what, in his own words, "is often thought to be the womb of the South's mystery, the Negro community of the Deep South," and the other of which led him into that violent and mysterious region evoked in the mind by the work of Margaret Mitchell, Wilbur J. Cash, and William Faulkner—a region cloaked by an "invisible mist" which not only blurred perspective but distorted justice and defied reason. Here *The Southern Mystique* relates a journey into the unknown, involving an *agon* of dangerous action, a reversal of purpose leading to a "revolution in perception," and a return to the North with what Mr. Zinn offers as a life-preserving message—i.e., his book.

For from his base in the Negro community—this "womb," this sanctuary, this place of growth, rebirth, and vision, resting in the "tranquil eye" of the South's hurricane of racial tensions—Mr. Zinn was to discover "those tiny circles of shadow out of sight, where people of several colors meet and touch as human beings . . ." And now he believes that contact between the races is a key to understanding and change, because contact—"intimate, massive and more than momentary—reshuffles all sensory memories and dissolves the mystique built upon the physical characteristics of the Negro." One gathers that, for him, contact, in a context of ameliorative action, produces a catharsis that is not only sensory and psychological, but intellectual and moral. Fear is exorcised, the errors springing from prejudice are corrected, and a redefinition of purpose, both personal and social, becomes possible. The assumption here is that social change is sparked by the concern of responsible individuals, and an overtone of individual salvation sounds throughout Mr. Zinn's book. He specifies, however, that interracial contact must be *equal*—which excludes most of the usual contacts between Negroes and whites, whether North or South. Thus, the coming together of whites and Negroes in the interest of change is change in itself, and therefore, threatening to those who fear the widening of American democracy.

In the "womb" of the Negro community, Mr. Zinn was moved to the passionate purpose of dispelling the mystique which he found cloaking the human realities of the South. After living there for seven intense years, he believes that he has discovered the reality underlying the Southern mystique (racial fear is its core). He sees the white Southerner not as a figure of horror but as an American who exhibits certain national characteristics in an exaggerated form. The South, he writes, "is still the most terrible place in America [but] because it is, it is filled with heroes." And yet, I must say that his perception (and he is conscious of this) has by no means been completely purified. Not when he can write that "every cliché uttered about the South, every stereotype attached to its people, white and Negro, is true"—even though he adds the qualification that "a thousand other characteristics, complex and subtle, are also true . . ."

For this, surely, is to concede too much to rhetorical strategy. The clichés and stereotypes attached to the South are no more "true" than those attached to any other region or people. What he means, perhaps, is that they contain an *element* of truth. Stereotypes are fabricated from fragments of reality, and it is these fragments that give them life, continuity, and availability for manipulation. Even this depends upon the psychological predisposition of those who accept them. Here, in fact, is the secret of the stereotypes' tenaciousness. Some people must feel superior on any ground whatsoever, and I'm afraid that for far too many, "whiteness" is the last desperate possibility. Unfortunately, this need has become contagious, and now, as should be expected, certain Negroes, who for years have been satisfied to be merely human and stake their chances upon individual attainment, are succumbing to *blackness* as a value.

As would be expected of a book involved with race and color in the United States, *The Southern Mystique* is concerned with seeing and non-seeing, with illusion and reality—but also with intellectual clarity. His own efforts to see clearly and act effectively lead Mr. Zinn to believe that certain key concepts influencing our view of personality tend to inhibit action in the field of civil rights. He is critical of Freudian psychology, for instance, because he feels that a concern with its categories leads to a "pervasive pessimism" about men in society. Agreeing with Sartre's "man is condemned at every instance to invent man," he suggests that in achieving change in the South, the point of departure is not a philosophical investigation of cause. Because "once you acknowledge *cause* as the core of a problem, you have built something into it that not only baffles people, but, worse, immobilizes them." (Evidently Mr. Zinn really believes that the devil appears only at man's bidding.)

He would therefore leave cause to the philosophers and, as an activist, concentrate on results. For after all, he argues, "A physicist may . . . not know what *really* lies behind the transformation of matter into energy, but if he has figured out how to release this energy, his achievement is stupendous." It is true that in many tightly controlled experiments the scientist must still play it by ear, and true again that civilizations have produced great art while leaving unsolved the problem of where babies come from, yet Zinn's argument makes me uneasy if for no other reason than that it evokes the myth of the sorcerer's apprentice. Not only does it blithely put aside the intractable fact that human beings are creatures of memory and spirit, as well as of conscious motivation, but it makes too much mystery of what, in its political aspects, is really a struggle for power, as white and Negro Southerners understand very well.

Nevertheless, Mr. Zinn's rejection of the gradualists' assumption that a change in thinking must precede changes in behavior seems justified by the actual dynamics of recent social changes in the South. Thus, his observation that "first you change the way people behave by legal or extralegal pressures of various kinds, in order to transform the environment which is the ultimate determinant of the way they think" seems valid not only on the basis of current events, but it describes what actually happened to Negroes following the betrayal of Reconstruction. Indeed, Mr. Zinn draws upon the researches of C. Vann Woodward to demonstrate how comparatively recent segregation has been a support of the "Southern way of life."

In answer to the fear that white Southerners will accept change and then retaliate violently, he considers this no reason to slow the pace of action. Today, he holds, neither change nor its approval depends upon the white Southerner's will but only upon his "quiescence." For now, he writes, what is called "intelligent white leadership . . . is really the exercise of influence by some whites to get other whites to follow, however grumblingly, the leadership of Negroes . . . whose decisions on tactics are the parents of those decisions on law that are made in the courts and announced in the headlines."

In other words, we've spiraled back to a situation similar to the one that followed the Hayes-Tilden Compromises;

and where the violence of sheriff's deputies and nightriders formed the force by which the white leadership then achieved its will, today the Negroes have converted their grievously acquired discipline in absorbing violence non-violently into a force for changing their condition. Perhaps we have made too much of the "moral" nature of the Negroes' struggle because their demands for freedom have *always* been moral; what is new is that their efforts now have sanction in national law. Thus, they can, if only in extreme instances, call upon the ultimate force of federal troops—a protection denied them since the end of Reconstruction.

Mr. Zinn points out, however, that except in rare instances change is being achieved in the South through a "mammoth internal convulsion," and that "in almost all cases where desegregation has occurred, the white South has made its own decision for acceptance." He explains this by noting a human fact long obscured by the Southern mystique (though not for Southern Negroes who have had to know better): the white Southerner has a "hierarchy of values, in which some things are more important than others, and segregation, while desirable, does not mean as much to him as certain other values [which] he has come to cherish." Thus he makes choices "with the guidance of some subconscious order of priorities, in a field of limited possibilities."

To his awareness of the relationship between the individual's hierarchy of values and Southern change, Mr. Zinn adds Kurt Lewin's dictum, derived from the "field theory" of theoretical physics, that "behavior depends neither upon the past nor the future, but on the present field"—a view which, if true, is true only in a highly qualified sense. Nevertheless, it allows Zinn a certain optimism in approaching Southern white behavior "not as the inevitable results of a fixed set of psychological traits, but as the response to a group atmosphere which is susceptible of manipulation."

Whatever the validity of applying "field theory" to human psychology, one of the strategies of the Negro freedom movement is to exert pressures in the social field that will move whites to make choices favorable to the Negroes' goals. This, actually, is a very old maneuver of Negro strategy, characterized by careful timing and flexibility within what, since the 1870s, has been a fairly rigid field. But theory is theory and practice is what we make it, while the past asserts itself regardless.

If Southern whites (who seem as unfamiliar with "field theory" as with Edmund Wilson's "sea slug" theory of the Civil War) respond to change as they have in the past—that is, often violently—then the Negroes have usually reacted as they did most frequently in their own past, namely, nonviolently. Today, however, the absorbing of blows has become a political technique, and thus a value. And a prime source of Negro morale is their knowledge that their forefathers survived so much violence (one of the major supports of the "American way of life," by the way) during times when the highest court in the land was against them. How, by the way, does one say "Negro American" without at once implying "slave" and, one hopes, "free man and equal and responsible citizen"?

But do not let me quibble here. For I am aware that theory has no necessary correspondence in action, nor means with results. Social change, nevertheless, involves the use of words, and words, even Mr. Zinn's words, are rooted deep in the realities of the past.

Zinn bolsters his argument with Harry Stack Sullivan's observation on the importance of the "significant other" in interpersonal relationships. And he suggests that intellectuals, scholars, and, especially, policy makers should be aware that in confronting (or failing to confront) problems of social change, they are no mere neutral observers but participants who modify the situation by affecting the field of social forces. In this sense, then, there is no escape; one acts even by not acting—a useful reminder for those who trouble over how to apply the concept of *engagement* to the current struggle, and one wishes to shout "Hear, Hear!" But his suggestion that an administration that recognizes its own activity as a force affecting white behavior might "map much bolder policies than one basing its moves on the passive situation represented by public opinion polls" seems far too charitable toward the politicians' motives.

For while the myths and mysteries that form the Southern mystique are *irrational* and even *primitive,* they are, nevertheless, real, even as works of the imagination are "real." Like all mysteries and their attendant myths, they imply—as Jane Harrison teaches us in *Themis,* her study of ancient Greek religion—a rite. And rites are *actions,* the goal of which is the manipulation of power; in primitive religions, magical power; in the South (and in the North), political power.

Further, in our own representative form of government the representatives of the white South (few of whom represent Negroes) are all too often the most dedicated, most magic-befouled manipulators of the mystique that surrounds American race prejudice. Neither Strom Thurmond nor Governors Johnson and Wallace have any intention of surrendering the power issuing from the Southern mystique out of the goodness of their hearts. They will give way only before the manifestation within the South of the broader, more human American myth of equality and freedom for all. Not even the presence in the White House of an even more significant Southern "other" has inhibited the celebrants of the rites of Southern prejudice, and now they have been joined by Senator Goldwater. Race remains an active political force because they make it so, and their techniques of manipulation are traditional.

"The most vicious thing about segregation—more deadly than its immediate denials of certain goods and services—is," in Mr. Zinn's opinion, "its perpetuation of the mystery of racial differences." I would have thought that the impact of segregation and discrimination upon individual and group alike would be more important. Most Negroes ignore the mystique of race differences, even as they comply with Southern law and custom. For they know through their own experience the superficiality of the evidence upon which the myth of white superiority rests. They also know that they haven't lived all these years as servants to a race of gods. The folk verse—"These white folk think/ That they so fine,/But their dirty linen stinks/Just like mine!"—while irreverent and a bit bawdy, is a sharp-nosed, clear-eyed observation of reality. No, it is less the mystique that harms us than the denial of basic freedom. It is not the myth that places dynamite in a Sunday School but terrorists carrying out a ritual of intimidation; for while the word slanders, the practice inflicts death. And if whites can accept change without surrendering their prejudices—and here Mr. Zinn sees quite clearly—so have Negroes existed under that prejudice without accepting its contentions.

I must leave it to more qualified critics to assess the broader implications of Mr. Zinn's theoretical approach, but I believe that his effort to see freshly and act constructively is, despite all objections, overwhelmingly important. His speculations have followed courageous action, and he is aware of how urgently the activities of the Negro Freedom Movement demand clarification in theoretical structuring. One source of the problem is our lack of any adequate definition of Negro life and experience, which is far from being as simple as many thinkers assume. And here Mr. Zinn's own urgency blurs his perception.

He believes that man has in his power the means to bring himself and society closer to a more human ideal, and his key term is *action.* His assault upon the viciousness committed in the name of instinct, race, and history makes him prefer theories that underplay the influence of the past—ironically, a tendency that reformers share with reactionaries and conservatives, who would repress all details of the past that would unmask their mythologies. Thus, Gordon Allport's hypothesis that "motives are contemporary . . . not bound functionally to historical origins or to early goals, but to present goals only" affords Zinn optimism in the field of action. But action does not imply insight, because the past is clearly present in the motivation of the Negroes with whom Zinn worked in the South. Perhaps in shrugging off the encumbrances of the past, he failed to observe them (or even to identify with them) in sufficient depth.

Zinn suggests that a half generation ago the Southern Negro personality was essentially that of the arch-stereotype of "Sambo" (that craven creation of nineteenth-century white Southern pseudo-sociology, recently reintroduced into what passes for intellectual discussion by Stanley M. Elkins) but was suddenly transformed by the Supreme Court Decision of 1954 into the "proud Negro demonstrator who appears in exactly those little towns and hamlets . . . that produced silence and compliance a half generation ago."

But here he's being taken in—both by Elkins and by his own need to re-create man, or at least Negro man, in terms of the expediencies of the historical moment. Didn't he notice that some of the older sharecroppers who are sheltering and advising the young Northern crusaders would seem to look, talk, and, when the occasion requires it, *act* like this alleged "Sambo"? He is perceptive when he notes that the terrible aspects of Southern life have made for many heroes, but he might also have noted that Southern life is the most dramatic form of life in the United States, and because it is, it is full of actors. In fact, the Southern mystique has assigned roles to whites as well as to Negroes —only, for Negroes the outcome of abandoning the role is frequently tragic, for it leads to terror, pitiful suffering, and death.

In concentrating on the mystery of race, Mr. Zinn overlooks the more intriguing mystery of culture (it is interesting how often, for an activist, *culture* means *politics!*). Still, the Southern Negroes who have *revealed* themselves since 1954 are not products of some act of legal magic—they are the products of a culture, a culture of the Southern states, and of a tradition that, ironically, they share with white Southerners. But with Negroes it developed out of slavery and through their experiences since the Civil War and the First Reconstruction. Thus, when Zinn writes, "There are two things that make a person a 'Negro': a physical fact and a social artifice," he misses the wonderful (and fortunate) circumstance that the Negro American is something more. He is the product of the synthesis of his blood mixture, his social experience, and what he has made of his predicament, i.e., his *culture.* And his quality of wonder and his heroism alike spring no less from his brutalization than from that culture.

Indeed, those Negroes whom Mr. Zinn has joined in action risk their lives out of a sense of life that has been expressed movingly in the blues but seldom on a more intellectually available level—even though, I believe, it is one of the keys to the meaning of American experience. For if Americans are by no means a *tragic* people, we might very well be a people whose fundamental attitude toward life is best expressed in the blues. Certainly, the Negro American's sense of life has forced *him* to go beyond the boundaries of the tragic attitude in order to survive. That, too, is the result of his past.

One needn't agree with Mr. Zinn that the initiative in the South is now in Negro hands (there is the matter of antagonistic cooperation to be considered), but many clues to action are to be found in their own dramatic experience. They've known for a long time, for instance, that you can change the white Southerner's environment without changing his beliefs because such changes have marked the fluctuations of Negro freedom. Negroes also know the counterpart of this fact—namely, that you prepare yourself for desegregation and the opportunities to be released thereby *before* that freedom actually exists. Indeed, it is in the process of preparation for an elected role that the techniques of freedom are discovered and that freedom itself is released.

The Negro Freedom Party of Mississippi, for instance, arose out of a mock political action, and as a mockery of the fraudulent democracy of the Democratic party of Mississippi. Its mockery took the form of developing techniques for teaching Negroes denied the right to vote how to form a political party and participate in the elective process. In the beginning it possessed all of the "artificiality" of a ritual, but the events, the "drama" acted out in Atlantic City, saw the transformation of their mockery and play-acting into a significant political gesture that plunged them into the realms of conscious history. Here the old slave proverb "Change the joke and slip the yoke" proved a lasting bit of wisdom. For Negroes, the Supreme Court Decision of 1954 and the Civil Rights Act of 1964 induced no sudden transformation of character; it provided the stage upon which they could reveal themselves for what their experiences have made them and for what they have made of their experiences. Here the past and the present come together, making possible a collaboration, across the years, between the old abolitionists and such contemporary activists as Howard Zinn. Nor should we forget that today Negroes are freeing themselves.

If I seem overly critical of *The Southern Mystique,* it is by no means out of a lack of respect for its author and what he has attempted to do. His is an act of intellectual responsibility in an area that has been cast outside the range of intellectual scrutiny through our timidity of mind in the face of American cultural diversity. Mr. Zinn has not only plunged boldly into the chaos of Southern change but he has entered that mazelike and barely charted area wherein twenty million Negro Americans impinge upon American society, socially, politically, morally, and therefore, culturally. One needn't agree with Zinn, but one cannot afford not to hear him out. And once we read him—and we must read him with the finest of our attention—we can no longer be careless in our thinking about the Negro Revolution, for he makes it clear that it involves us all.

—Review in *Book Week* (N. Y. *Herald Tribune*),
November 8, 1964

What America Would Be Like Without Blacks

The fantasy of an America free of blacks is at least as old as the dream of creating a truly democratic society. While we are aware that there is something inescapably tragic about the cost of achieving our democratic ideals, we keep such tragic awareness segregated to the rear of our minds. We allow it to come to the fore only during moments of great national crisis.

On the other hand, there is something so embarrassingly absurd about the notion of purging the nation of blacks that it seems hardly a product of thought at all. It is more like a primitive reflex, a throwback to the dim past of tribal experience, which we rationalize and try to make respectable by dressing it up in the gaudy and highly questionable trappings of what we call the "concept of race." Yet, despite its absurdity, the fantasy of a blackless America continues to turn up. It is a fantasy born not merely of racism but of petulance, of exasperation, of moral fatigue. It is like a boil bursting forth from impurities in the bloodstream of democracy.

In its benign manifestations, it can be outrageously

comic—as in the picaresque adventures of Percival Brownlee who appears in William Faulkner's story "The Bear." Exasperating to his white masters because his aspirations and talents are for preaching and conducting choirs rather than for farming, Brownlee is "freed" after much resistance and ends up as the prosperous proprietor of a New Orleans brothel. In Faulkner's hands, the uncomprehending drive of Brownlee's owners to "get shut" of him is comically instructive. Indeed, the story resonates certain abiding, tragic themes of American history with which it is interwoven, and which are causing great turbulence in the social atmosphere today. I refer to the exasperation and bemusement of the white American with the black, the black American's ceaseless (and swiftly accelerating) struggle to escape the misconceptions of whites, and the continual confusing of the black American's racial background with his individual culture. Most of all, I refer to the recurring fantasy of solving one basic problem of American democracy by "getting shut" of the blacks through various wishful schemes that would banish them from the nation's bloodstream, from its social structure, and from its conscience and historical consciousness.

This fantastic vision of a lily-white America appeared as early as 1713, with the suggestion of a white "native American," thought to be from New Jersey, that all the Negroes be given their freedom and returned to Africa. In 1777, Thomas Jefferson, while serving in the Virginia legislature, began drafting a plan for the gradual emancipation and exportation of the slaves. Nor were Negroes themselves immune to the fantasy. In 1815, Paul Cuffe, a wealthy merchant, shipbuilder, and landowner from the New Bedford area, shipped and settled at his own expense thirty-eight of his fellow Negroes in Africa. It was perhaps his example that led in the following year to the creation of the American Colonization Society, which was to establish in 1821 the colony of Liberia. Great amounts of cash and a perplexing mixture of motives went into the venture. The slaveowners and many Border-state politicians wanted to use it as a scheme to rid the country not of slaves but of the militant free Negroes who were agitating against the "peculiar institution." The abolitionists, until they took a lead from free Negro leaders and began attacking the scheme, also participated as a means of righting a great historical injustice. Many blacks went along with it simply because they were sick of the black and white American mess and hoped to prosper in the quiet peace of the old ancestral home.

Such conflicting motives doomed the Colonization Society to failure, but what amazes one even more than the notion that anyone could have believed in its success is the fact that it was attempted during a period when the blacks, slave and free, made up eighteen percent of the total population. When we consider how long blacks had been in the New World and had been transforming it and being Americanized by it, the scheme appears not only fantastic, but the product of a free-floating irrationality. Indeed, a national pathology.

Nevertheless, some of the noblest of Americans were bemused. Not only Jefferson but later Abraham Lincoln was to give the scheme credence. According to historian John Hope Franklin, Negro colonization seemed as important to Lincoln as emancipation. In 1862, Franklin notes, Lincoln called a group of prominent free Negroes to the White House and urged them to support colonization, telling them, "Your race suffers greatly, many of them by living among us, while ours suffers from your presence. If this is admitted, it affords a reason why we should be separated."

In spite of his unquestioned greatness, Abraham Lincoln

was a man of his times and limited by some of the less worthy thinking of his times. This is demonstrated both by his reliance upon the concept of race in his analysis of the American dilemma and by his involvement in a plan of purging the nation of blacks as a means of healing the badly shattered ideals of democratic federalism. Although benign, his motive was no less a product of fantasy. It envisaged an attempt to relieve an inevitable suffering that marked the growing pains of the youthful body politic by an operation which would have amounted to the severing of a healthy and indispensable member.

Yet, like its twin, the illusion of secession, the fantasy of a benign amputation that would rid the country of black men to the benefit of a nation's health not only persists; today, in the form of neo-Garveyism, it fascinates black men no less than it once hypnotized whites. Both fantasies become operative whenever the nation grows weary of the struggle toward the ideal of American democratic equality. Both would use the black man as a scapegoat to achieve a national catharsis, and both would, by way of curing the patient, destroy him.

What is ultimately intriguing about the fantasy of "getting shut" of the Negro American is the fact that no one who entertains it seems ever to have considered what the nation would have become had Africans *not* been brought to the New World, and had their descendants not played such a complex and confounding role in the creation of American history and culture. Nor do they appear to have considered with any seriousness the effect upon the nation of having any of the schemes for exporting blacks succeed beyond settling some fifteen thousand or so in Liberia.

We are reminded that Daniel Patrick Moynihan, who has recently aggravated our social confusion over the racial issue while allegedly attempting to clarify it, is co-author of a work which insists that the American melting pot didn't melt because our white ethnic groups have resisted all assimilative forces that appear to threaten their identities. The problem here is that few Americans know who and what they really are. That is why few of these groups—or at least few of the children of these groups—have been able to resist the movies, television, baseball, jazz, football, drum-majoretting, rock, comic strips, radio commercials, soap operas, book clubs, slang, or any of a thousand other expressions and carriers of our pluralistic and easily available popular culture. And it is here precisely that ethnic resistance is least effective. On this level the melting pot did indeed melt, creating such deceptive metamorphoses and blending of identities, values, and life-styles that most American whites are culturally part Negro American without even realizing it.

If we can resist for a moment the temptation to view everything having to do with Negro Americans in terms of their racially imposed status, we become aware of the fact that for all the harsh reality of the social and economic injustices visited upon them, these injustices have failed to keep Negroes clear of the cultural mainstream; Negro Americans are in fact one of its major tributaries. If we can cease approaching American social reality in terms of such false concepts as white and nonwhite, black culture and white culture, and think of these apparently unthinkable matters in the realistic manner of Western pioneers confronting the unknown prairie, perhaps we can begin to imagine what the United States would have been, or not been, had there been no blacks to give it—if I may be so bold as to say—color.

For one thing, the American nation is in a sense the product of the American language, a colloquial speech that began emerging long before the British colonials and Africans were transformed into Americans. It is a language that evolved from the king's English but, basing itself upon the realities of the American land and colonial institutions—or lack of institutions, began quite early as a vernacular revolt against the signs, symbols, manners, and authority of the mother country. It is a language that began by merging the sounds of many tongues, brought together in the struggle of diverse regions. And whether it is admitted or not, much of the sound of that language is derived from the timbre of the African voice and the listening habits of the African ear. So there is a *de'z* and *do'z* of slave speech sounding beneath our most polished Harvard accents, and if there is such a thing as a Yale accent, there is a Negro wail in it—doubtlessly introduced there by Old Yalie John C. Calhoun, who probably got it from his mammy.

Whitman viewed the spoken idiom of Negro Americans as a source for a native grand opera. Its flexibility, its musicality, its rhythms, freewheeling diction, and metaphors, as projected in Negro American folklore, were absorbed by the creators of our great nineteenth-century literature even when the majority of blacks were still enslaved. Mark Twain celebrated it in the prose of *Huckleberry Finn;* without the presence of blacks, the book could not have been written. No Huck and Jim, no American novel as we know it. For not only is the black man a co-creator of the language that Mark Twain raised to the level of literary eloquence, but Jim's condition as American and Huck's commitment to freedom are at the moral center of the novel.

In other words, had there been no blacks, certain creative tensions arising from the cross-purposes of whites and blacks would also not have existed. Not only would there have been no Faulkner; there would have been no Stephen Crane, who found certain basic themes of his writing in the Civil War. Thus, also, there would have been no Hemingway, who took Crane as a source and guide. Without the presence of Negro American style, our jokes, our tall tales, even our sports would be lacking in the sudden turns, the shocks, the swift changes of pace (all jazz-shaped) that serve to remind us that the world is ever unexplored, and that while a complete mastery of life is mere illusion, the real secret of the game is to make life swing. It is its ability to articulate this tragic-comic attitude toward life that explains much of the mysterious power and attractiveness of that quality of Negro American style known as "soul." An expression of American diversity within unity, of blackness with whiteness, soul announces the presence of a creative struggle against the realities of existence.

Without the presence of blacks, our political history would have been otherwise. No slave economy, no Civil War; no violent destruction of the Reconstruction; no K.K.K. and no Jim Crow system. And without the disenfranchisement of black Americans and the manipulation of racial fears and prejudices, the disproportionate impact of white Southern politicians upon our domestic and foreign policies would have been impossible. Indeed, it is almost impossible to conceive of what our political system would have become without the snarl of forces—cultural, racial, religious—that make our nation what it is today.

Absent, too, would be the need for that tragic knowledge which we try ceaselessly to evade: that the true subject of democracy is not simply material well-being but the extension of the democratic process in the direction of perfecting itself. And that the most obvious test and clue to that perfection is the inclusion—*not* assimilation—of the black man.

Since the beginning of the nation, white Americans have suffered from a deep inner uncertainty as to who they really are. One of the ways that has been used to simplify the answer has been to seize upon the presence of black Americans and use them as a marker, a symbol of limits, a metaphor for the "outsider." Many whites could look at the social position of blacks and feel that color formed an easy and reliable gauge for determining to what extent one was or was not American. Perhaps that is why one of the first epithets that many European immigrants learned when they got off the boat was the term "nigger"—it made them feel instantly American. But this is tricky magic. Despite his racial difference and social status, something indisputably American about Negroes not only raised doubts about the white man's value system but aroused the troubling suspicion that whatever else the true American is, he is also somehow black.

Materially, psychologically, and culturally, part of the nation's heritage is Negro American, and whatever it becomes will be shaped in part by the Negro's presence. Which is fortunate, for today it is the black American who puts pressure upon the nation to live up to its ideals. It is he who gives creative tension to our struggle for justice and for the elimination of those factors, social and psychological, which make for slums and shaky suburban communities. It is he who insists that we purify the American language by demanding that there be a closer correlation between the meaning of words and reality, between ideal and conduct, our assertions and our actions. Without the black American, something irrepressibly hopeful and creative would go out of the American spirit, and the nation might well succumb to the moral slobbism that has ever threatened its existence from within.

When we look objectively at how the dry bones of the nation were hung together, it seems obvious that some one of the many groups that compose the United States had to suffer the fate of being allowed no easy escape from experiencing the harsh realities of the human condition as they were to exist under even so fortunate a democracy as ours. It would seem that some one group had to be stripped of the possibility of escaping such tragic knowledge by taking sanctuary in moral equivocation, racial chauvinism, or the advantage of superior social status. There is no point in complaining over the past or apologizing for one's fate. But for blacks, there are no hiding places down here, not in suburbia or in penthouse, neither in country nor in city. They are an American people who are geared to what *is* and who yet are driven by a sense of what it is possible for human life to be in this society. The nation could not survive being deprived of their presence because, by the irony implicit in the dynamics of American democracy, they symbolize both its most stringent testing and the possibility of its greatest human freedom.

—From *Time,* April 6, 1970

Portrait of Inman Page: A Dedication Speech

When confronted by such an unexpected situation as this, what does one say? It's not that I haven't been aware of Dr. Page's influence upon my life, for after all these many years he is apt to be conjured up by a wide variety of contacts and situations. And he was so dominant a figure during my school days that his voice and image are still evoked by certain passages of the Bible. I remember him in a context of ceremonies, in most of which he acted as the celebrant—but never in my wildest fantasies would I have anticipated my being called upon to play a role in a ceremony dedicated to his memory. Such a development would have seemed impossible because in my mind my relationship with Dr. Page has remained what it was back in the 1930s, which was that of a boy to a grand, dignified elder. In my scheme of things there remained between us a fixed hierarchal distance that had been dictated by age, accomplishment, and authority. So while I would have had no problem in imagining myself witnessing such a ceremony as this, the idea of my having an active role in it would have been in the realm of the impossible. And now that I find myself standing here, it is as though a preordained relationship has been violated, and as a result, my sense of time has begun leaping back and forth over the years in a way which assaults the logic of clock and calendar, and I am haunted by a sense of the uncanny.

And all the more so as I look at these portraits in which Richard Yarde depicted Dr. Page as he appeared when a student here at Brown. He was a much older man when I came to know him, but the dignified educator with whom I was familiar is prefigured in the portraits, especially in the cast of the eyes. This makes for a pleasant surprise, because during my school days it never occurred to me that Inman Page had ever been a *young* man. To me he was always lofty and enigmatic, a figure of authority and penetrating vision. Perhaps that is why I am haunted by a feeling that somehow Dr. Page must have prearranged today's proceedings years ago, with the foreknowledge that at some predestined time and place they would culminate, at least for me, in a moment of astonishment and instruction.

Now, I don't know whether Dr. Page ever indulged in the old American pastime of practical joking when he was a student here, but I *do* know that practical jokes can be used as agencies of instruction, and that they can indeed be calculated to challenge one's wits and test one's alertness. I also know that they can be staged in such a way that a narrowing of the hierarchal distance between those of lowly status and their superiors is brought about. Not necessarily by effecting a ritual deflation of those who are glamorous and exalted (as happens in the celebration of Mardi Gras), but by way of elevating the lowly for a brief moment to the level of their superiors, and thus initiating them into the mysterious processes of time and authority. Because they sponsor a sense of equality, such symbolic elevations have an important function in our democracy and are likely to be operating when we least expect. I say this because if there is such a joke at play in these proceedings, doubtlessly it is asserting its presence by forcing me to respond to the implication of this ceremony in spontaneous words. Perhaps that is why it is as though I am once again undergoing an examination which this time Dr. Page is conducting from a point beyond time and space.

But such speculations aside, how could such an occasion as this come about? Through the medium of time, of course. And through the interplay, both intentional and accidental, between certain American ideals and institutions and their human agents. More specifically, it has come about through the efforts exerted by the members of one generation of Americans in the interest of the generations which were to follow. Such occasions are a product of the living continuity of earlier historical contacts and relationships which were initiated during the turbulent days of our nineteenth century, and which have persisted even when their origins have been forgotten or ignored. Such occasions are made possible because ideas and ideals retain their vitality by being communicated from concerned individuals to other (and sometimes resistant) individuals. And when these ideas and ideals succeed in finding embodiment in receptive personalities they become linkages which have the power to shape obscure destinies in unexpected ways. Sometimes they manage to affirm our faith by reversing our expectations. Thus we are gathered here today as the result of such linkages between ideals and personalities which were forged and began forming a chain of cause and effect more than a hundred years ago.

Which is to suggest that from the period of the Emancipation there has been transmitted throughout the Afro-American areas of this country a continuing influence that sprang from the early New England tradition of education. That tradition, which has contributed so much to this nation's vitality, was introduced into the areas of the South from which I spring by young graduates of New England colleges who went south to teach the newly freed slaves. I am, incidently, the grandson of a freedman—which would appear to be something of an irony of history. But despite the rapid acceleration of historical change in the United States, the period of slavery isn't so far in the past as it might seem. Inman Page, who was himself a slave and who left this campus at a time when the dismantling of the Reconstruction was well under way, was a bearer of that same tradition of New England education of which I speak. And through him its standards were imparted to many, many ex-slaves and their descendants. And since that transmitted tradition is still alive, I think it a good idea to keep this historical circumstance in mind when we hear glib talk of a "white culture" and a "black culture" in the United States. Because the truth of the matter is that between the two racial groups there has always been a constant exchange of cultural, of stylistic elements. Whether in the arts, in education, in athletics, or in certain conceptions and misconceptions of democratic justice, interchange, appropriation, and integration—not segregation—have been the constants of our developing nation. So at this particular moment of our history I think it very important that we keep in mind that the culture of the United States is a composite, pluralistic culture-of-cultures, and that all of its diverse elements have been to some extent inspirited by those ideals which were enshrined during the founding of this nation. In our embrace of these ideals we are one and yet many, and never more so than after they led to the Civil War, the Emancipation, and the Reconstruction. It was these ideals which inspired the many examples of personal courage such as can be seen in the life of Inman E. Page. For certainly his act of implanting the ideals of New England education out in the "Territory," that then young wild state of Oklahoma, called for both courage and a dedication to education. Because by the time he graduated from Brown the Reconstruction, which had promised full citizenship to the freedmen, was, as I've said, well on the way toward betrayal. It was a most pessimistic period for his people but he did his best, and therefore, thanks to Inman Page—and no matter how incongruously—I am here.

I must confess, however, that as a student I always found the man forbidding. I realize now that much of my intimidation was due to his sheer personal style, his quality of command. At Brown he was chosen the orator of his class, and during my school days he was indeed eloquent.

I can still hear him reading from Saint Paul's Letters to the Corinthians, as he did so often during our daily chapel exercises. Just listening to him taught one the joy and magic of words. He made one believe in his message, because he expressed authority in the smallest gesture. I don't mean that he was pompous, for indeed he was quite fatherly. But for me at least he possessed an aura of the untouchable. In his presence one was careful of one's manners, and since it was his role to punish those guilty of serious misconduct with a strapping, personal contact with him was to be avoided. Usually I managed to keep out of his way, but one memorable day I failed, and it was at a time when the student body was gathering in the school's auditorium for chapel services.

During these exercises the junior and senior high school boys were seated on the platform behind the lectern from which Dr. Page conducted the religious services. This platform was actually a stage that was used for concerts and theatricals and was equipped with a curtain that could be raised and lowered by ropes that were lashed to the floor on either side. We took our places on the stage left and right by marching up short flights of stairs, which were favorite sites for horseplay. This involved much pushing and shoving, not to mention other attacks upon one's anatomy. Sometimes these could be both painful and degrading, and therefore, being on this occasion somewhat out of sorts, I told myself that if some guy pushes me, I'm going to swing on him and start punching.

Well, I got pushed, and went into action, but unfortunately for me, it wasn't a student who took my punch, it was Dr. Page. And before I realized what was happening, Dr. Page had grabbed me, I grabbed the ropes of the stage curtain, and the two of us went swinging in a tight circle that carried us around and around over the platform and steps until I lost my grip and caused the two of us to fall —with me landing on top of Dr. Page.

Well, Dr. Page was probably as shocked by this sudden eruption of chaos as I was, but he was still in command.

"What do you think you're doing, boy," he roared. "What do you think you're doing!"

Even today I'm unsure of my reply, but for years afterward a good friend used to remind me of the incident by suddenly breaking out with high-pitched cries of "We fell, Mister Page! Mister Page, we *fell!*"

I'm still unsure of what I said, because I was too excited. But as Dr. Page pushed me off and snatched me to my feet a most amazing thing occurred: In spite of my fear and excitement and the teeth-rattling shaking he was giving me, I could hear Dr. Page chuckling under his breath. But then he was chasing me, literally, straight up the aisle and out of the auditorium. And as I was heading up a flight of stairs to the walk, with him right behind me, I could hear him thundering, "And don't come back! Don't you *dare* come back!"

It was a rough moment for me, a fall into chaos and disgrace, with the student body roaring its delight. And all the more so because of that mysterious chuckle, a chuckle which was so incongruous that I could not be certain I had heard it. But I had, because the next day Dr. Page relented and got word to me that I hadn't been permanently expelled. In fact, I returned and managed to keep out of serious trouble from that day until I graduated. That one chaotic contact with authority was enough for me.

And now I'll bring these remarks to a close by suggesting that if Dr. Page is present with us in spirit—and I'm sure he is—no doubt he is still chuckling as he did on the day he chased me from school. Because here, once again, he finds himself a participant in another most incongruous juxtaposition. A juxtaposition in which his old student Ralph Ellison is linked unexpectedly to the exaltation of *his* principal.

—From *The Carleton Miscellany,* Winter 1980;
address given September 19, 1979, at the
Ralph Ellison Festival at Brown University

Going to the Territory

Once again I must wonder at the sheer unexpectedness of life in these United States. Even the most celebrated of writers would find this scene exhilarating, but for me—well, it is simply overwhelming. It's as though I am being rebuked—even if ever so gently—for every instance in which I doubted the possibility of communicating my peculiar vision to my fellow Americans. Now I realize how fortunate I am to have held on to literature as a medium for transcending the divisions of our society, for your presence affirms that faith most generously.

But Lord knows I had no idea that such emotional turmoil would be the price for becoming the focus of such a scene. It reminds me of how often I've been told that extremes will meet, and it proves the correctness of those who advised me that in this country it is always wise to expect the unexpected. I say this because your campus has become the scene in which certain lines of interpersonal, institutional, and even historical relationships have not only come together but have collided in a way which I find most confounding. And it all began yesterday with the ceremony in

Rockefeller Library during which I was presented with one of Richard Yarde's portraits of Dr. Inman E. Page. And now here in Sayles Hall the shock wave set off by that collision appears on its way toward a rousing, Wagnerian crescendo of the unexpected.

Since Inman Page was the first Afro-American to graduate from Brown University, the honor paid him here last September wasn't surprising—but that it should be *my* fate to be honored a year later with the presentation of his portrait is an example of the unexpected outdoing itself in demonstrating its power to surprise. Because in yesterday's ceremony two lines of destiny, which had touched during the early 1920s and then diverged rather abruptly during the Great Depression, were brought together again under circumstances which in those days would have been unimaginable. It is true that their divergence began with an educational ceremony, but no one would have been so rash as to predict that a recapitulation would occur, not even at a point in what was then the far distant future. In other words, yesterday's ceremony would have been unthinkable —even as a comic, practical-joking inflation of the original. And yet all of the elements were already in motion.

One of Dr. Page's many roles after his graduation from Brown was that of supervisor of education for Negroes and principal of old Douglass High School in Oklahoma City. I attended old Douglass (which was named in honor of Frederick Douglass, the ex-slave abolitionist) from the first grade through the twelfth, and at my graduation Dr. Page presented me with my diploma. Thus ended—or appeared to end—our years of relationship. I went south to college, and except for the summer vacation of my sophomore year, I was not to return home again for some seventeen years. On my return I was to see Dr. Page for the last time, and with my attention turned elsewhere, I thought his influence upon my life had concluded.

But for me as for most members of our community, students and adults alike, Dr. Page served as a representative figure. As such he inspired the extremes of ambivalent emotion: love and hate, admiration and envy, fear and respect. He moved many of his students to secret yearnings to possess some of his implicit authority, some of his wisdom and eloquence. And in fact, quite a number became teachers and community leaders. Today his influence is such that although he passed away some forty years ago, one has only to bring a group of his old students together and immediately he lives again in apotheosis. This has been happening out in the Southwest for many years, but I have no doubt that much of the turmoil which I feel this evening springs from the unexpectedness of finding his personality such a powerful presence in a place so far from where I knew him. So perhaps that which we term the "unexpected" is really a product of that which we do not know or fail to take into account. Learn enough about a given phenomenon and the "unexpected" becomes fairly predictable.

Which suggests that although Dr. Page spent his life working in segregated institutions and thus was overlooked by those who record the history of American education, he was nonetheless a figure of national importance, and one who influenced history despite having been forced to work outside its rather arbitrarily drawn framework. If so, the honor paid him here last year celebrated not only his relationship with Brown but marked the recognition of his national significance as an educator. At any rate, once in a while the veil which shrouds the details of our unwritten history is thrown back, and not only do the deserving find belated recognition, but sometimes marvelous interconnections between the past and the present spring to light.

And so, thanks to the administrators of Brown University, thanks to Michael Harper and his assistants, and thanks to the intricate relationship which obtains between Brown and American history generally, an attempt was made to rediscover some of the more obscure connections through which the past has become a part of the living present. And somehow, in that process of retrieval an Oklahoma boy was found whose life was profoundly influenced by Inman E. Page—and so I stand before you.

And yet, considering the ironic fact that Americans continue to find themselves stumbling into (as well as over) details of their history, tonight's is a most *American* occasion. For it is one in which by seeking to move forward we find ourselves looking back and discovering with some surprise from whence we've come. Perhaps this is how it has to be. For given the circumstances of our national origins, given our vast geopolitical space and the improvised character of our society, and given the mind-boggling rapidity of our national growth—perhaps it is understandably difficult for Americans to keep in touch with what has happened to them. At any rate, in the two hundred years of our national existence a great deal has been overlooked or forgotten. Some developments become obscure because of the sheer rush and density of incidents which occur in any given period of time; others fade through conscious design, either because of an unwillingness to solve national dilemmas or because we possess such a short attention span and are given to a facile waning of our commitments. Then too, having had no adequate model to guide us in establishing what we told ourselves was to be a classless society, it has often been difficult for us to place people and events in a proper perspective of national importance. So it is well that we keep in mind the fact that not all of American history is recorded. And in some ways we are fortunate that it isn't, for if it were, we might become so chagrined by the discrepancies which exist between our democratic ideals and our social reality that we'd soon lose heart. Perhaps this is why we possess two basic versions of American history: one which is written and as neatly stylized as ancient myth, and the other unwritten and as chaotic and full of contradictions, changes of pace, and surprises as life itself. Perhaps this is to overstate a bit, but there's no denying the fact that Americans can be notoriously selective in the exercise of historical memory.

Surely there must be some self-deceptive magic in this, for in spite of what is left out of our recorded history, our unwritten history looms as its obscure alter ego, and although repressed from our general knowledge of ourselves, it is always active in the shaping of events. It is always with us, questioning even when not accusing its acclaimed double, and with the two locked in mute argument which is likely to shock us when it becomes visible during periods of national stress. Meanwhile, yearning and thirsting for a rational social order, and being forced as human beings to live in what we like to identify as the "present," we go on struggling against the built-in conditions which comprise the pathology of American democracy. Perhaps it is our need to avoid the discouraging facts of our experience that accounts for the contradiction between those details of our history which we choose to remember and those which we ignore or leave unstated.

But no matter how we choose to view ourselves in the abstract, in the world of work and politics Americans live in a constant state of debate and contention. And we do so no matter what kinds of narrative, oral or written, are made in the reconstruction of our common experience. American democracy is a most dramatic form of social organization, and in that drama each of us enacts his role by asserting his own and his group's values and traditions against those of his fellow citizens. Indeed, a battle-royal conflict of interests appears to be basic to our conception of freedom, and the drama of democracy proceeds through a warfare of words and symbolic actions by which we seek to advance our private interests while resolving our political differences. Since the Civil War this form of symbolic action has served as a moral substitute for armed warfare, and we have managed to restrain ourselves to a debate which we carry on in the not always justified faith that the outcome will serve the larger interests of democracy. Unfortunately, this doesn't always work out, and when it doesn't, the winners of a given contention are likely to concern themselves with only the fruits of victory, while leaving it to the losers to grapple with the issues that are left unresolved.

Something like this was taking place at the time Inman Page was graduating from Brown, and it set the tone of the scene in which he was to act. Having won its victory, the North could be selective in its memory as well as in its priorities, while leaving it to the South to struggle with the national problems which developed following the end of the Reconstruction. And even the South became selective in its memory of the incidents that led to its rebellion and defeat. And of course, a defenseless scapegoat was easily at hand. But my point here is that by pushing significant details of our experience into the underground of unwritten history, we not only overlook much which is positive, but we blur our conceptions of where and who we are. Not only do we confuse our moral identity, but by ignoring such matters as the sharing of bloodlines and cultural traditions by groups of widely differing ethnic origins, and by overlooking the blending and metamorphosis of cultural forms which is so characteristic of our society, we misconceive our cultural identity. It is as though we dread to acknowledge the complex, pluralistic nature of our society, and as a result we find ourselves stumbling upon our true national identity under circumstances in which we least expect to do so. This is because some of our brightest achievements have been as lights hidden under a basket of myths. Who would have expected that through one of the members of the class of 1877, Brown University would play a role in the fate of a writer from Oklahoma? More important, who would have thought that Brown's standards of education would affect the outlook of so many thousands who would never see it?

Thus, in the underground of our unwritten history much of that which is ignored defies our inattention by continuing to grow and have consequences. This happens through a process of apparently random synthesis; a process which I see as the unconscious logic of the democratic process. Set in motion over two hundred years ago with the founding of this nation, it is an irrepressible force which draws its power from those fateful promises that were made in Philadelphia, and it moves all too slowly, but steadily, against and around those forces which would thwart our progress toward the fulfillment of the democratic ideal. An aspect of the democratic principles which inspirit our institutions and social processes, it expresses itself in the unremarked contacts between individuals of differing status and background and through the impact, accidental or intended, which significant individuals exert upon our institutions. Ever at work in our lives, it reveals itself in those gestures and elements of style through which we find our definition as Americans. This includes the way we walk, talk, and move; but, ironically, it is likely to become our conscious possession during those moments when events force us to measure that which we have been taught formally, abstractly, against that which we've learned through hard experience. And sometimes when this happens we discover that we're a bit worse than we've been taught, but then again, much better than we'd dare believe.

Sometimes we become aware of the underground logic of the democratic process quite consciously, but are likely to perceive the rightness of its products with a feeling of unease. Because our perception of justice attained doesn't always square with our conception of that which is best for our own interests. Sometimes it works its transformations of society so quietly (as during periods of war or economic depression) that we fail to realize that in such interruptions of normal order, injustices that have been long accepted have been resolved. Let's face it, no matter what motives are ascribed as leading to the Civil War, it took that conflict for Inman Page to be able to come to Brown. And so it is often on this unrecognized level that our democratic ideals are most successful in nudging us toward our goal.

And so it is that we go on striving. We take chances—and are taken by the random working of the democratic impulse—and we continue to assert the old received values, modifying them as seems necessary, but seeking to affirm them nevertheless. This we do out of our individual yearnings, out of our individual passions, and out of our often half-hearted hopes that some day we'll achieve the transcendent dream which was projected by the Founding Fathers when they committed their conception of an ideal society to paper.

That conception was arrived at, remember, through strenuous debate, and we have been arguing with one another ever since. Still, ours is a debate, a contention, in which we seek to make our conception of democracy manifest in every detail of our living. Not only in flags and emblems, or in words and rituals, but even in such details as the architecture of your magnificent buildings—which are among the glories of your campus—and in such minor artifacts as the blue jeans which parade the names of heiresses on the hip pocket. There has to be a powerful democratic magic in the latter, because for Inman Page's generation education was seen as a way of *not* having to live in blue jeans. But as I say, extremes meet—and this in more ways than one. For in this country we seem to go to any extreme in promoting our notions of excellence, and this can lead to incongruous juxtapositions. There is also the fact that anyway one takes it, democracy is a leveling process which moves in any direction along the scale of taste. And there is also the fact that in order for democratic principles and ideals to remain vital, they must be communicated not only across the built-in divisions of class, race, and religion, but across the divisions of aesthetic styles and tastes as well. And when this is achieved, not only do we find communication and communion, but we learn a bit more about how to live within the mystery which haunts American experience, and that is the mystery of how we are many and yet one. I suppose that when used as costume, blue jeans are a way of dramatizing our basic unity.

Which reminds me that since arriving on campus I've had the pleasure of listening to a number of discussions of my fiction, and I've been amazed to discover how much of what I conceived to be a basic pattern of American experience appears to have been communicated to readers who originate on opposite sides of the color line. To me this is most important, not only because I wish to be understood, but because race and color have been basic determinants in structuring what is one of the most aggravating barriers to free communication in this society. Approach the reality of racial differences, and our dictionary of democratic terminology can be thrown into confusion, with such common terms as "equality" and "freedom" turning into their opposites. But in listening to these discussions this didn't happen. It was as though my novel had become a lens through which readers of widely differing backgrounds were able to see elements of their own experience brought to a unifying focus. And in some instances I found this a bit bewildering, even though I am aware that a novel can come alive only through the collaboration of its readers' imaginations, and it was quite evident that the students who participated with the panelists had been taught to read. But something more was taking place, for it was as though a group of sophisticated minds were functioning like a group of jazz musicians and were working in a spirit of antagonistic cooperation to explore its hidden possibilities. In a jam session this process works in such a way that not only is the original theme enhanced, but the listener is compelled to experience a feeling of catharsis.

Let me hasten to say that I don't mean to flatter myself by implying that those involved in these discussions were *themselves* undergoing a catharsis. But *I* certainly did, and it left me not only intellectually gratified but physically weak. And perhaps this was because when one works with words and situations that are commonly charged with divisive emotions it is gratifying to discover that despite this, you've been able to communicate. And all the more when you know that in this country effective artistic communication requires a symbolic sharing of emotions and situations which have usually blocked communication in the world of work and politics. What is important in all this lies in the fact that the ground terms which allow for communication are the same which we use to spell out our democratic ideals. They're the same terms which inspired Inman Page to take his chances here at Brown, and thus my being here tonight is not only an occasion in which certain details of our common history have come together, but it is also one in which there is revealed something of the fate of those principles in whose name we struggle and in whose spirit we have often died. I say *struggle* because for all our many achievements as a nation, we've never been able to make our principles adequately manifest in either our conduct or in our social structure. And yet, once in a while, we have been capable of enormous efforts. Today many agree that the ideals of the Great Society—which were a restatement of the ideals of the Reconstruction—have proved to be dross. I'd say that this depends upon where one looks. For here in an area that is somewhat buffered against the contentions of politics, there is evidence that at least some of our efforts have found a measure of success, even as did certain efforts that were launched during the period when Inman Page came to Brown.

Inman Page arrived at Brown University at a time when the optimism which was released among the former slaves by their emancipation was still buoyed by the promises of the already fading Reconstruction. For the first time Afro-Americans were participating as a group in political affairs and their right to do so was being protected by federal troops. Thus the nation's tragic drama of sectional warfare appeared to have ended their subjugation. We know now, however, that the freedmen were actors within a play-within-a-play, and that theirs was a tragic action within a larger drama in which events would convert tragedy into a farce. And if the larger drama was resolved in the ambiguous victory of the North, theirs would proceed through an abrupt reversal of their group expectations to social and political defeat. Because after the Hayes-Tilden Compromise they were forced to live under a system which was close to, and in some ways worse than, slavery. Here, surely, is an example of the rapidity of historical change of which I have spoken. Within thirteen years Afro-Americans were swept from slavery to a brief period of freedom, to a condition of second-class citizenship. And from a condition of faint hope, through a period of euphoric optimism, to a condition of despair. The familiar world of slavery was gone, but now they faced a world of ambiguity in which their access to even the most fundamental of life's necessities was regulated strictly on the basis of race and color.

Such was the general picture, but in spite of these dismal developments, there were still reasons for cautious optimism. And this lay in the physical fact that they were now the owners of their own bodies and had the freedom to express something of their aspirations as individuals. As slaves they had long been aware that for themselves, as for most of their countrymen, geography was fate. Not only had they observed the transformation of individual fortune made possible by the westward movement along the frontier, but the Mason-Dixon Line had taught them the relationship between geography and freedom. They knew that to be sold down the Mississippi River usually meant that they would suffer a harsher form of slavery. And they knew that to escape across the Mason-Dixon Line northward was to move in the direction of a greater freedom. But freedom was also to be found in the West of the old Indian Territory. Bessie Smith gave voice to this knowledge when she sang of "Goin' to the Nation, Going to the Terr'tor'," and it is no accident that much of the symbolism of our folklore is rooted in the imagery of geography. For the slaves had learned through the repetition of group experience that freedom was to be attained through geographical movement, and that freedom required one to risk his life against the unknown. And geography as a symbol of the unknown included not only places, but conditions relating to their racially defined status and the complex mystery of a society from which they'd been excluded. Emancipation had intensified their awareness of the mystery which cloaked the larger society, and they realized that education, the freeing of the mind, was necessary if they were to make the most of their change in legal status. It was out of such circumstances that Inman Page chose to enhance his freedom by coming to Brown, and it was here that he was able to establish his individual worth and prepare himself for his liberating role as an educator. This much of his story I've known since I was a child, but I am still amazed by the extent to which his willingness to take his chances in unknown territories has affected my own life. The theme of this festival is "Goin' to the Territory"—well, I met Dr. Page in what was first known as the Indian Territory, and then the Oklahoma Territory. Long before it became the State of Oklahoma the Territory had been a sanctuary for runaway slaves who sought there the protection of the Five Great Indian Nations. Dr. Page went to the Territory in 1898 to become president of what is now Langston University, and by the time he became the principal of my old school he was a man in his seventies. At that time the state of Oklahoma had attracted many of the descendants of the freed slaves, who considered it a territory of hope and a place where they could create their own opportunities. It was a magnet for many individuals who had found disappointment in the older area of the country, white as well as black, but for Negroes it had a traditional association with freedom which had entered their folklore. Thus the uneducated and educated alike saw Oklahoma as a land of opportunity. In fact, as principal of old Douglass High School, Dr. Page was to succeed a former West Point cadet. This was Professor Johnson Chestnut Whittaker, whose experiences as a cadet led to a cause célèbre that brought the dismissal of West Point's superintendent.

Professor Whittaker was a *white* black man. Which is to say that visually he was whiter than almost anyone here in Sayles Hall. But by birth and native background he was a South Carolina slave who had been born the property of the family of U. S. Senator James Chestnut, Jr. His mother was the personal servant of Mary Boykin Chestnut, the author of *A Diary From Dixie,* a famous work of the Civil War period in which the Whittaker family is mentioned. A year before Inman Page graduated from Brown, Johnson C. Whittaker was appointed to West Point—which is an example of the type of transformations that were made possible by Emancipation. But it was also an example of the reversal of expectations wrought by the betrayal of the Reconstruction. For Whittaker's career ended in a racial attack during which he was seized by other cadets who tied him to his cot and notched his ear. My mother, who knew Professor Whittaker in South Carolina, told me that this was done so that he could not measure up to a West Point tradition which held that its graduates had to be physically perfect. This incident caused much indignation in the North, but Cadet Whittaker had to leave the Point, and thus the Army's loss was to become the Territory's gain. For after taking a law degree and practicing in South Carolina, Professor Whittaker became the principal of Douglass High School, where he was to introduce elements of West Point discipline and military style to young Oklahoma Negroes. Thus once again we have an example of the unnoticed logic of the democratic process.

I hope you'll understand that I haven't mentioned this unpleasant incident just to shock you. I do so to suggest that our unknown history doesn't stop having consequences even though we ignore them, and I *am* trying to give you some idea of the scene and the political and social climate which led such people as Dr. Page and my parents from the southeastern part of the country to make a life out in the Old Territory. Geography is fate, and in moving west they were repeating a pattern begun by runaway slaves and by the Negroes who accompanied the Indian tribes along the death march which took so many lives that it became known as "The Trail of Tears," a march initiated by Andrew Jackson in fulfillment of the treaty of Dancing Rabbit.

Thus it was that Dr. Page first became a representative figure in the Territory and later in the new state, where we were very much aware that he was a graduate of Brown. It is understandable that this university occupies a warm place in our hearts, since we felt a tie to you through our principal. And so it was that certain ideals which Dr. Page gained here and certain testings of his manhood and faith which were affirmed here became a part of my own heritage as an Oklahoman. This came about through his role as educator, but there was a more important link between us, and this had to do with my introduction to the arts and, ultimately, with my becoming a writer.

Dr. and Mrs. Page were the parents of a most wonderful daughter whose name was Zelia N. Breaux, and her impact upon our community was in some ways as profound as that of her father. We are now in the area of culture where we may see how the generation which came between Dr. Page's and my own functioned in structuring the cultural life of the then wild territory of Oklahoma—and I assure you that it was wild! Yes, but wild mainly in the sense of its being a relatively unformed frontier state. I have stressed that in this country geography has performed the role of fate, but it is important to remember that it is not geography alone which determines the quality of life and culture. These depend upon the courage and personal culture of the individuals who make their homes in any given locality. In his *The Oregon Trail,* Francis Parkman writes of his surprise at coming upon a snug little cottage, far on the other side of the great prairie, wherein he discovered vintage French wines and the latest French novels.

Well, those cultural artifacts didn't get there by magic; they were transported there to supply the cultural tastes of the cottage's owner. Thus they formed a cultural synthesis between the culture of France and the prairie. But of course, such apparently incongruous juxtapositions are a norm on the frontiers of American society. Today most of the geographical frontier is gone, but the process of cultural integration continues along the lines that mark the hierarchal divisions of the United States.

Be that as it may, Mrs. Breaux was a musician and a teacher of music. By the time I entered the primary grades she was supervisor of music for Oklahoma City's Negro schools, and the connection between Mrs. Breaux and my presence here began in a second-grade classroom. At the time we were dancing and singing to a little nursery-type tune which went, "Oh busy squirrel with bushy tail and shiny eyes so round/Why do you gather all the nuts that fall upon the ground." There were quite a number of us hopping about, but she must have been struck by the way this particular little nut was doing his squirrel act, because she gathered me up for special attention. And so began one of the most important relationships in my life. For more than ten years Mrs. Breaux was a sort of second mother. Naturally, I had my own mother and I loved her very much, but between us there arose the usual conflicts which affect the relationships between parent and child, and when this happened, Mrs. Breaux was always there to be turned to. Better still, she was an agent of music, which soon became the main focus of my attempts to achieve my own identity.

This was during the 1920s, the period in which what was known as the Public School Music Program was sweeping the nation. Mrs. Breaux was a leader in that movement which did so much to broaden and enrich the nation's musical culture. She did so by teaching musical theory and by training what became famous marching bands. She organized school orchestras and choral groups, she staged and directed operettas, and she was responsible for the high quality of our music-appreciation program. Thanks to her, ours became a music-centered culture which involved as many of the other arts as was possible in a system that was limited in budget and facilities. On May Day children from all of the Negro schools were assembled on the playing field of the old Western League baseball stadium, the girls in their white dresses and the boys in blue serge knickers and white shirts, and there to the music of the Douglass High School Band, we competed in wrapping dozens of maypoles and engaged in the mass dancing of a variety of

European folk dances. As was to be expected, there were those who found the sight of young Negroes dancing European folk dances absurd, if not comic, but their prejudiced eyes missed the point of this exercise in democratic education. For in learning such dances, we were gaining an appreciation of the backgrounds and cultures of our fellow Americans whose backgrounds lay in Europe. And not only did it narrow the psychological distance between them and ourselves, but we saw learning their dances as an *artistic* challenge. And while there were those who thought that we were stepping out of the role assigned Negroes and were expressing a desire to become white, we ignored them. For we knew that dancing such dances would no more alter our racial identity or social status than would our singing of Bach chorales. Our interest lay in competing to master the steps, and our reward came in the form of a painless absorption of information which we might otherwise have found uninteresting. And thanks to Mrs. Breaux, we were being introduced to one of the most precious of American freedoms, which is our freedom to broaden our personal culture by absorbing the cultures of others. Even more important was the fact that we were being taught to discover and exercise those elements of freedom which existed unobserved (at least by outsiders), within our state of social and political unfreedom. And this gift, this important bit of equipment for living, came through the efforts of a woman educator who by acting as agent of the broader American culture was able to widen our sense of possibility and raise our aspirations.

Nor was this all, for while I was to become a writer instead of a musician, it was Mrs. Breaux who introduced me to the basic discipline required of the artist. And it was she who made it possible for me to grasp the basic compatibility of the mixture of the classical and vernacular styles which were part of our musical culture. She was one of the owners of what for many years was the only Negro theater in Oklahoma City, and it was here that she made valuable contributions to the popular arts. For while she discouraged her students from playing jazz, she also saw to it that our community was provided the best of Negro entertainers. In her Aldridge Theater one could see and hear the great blues singers, dancers, and comedians, the famous jazz orchestras and such repertory drama groups as the Lafayette Players. In other words, just as she taught the Negro spirituals along with Bach and Handel, she provided a cultural nexus in which the vernacular art forms could be encountered along with the classical. So just as her father transmitted the ideals which he'd gained at Brown University across the color line and down the annals of our unwritten history, so did his daughter bring together and make possible an interaction of art forms, styles, and traditions. Interesting enough, it wasn't until years later that I learned how unusual this was, or the extent to which it cleared away the insidious confusion between race and culture which haunts this society.

Today we hear much discussion of what is termed "Black English," a concept unheard of during my school days. And yet we were all the grandchildren of slaves and most of us spoke in the idioms that were native to the regions from which our families had migrated. Still, no one, much less our teachers, suggested that standard American English was beyond us; how could they with such examples as Dr. Page before us? He could make the language of Shakespeare and the King James version of the Bible resound within us in such ways that its majesty and beauty seemed as natural and as normal coming from one of our own as an inspired jazz improvisation or an eloquently sung spiritual. By daily examples he made us aware that great poetry and fluent English were a part of our heritage; thus we developed an ear for a variety of linguistic idioms. And with so many other masters of America's nineteenth-century oratorical style—many of them preachers—living among us, we had no difficulty in grasping how elevated styles of speech related to the spoken vernacular. For example, as a boy I heard the debate team of Wiley College, which was coached by the late Afro-American poet Melvin Tolson, defeat the team of England's Oxford University, who did not disdain to debate with Negroes. Tolson's team was made up of young men whose backgrounds were similar to our own and they appeared to have no difficulty in mastering the king's English.

No, being of a people whose backgrounds were in slavery, we were taught that it was necessary to acquire the skills needed for communicating in a mixed society, and we knew from experience that this required a melting and blending of vernacular and standard speech and a grasp of the occasions in which each, or both, were called for. So instead of clinging defensively to our native idiom, we sought consciously to extend its range. Actually, language was our most easily available toy and we played with its capacity to create the unexpected and to blunt its capacity to surprise. The ever-present conflict of American linguistic styles was a source of comedy which sharpened our eye for the incongruous; a matter encouraged both by our condition as boys and as members of a group whose social situation was most ambiguous. Verbal comedy was a way of confronting social ambiguity. And being familiar with racial violence—we were living in the aftermath of the race riots that followed World War I, remember—we learned quite early that laughter made the difficulties of our condition a bit more bearable. We hadn't read Henry James at that time, but we realized nevertheless that American society contained a built-in joke, and we were aware even if James wasn't—or did not choose to admit—that that joke was in many ways centered in our condition. So we welcomed any play on words or nuance of gesture which gave expression to our secret sense of the way things really were. Usually this took the comic mode, and it is quite possible that one reason the popular arts take on an added dimension in our democracy lies in an unspoken, though no less binding, agreement that popular culture is not to be taken seriously. Thus the popular arts have become an agency through which Americans can contemplate those aspects of our experience that are deemed unspeakable.

Perhaps that is why it was left to such comedians as Redd Foxx to notify us that since the 1950s a major change has occurred in our attitudes toward racial minorities. Thus when he, a black comedian, makes remarks about ugly white women which once were reserved only for black women, he allows us to bring attitudes and emotions that were once tabooed into the realm of the rational, where, protected by the comic mode, we may confront our guilt and prejudices and, perhaps, resolve them.

Today I've heard some very interesting discussions of the American vernacular style in literature, and found them most informative. Because it seems to me that our most characteristic American style *is* that of the vernacular. But by "vernacular" I mean far more than popular or indigenous language. I see the vernacular as a dynamic *process* in which the most refined styles from the past are continually merged with the play-it-by-eye-and-by-ear improvisations which we invent in our efforts to control our environment and entertain ourselves. And this not only in language and literature, but in architecture and cuisine, in music, costume, and dance, and in tools and technology. In it the styles and techniques of the past are adjusted to the needs of the present, and in its integrative action the high styles of the past are democratized. From this perspective the vernacular is, no less than the styles associated with aristocracy, a gesture toward perfection.

Which is to suggest that although the perfection toward which it moves is democratic rather than aristocratic, there is no necessary contradiction between our vernacular style and the pursuit of excellence. After all, "democracy" is our term for social perfection (or a perfect society), while "excellence" is a general term for perfect quality. And while the vernacular is shy of abstract standards, it still seeks perfection in the form of functional felicity. That is why considerations of function and performance figure so prominently in the scale of vernacular aesthetics. Perfection is arrived at through a process of refinement, elimination, and integration in which form and function become aesthetically one.

Today there is much discussion of a supposedly unresolvable conflict between elitist and populist values. But this assumes that the vernacular process destroys the so-called elitist styles, when in truth past standards of excellence remain to be used again and again, and indeed often undergo metamorphosis as they contribute to the needs of the present. In a sense jazz, which is an amalgam of past musical styles, may be seen as a rejection of a music which expressed the values of a social elite, but let me say that although jazz musicians are practitioners of a vernacular style, they are also unreconstructed elitists when it comes to maintaining the highest standards of the music which expresses their sense of the American experience. And so was Mark Twain, who transformed elements of regional vernacular speech into a medium of uniquely American literary expression and thus taught us how to capture that which is essentially American in our folkways and manners. For indeed the vernacular process is a way of establishing and discovering our national identity.

But wherever we find the vernacular process operating

we also find individuals who act as transmitters between it and earlier styles, tastes, and techniques. In the United States all social barriers are vulnerable to cultural styles. Therefore, Dr. Page and Mrs. Breaux—and there were many others, both white and black—worked to maintain high standards, wherever they originated. And they tried to give their students a sense of the fact that as Americans, they too were heirs to the culture of all the ages. Their type of teaching was both an act of individual idealism and a fulfillment of their faith in democracy. It was also a great, if unrecognized, service to this nation. For while preparing us for the next stage in our education, they were conditioning us to take advantage of such opportunities as the built-in-logic of the democratic process would throw our way.

There was a time when a Negro singer of classical music was viewed as a mere exotic, so if you're surprised that there are now so many Afro-American opera and concert singers, I'd remind you that it didn't happen accidentally. God didn't reach down and say, "All right, Leontyne Price, Shirley Verrett, Betty Allen, Jessie Norman, Simon Estes, you may now sing opera as well as your native Negro spirituals." No, this came about because there were agents of culture among us who embraced the ideals of art and found ways of imparting them to their students.

I am saying that within an area of our society which has been treated as though it were beyond the concerns of history, the democratic process has been made to operate by dedicated individuals—at least on the level of culture; and that it has thus helped to define and shape the quality of the general American experience. Which is something that those who were charged with making our ideals manifest on the political level were not doing. But fortunately, American culture is of a whole, for that which is essentially "American" in it springs from the synthesis of our diverse elements of cultural style. It is the product of a process which was in motion even before the founding of this nation, and it began with the interaction between Englishmen, Europeans, and Africans and American geography. When our society was established this "natural" process of Americanization continued in its own unobserved fashion, defying the social, aesthetic, and political assumptions of our political leaders and tastemakers alike. This, as I say, was the vernacular process, and in the days when our leaders still looked to England and the Continent for their standards of taste, the vernacular stream of our culture was creating itself out of whatever elements it found useful, including the Americanized culture of the slaves. So in this sense the culture of the United States has always been more "democratic" and "American" than the social and political institutions in which it was emerging. Ironically, it was the vernacular which gave expression to that very newness of spirit and outlook of which the leaders of the nation liked to boast. Such Founding Fathers as Franklin and Webster feared the linguistic vernacular as a disruptive influence and sought to discourage it, but fortunately, they failed. For otherwise there would have been no Mark Twain.

They failed because thanks to the pluralistic character of our society, there is no way for any one group to discover by itself the intrinsic forms of our democratic culture. This has to be a cooperative effort, and it is achieved through contact and communication across our divisions of race, class, religion, and region. In the past the cultural contributions of those who were confined beneath the threshold of social hierarchy—which is to say outside the realm of history—were simply appropriated without credit by those who used them to their own advantage. But today we've reached a stage of general freedom in which it is no longer possible to take the products of a slave or an illiterate artist without legal consequence. For today the vernacular artist knows his own value, and thanks to our increased knowledge of our cultural pluralism, such artists are identified less by their race or social status than by the excellence of their art. Our awareness of what we are culturally is still inadequate, but the process of synthesis through which the slaves took the music and religious lore of others and combined them with their African heritage in such ways as to create their own cultural idiom continues. Through the democratizing action of the vernacular, almost any style of expression may be appropriated, and today such appropriation continues at an accelerating pace. I must confess, however, that I find some of its products incongruous if not unexpected. As when I hear a group of middle-class white kids doing their best to sound like members of an old-fashioned black Baptist congregation. They'd probably find the churches in which such sounds are a form of religious exaltation bizarre, but I recognize that by appropriating the style—and profaning it, as it were—they are simply trying to attain some vague ideal of perfection. In this country it is in the nature of cultural styles to become detached from their places of origin, so it is possible that in their frenzy the kids don't even realize that they are sounding like black Baptists. Being Americans who are influenced by the vernacular, it is natural for them to seek out those styles which provide them with a feeling of being most in harmony with the undefined aspects of American experience. In other words, they're seeking the homeness of home.

In closing, let me say that our pluralistic democracy is a difficult system under which to live, our guarantees of freedom notwithstanding. Socially and politically we have yet to feel at ease with our principles, and on the level of culture no one group has managed to create the definitive American style. Hence the importance of the vernacular in the ongoing task of naming, defining, and creating a consciousness of who and what we have come to be. Each

American group has dominated some aspect of our corporate experience by reducing it to form; thus we might well make a conscious effort to seek out and explore such instances of domination and make them our conscious possession. I say "conscious" because in pursuing our democratic promises, we do this even when we're unaware. What is more, our unwritten history is always at work in the background to provide us with clues as to how this process of self-definition has worked in the past. Perhaps if we learn more of what has happened and *why* it happened, we'll learn more of who we really are. And perhaps if we learn more about our unwritten history, we won't be so vulnerable to the capriciousness of events as we are today. And in the process of becoming more aware of ourselves we will recognize that one of the functions of our vernacular culture is that of preparing for the emergence of the unexpected, whether it takes the form of the disastrous or the marvelous. Such individuals as Dr. Page and his daughter worked, it seems to me, to such an end. Ultimately, theirs was an act of faith: faith in themselves, faith in the potentialities of their own people, and despite their social status as Negroes, faith in the potentialities of the democratic ideal. Coming so soon after the betrayal of the Reconstruction, theirs was a heroic effort. It is my good fortune that their heroism became my heritage, and thanks to Inman Page and Brown University, it is also now a part of the heritage of all Americans who would become conscious of who they are.

—From *The Carleton Miscellany,* Winter 1980;
address given September 20, 1979, at the
Ralph Ellison Festival at Brown University

An Extravagance of Laughter

In December 1983 the good news that Erskine Caldwell had reached his eightieth birthday reminded me that although I have had the pleasure of seeing him on and off for some twenty years, I have never been able to offer him an apology for an offense of which I was guilty back in the 1930s. Perhaps I failed because my offense took the form of laughter—or, to be more precise, of a particular quality and an *extravagance* of laughter; which, since it came at the expense of Caldwell's most famous work of comedy, may explain both my confusion and my reluctance. And since the work in question was *designed* and intended to evoke laughter, any account of why I should term my particular laughter "offensive" will require a bit of autobiographical exploration which may well enable me both to understand my failure to apologize and to clarify the role which that troublesome moment of laughter was to play in my emotional and intellectual development.

Charles Baudelaire observed that "the wise man never laughs but that he trembles." Therefore, for the moment let it suffice to say that being both far from wise and totally unaware of Baudelaire's warning, I not only laughed extravagantly but trembled even *as* I laughed; and thus I found myself utterly unprepared for the Caldwell-inspired wisdom which erupted from that incongruous juxtaposition of mirth and quaking. This is no excuse, however, because Aesop and Uncle Remus have taught us that comedy is a disguised form of philosophical instruction; and especially when it allows us to glimpse the animal instincts operating beneath the surface of our civilized affectations. For by allowing us to laugh at that which is normally *un*-laughable, comedy provides an otherwise unavailable clarification of vision that calms the clammy trembling which ensues whenever we pierce the veil of conventions that guard us from the basic absurdity of the human condition. During such moments the world of appearances is turned upside down, and in my case Caldwell's comedy plunged me quite unexpectedly into the deepest levels of a most American realm of the absurd while providing me with the magical wings with which to ascend back to a world which, for all his having knocked it quite out of kilter, I then found more rational. Caldwell had no way of knowing what I was experiencing, but even though I caused unforeseen trouble, he was a wise and skillful guide, and thus it is that I offer him both my apologies and, for reasons to be made clear a bit later, my heartfelt thanks.

It all began in 1936, a few weeks after my arrival in New York, when I was lucky enough to be invited by an old hero and new-found friend, Langston Hughes, to be his guest at what would be my introduction to Broadway theater. I was so delighted and grateful for the invitation that I failed to ask my host the title of the play, and it was not until we arrived at the theater that I learned that it would be Jack Kirkland's dramatization of Erskine Caldwell's famous novel *Tobacco Road.* No less successful than in its original form, the play was well on its way to a record-breaking seven-year run in the theater, and that alone was enough to increase my expectations. And so much so that I failed to note the irony of circumstance that would have as my introduction to New York theater a play with a Southern setting and characters that were based upon a type and class of whites whom I had spent the last three years trying to avoid. Had I been more alert, it might have occurred to me that somehow a group of white Alabama farm folk had learned of my presence in New York, thrown together a theatrical troupe, and flown north to haunt me. But being dazzled by the lights, the theatrical atmosphere, the babble of the playgoing crowd, it didn't. And yet that irony arose precisely from the mixture of motives—practical, educational, and romantic—that had brought me to the North in the first place.

Among these was my desire to enjoy a summer free of the South and its problems while meeting the challenge of being on my own for the first time in a great Northern city. Fresh out of Alabama, with my junior year at Tuskegee Institute behind me, I was also in New York seeking funds with which to complete my final year as a music major—a goal at which I was having less success than I had hoped. However, there had been compensations. For between working in the Harlem YMCA cafeteria as a substitute for vacationing waiters and countermen and searching for a more profitable job, I had used my free time exploring the city's many cultural possibilities, making new acquaintances, and enjoying the many forms of social freedom that were unavailable to me in Alabama. The very idea of being in New York was dreamlike, for like many young Negroes of the time, I thought of it as the freest of American cities and considered Harlem as the site and symbol of Afro-American progress and hope. Indeed, I was both young and bookish enough to think of Manhattan as my substitute for Paris and of Harlem as a place of Left Bank excitement. So now that I was there in its glamorous scene, I meant to make the most of its opportunities.

Yes, but I had discovered, much to my chagrin, that while I was physically out of the South, I was restrained—sometimes consciously, sometimes not—by certain internalized thou-shalt-nots that had structured my public conduct in Alabama. It was as though I had come to the Eden of American culture and found myself indecisive as to which of its fruits were free for my picking. Thus, for all my bright expectations, my explorations had taken on certain aspects of an unanticipated and amorphous rite of initiation in which the celebrant—if indeed one existed—remained mute and beyond my range of ear and vision. Therefore, I found myself forced to act as my own guide and instructor, and had to enact, touch-and-go, the archetypical American role of pioneer in what was our most sophisticated and densely populated city. And in the process I found myself being compelled, as it were, to improvise a makeshift map of the city's racially determined do's-and-don'ts and impose it upon the objective scene by dealing consciously with such complications of character and custom as might materialize in the course of my explorations.

I missed, in brief, a sense of certainty which the South imposed in the forms of signs and symbols that marked the dividing lines of racial segregation. This was an embarrassing discovery, so given what I assumed would be the shortness of my visit, I tried to deal with it and remained quite eager to take the risks necessary to achieve New York's promises. After certain disappointments, however, I had been going about it in the manner of one learning to walk again upon a recently mended leg that still felt strange without the protective restraint of a plaster cast now left happily behind. So there were moments when I reminded myself of the hero of the old Negro folktale who, after arriving mistakenly in heaven and being issued a pair of wings, was surprised to learn that there were certain earth-like restrictions which required people of his complexion to fly with one wing strapped to their sides. But, while surprised, the new arrival came to the philosophical conclusion that even in heaven, that place of unearthly perfection, there had to be rules and regulations. And since rules were usually intended to make one think, no less than to provide guidance, he decided to forgo complaint and get on with the task of mastering the challenge of one-wing flying. As a result, he soon became so proficient at the art that by the time he was cast out of heaven for violating its traffic regulations, he could declare (and so truthfully that not even Saint Peter could say him nay) that he was the most skillful one-winged flyer ever to have been grounded by heavenly decision.

So, following the example of my legendary ancestor, I determined to master my own equivalent of one-winged flying in such a manner as to do the least violence to myself or to such arcane rules of New York's racial arrangements as I might encounter. Which meant that I would have to mask myself and confront its mysteries with a combination of uncertainty and daring. Thus it was that by the time I stumbled onto *Tobacco Road,* I had been nibbling steadily at the "Big Apple"—which even in those days was the Harlemite's fond name for the city—and in the process had discovered more than an ambiguous worm or two. Nevertheless, it should be remembered that worms teach small earthly truths even as serpents teach theology.

Beyond the borders of Harlem's brier patch—which seemed familiar because of my racial and cultural identification with the majority of its people and the lingering spell that had been cast nationwide by the music, dance, and literature of the so-called Harlem Renaissance—I viewed

New Yorkers through the overlay of my Alabama experience. Contrasting the whites I encountered with those I had observed in the South, I weighed class against class and compared Southern styles with their Northern counterparts. I listened to diction and noted dress, and searched for attitudes in inflections, carriage, and manners. And in pursuing this aspect of my extracurricular education, I explored the landscape.

I crossed Manhattan back and forth from river to river and up, down, and around again, from Spuyten Duyvil Creek to the Battery, looking and listening and gadding about; rode streetcar and el, subway and bus; took a hint from Edna Millay and spent an evening riding back and forth on the Staten Island Ferry. For given my Oklahoma-Alabama perspective, even New York's forms of transportation were unexpected sources of education. From the elevated trains I saw my first penthouses with green trees growing atop tall buildings, caught remote glimpses of homes, businesses, and factories while moving above the teeming streets, and felt a sense of quiet tranquillity despite the bang and clatter. Yes, but the subways were something else again.

In fact, the subways were utterly confusing to my Southern-bred idea of good manners, and especially the absence of a certain gallantry that men were expected to extend toward women. Subway cars appeared to be underground arenas in which Northern social equality took the form of an endless shoving match in which the usual rules of etiquette were turned upside down—or so I concluded after watching a five-o'clock foot race in a crowded car.

The contest was between a huge white woman who carried an armful of bundles, and a small Negro man who lugged a large suitcase. At the time I was standing against the track-side door, and when the train stopped at a downtown station I saw the two come charging through the opening doors like race horses leaving the starting gate at Belmont. And as they spied and dashed for the single empty seat, the outcome appeared up for grabs, but it was the woman, thanks to a bustling, more ruthless stride (and more subway know-how) who won—though but by a hip and a hair. For just as they reached the seat she swung a well-padded hip and knocked the man off stride, thus causing him to lose his balance as she turned, slipped beneath his reeling body, and plopped into the seat. It was a maneuver which produced a startling effect—at least on me.

For as she banged into the seat it caused the man to spin and land smack-dab into her lap—in which massive and heaving center of gravity he froze, stared into her face nose-tip to nose, and then performed a springlike leap to his feet as from a red-hot stove. It was but the briefest conjunction, and then, as he reached down and fumbled for his suitcase, the woman began adjusting her bundles, and with an elegant toss of her head she looked up into his face with the most ladylike and triumphant of smiles.

I had no idea of what to expect next, but to her sign of good sportswomanship the man let out with an exasperated "Hell, you can have it, I don't want it!" A response which evoked a phrase from an old forgotten ditty to which my startled mind added the unstated line—"Sleeping in the bed with your hand right on it"—and shook me with visions of the train screeching to a stop and a race riot beginning . . .

But not at all. For while the defeated man pushed his way to another part of the car the crowd of passengers simply looked on and laughed. The interracial aspects of the incident with its evocation of the naughty lyric left me shaken, but I was learning something of the truth of what Henry James meant by the arduousness of being an American. And that went double for a Tuskegee student who was trying to adjust to the New York underground. I never knew what to expect, because there appeared to be no agreed-upon rules of conduct. Indeed, in the subways the operating slogan appeared to be "Every Man and Woman for Themselves." Or perhaps it was "Hurray for Me and Phoo-phoo on You!" But *whatever* its operating principle, whenever I rode the subway trains something I had never seen before seemed fated to happen.

As during a trip in another crowded car when I found myself standing beside a Negro man who stood just in front of a seat that was about to be vacated—when suddenly from on his other side a woman decided to challenge him for its possession. This time, however, it was the man who won. For in a flash the man folded his arms, dropped into the posture of a Cossack dancer, and was in the seat before the woman could make her move. Then, as she grabbed a handhold and glared down into his face, he restored something of my sense of reality by saying, "Madam, all you had to do was risk the slight possibility that I just *might* be a gentleman. Because if you had, I would have been *compelled* to step aside."

And then, opening a copy of *The Wall Street Journal,* he proceeded to read.

But for all their noise and tension, it was not the subways that most intrigued me. For although a pleasant way to explore the city, my rides in New York buses soon aroused questions about matters that I had hoped to leave behind. And yet the very fact that I encountered little on Northern buses that was distressing allowed me to face up to a problem which had puzzled me down South: the relationship between Southern buses and racial status. In the South you occupied the back of the bus, and nowhere *but* the back, or so help you God. So being in the North and encouraged by my anonymity, I experimented by riding all *over* New York buses, excluding only the driver's seat—front end, back end, right side, left side, sitting or standing as the route and flow of passengers demanded. *And,* since those were the glorious days of double-deckers, both enclosed and open, I even rode *top*side.

Thus having convinced myself that no questions of racial status would be raised by where I chose to ride, I asked myself whether a seat at the back of the bus wasn't actually more desirable than one at the front. For not only did it provide more leg room, it offered a more inclusive perspective on both the interior and exterior scenes. I found the answer obvious and quite amusing, but then, as though to raise to consciousness more serious questions that I had too long ignored, the buses forced a more troubling contradiction upon my attention. Now that I was no longer forced by law and compelled by custom to ride at the back and to surrender my seat to any white who demanded it, what was more desirable—the possibility of exercising what was routinely accepted in the North as an abstract, highly symbolic (even trivial) form of democratic freedom, or the creature comfort which was to be had by occupying a spot from which more of the passing scene could be observed? And in my own personal terms, what was more important —my own individual comfort, or the exercise of the democratic right to be squeezed and jostled by strangers? The highly questionable privilege of being touched by anonymous whites—not to mention reds, browns, blacks, and yellows—or the minor pleasure afforded by having a maximum of breathing space? Such questions were akin to that of whether you lived in a Negro neighborhood because you were forced to do so, or because you preferred living among those of your own background. Which was easy to answer, because having experienced life in mixed neighborhoods as a child, I preferred to live where people spoke my own version of the American language, and where misreadings of tone or gesture were less likely to ignite lethal conflict. Segregation laws aside, this was a matter of personal choice, for even though class and cultural differences existed among Negroes, it was far easier to deal with hostilities arising between yourself and your own people than with, say, Jeeter Lester or, more realistically, Lester Maddox. And that even though I would have found it far better to be Lestered by Jeeter than mattock-handled by Maddox, that most improbable governor of a state that I had often visited!

But my interrogation by the New York scene (for that is what it had become) was not to stop there, for once my mind got rolling on buses, it was difficult to stop and get off. So I became preoccupied with defining the difference between Northern and Southern buses. Of the two, New York buses were simpler, if only for being earthbound. They were merely a form of transportation, an inflated version of a taxicab or passenger car which one took to get from one locality to another. And as far as one's destination and motives were concerned they were neutral. But this was far from true of Southern buses. For when compared with its New York counterparts, even the most dilapidated of Southern buses seemed (from my New York perspective) to be a haunted form of transportation.

A Southern bus was a contraption contrived by laying the South's social pyramid on its side, knocking out a few strategic holes, and rendering it vehicular through the addition of engine, windows, and wheels. Thus converted, with the sharp apex of the pyramid blunted and equipped with fare box and steering gear, and its sprawling base curtailed severely and narrowly aligned (and arrayed with jim-crow signs), a ride in such a vehicle became, at least for Negroes, as unpredictable as a trip in a spaceship doomed to be caught in the time warp of history—that man-made "fourth dimension" which ever confounds our American grasp of "real," or *actual,* time or duration.

For blacks and whites alike, Southern buses were places of hallucination, but especially for Negroes. Because once inside, their journey ended even before the engine fired and the wheels got rolling. Then, as with a "painted ship upon a painted ocean," the engine chugged, the tires scuffed, and the scenery outside flashed and flickered, but they themselves remained, like Zeno's arrow, ever in the same old place. Thus the motorized mobility of the social pyramid did little to advance the Negroes' effort toward equality. Because although they were allowed to enter the section that had been—in its vertical configuration—its top, any semblance of upward mobility ended at the fare box—from whence, once their fares were deposited, they were sent, forthwith, straight to the rear, or horizontalized bottom. And along the way almost *anything* could happen, from push to shove, assaults on hats, heads, or aching corns, to unprovoked tongue-lashings from the driver or from any white passenger, drunk or sober, who took exception to their looks, attitude, or mere existence. Nor did the perils of this haunted, gauntletlike passage end at the back of the bus. For often it was so crowded that there was little breathing space, and since the segregated passengers were culturally as "Southern" as the whites, the newcomer might well encounter a few contentious Negroes who would join in the assault—if only because he appeared uneasy in his command of the life-preserving "cool" which protected not only the individual Negro but each member of the group in his defenseless, nonindividualized status. In brief, all were faceless nobodies caught up in an endless trip to nowhere—or so it seemed to me in my Northern sanctuary.

For even as the phantomized bus went lurching and fuming along its treadmill of a trajectory, the struggle within scuffled and raged in fitful retrograde. Thus, as it moved without moving, those trapped inside played out their roles like figures in dreams—with one group ever forcing the other to the backmost part, and the other ever watching and waiting as they bowed to force and clung to sanity. And indeed the time would come when such bus en-scened pantomime would erupt in a sound and fury of action that would engulf the South and change American society. And most surprising and yet most fittingly, it would begin when a single tired Negro woman refused to go on with what had now become an unbearable farce. Then would come fire and gunshot, cattle prods and attack dogs, but the enchantment would end, and at last the haunted bus would shift gears and move on to the road of reality and toward the future . . .

But of this I had no way of knowing at the time. I only knew that Southern bus rides had the power to haunt and confuse my New York passage. Moreover, they were raising the even more troublesome question of to what extent had I failed to grasp a certain degree of freedom that had always existed in my group's state of unfreedom? Of what had I neglected to avail myself through fear or lack of interest while sitting silently behind jim-crow signs? For after all, a broad freedom of expression within restrictions could be heard in jazz and seen in sports, and that freedom was made movingly manifest in religious worship. There was an Afro-American dimension in Southern culture, and the lives of many black Southerners possessed a certain verve and self-possessed fullness—so to what extent had I overlooked similiar opportunities for self-discovery while accepting a definition of possibility laid down by those who would deny me freedom?

Thus, while I enjoyed my summer, such New York-provoked questions made for a certain unease which I tried to ignore. Nevertheless, they made me aware that whatever its true shape turned out to be, Northern freedom could be grasped only by my running the risk of the unknown and by acting in the face of uncertainty. Which meant that I would have to keep moving into racially uncharted areas. Otherwise I would remain physically in Harlem and psychologically in Alabama—neither of which was acceptable. Harlem was "Harlem," a dream place of glamour and excitement—what with its music, its dance, its style. But it was all of this because it was a part of (and apart *from*) the larger city. Harlem, I came to feel, was the shining transcendence of a national negative, and it took its fullest meaning from that which it was not, and without which I would have regarded it as less interesting than, say, Kansas City, Missouri—or South Side Chicago. Harlem, whose ironic inhabitants described it a thousand times a day as being "nowhere," took much of its meaning from the larger metropolis; so I could only achieve the fullest measure of its attractions by experiencing that which it was not. Which meant, in the broadest sense, that I would have to use Harlem as a base and standard of measurement from which to pursue, in all its plenitude, that which was denied me in the South. In brief, if I were to grasp American freedom, I was compelled to continue my explorations of downtown Manhattan.

Yes, but as I say, my explorations of the city were rendered uncertain by the ongoing conflict between the past and the present as they existed within me: between the dream in my head and the murky, seek-and-find-it shiftings of the New York scene; between the confounding complexity of America's racial arrangements as they coincided and differed according to the customs, laws, and values fostered by both North and South. I still clung to the Southern Negro's conception of New York as the freest of American cities, but although now far removed from the geographical region where old-time things are defiantly not forgotten, I was learning that even here, where memories of the past were deliberately repressed, if not forgotten, the past itself continued to shape perceptions and attitudes. And it appeared that for some New Yorkers, I *myself* constituted a living symbol of that complexity of American experience which they had never known, and a disquieting reminder of their involvement in certain unsavory aspects of America's social reality that they preferred to ignore.

And yet, given my persistent questing, how could they? For I, who was an unwilling and not always conscious embodiment of that historical complexity, and a symbol of the Civil War's sacrificial bloodshed, kept showing up in areas of culture where few of my people were to be seen. Thus, in my dark singularity I often appeared to be perceived more as a symbol than as an individual, more as a threatening sign (a dark cloud no larger than a human hand, but somehow threatening) than as a disinterested seeker after culture. This made for problems because I had no way of anticipating the response to my presence.

Prior to stumbling onto *Tobacco Road*—at which I shall presently arrive—I had already encountered some of the complexity evoked by my probings. As the guest of a white female friend who reported musical events for a magazine, I had occupied a seat in the orchestra section of Carnegie Hall without inciting protest. But shortly thereafter I had been denied admission to a West Side cinema house that featured European movies. Then I had learned that while one midtown restaurant would make you welcome, in another (located in Greenwich Village, Harlem's twin symbol of Manhattan's freedom), the waiters would go through the polite motions of seating you but then fill your food with salt. And to make certain that you got the message, they would enact a rite of exorcism in which the glasses and crockery, now considered hopelessly contaminated by your touch, were enfolded in the tablecloth and smithereened in the fireplace.

Or again, upon arriving at a Central Park West apartment building to deliver a music manuscript for the Tuskegee composer William L. Dawson, you encountered a doorman with a European accent who was so rude that you were tempted to break his nose. Fortunately, you didn't, for after you refused to use the servant's elevator he rang up the tenant into whose hands alone you were instructed to make the delivery, Jacques Gordon of the Gordon String Quartet, who hurried down and invited you up to his apartment. Where, to your surprise and delight, he talked with you without condescension about his recordings, questioned you sympathetically about your musical background, and encouraged you in your ambitions to become a composer. So if you weren't always welcome to break bread in public places, an interest in the arts *could* break down social distance and allow for communication that was uninhibited by questions of race—or so it seemed.

As on a Madison Avenue bus when an enthusiastic, bright-eyed little old Jewish lady, fresh from an art exhibition with color catalogue in hand, would engage you in conversation and describe knowingly the styles and intentions of French painters of whom you'd never heard.

"Then you must go to galleries," she insisted.

"Stir yourself and go to museums," she demanded.

"This is one of the world's great centers of art, so learn about them! Why are you waiting? Enough already!" she exhorted.

And eventually, God bless her, I did.

But then, on another bus ride, a beautifully groomed and expensively dressed woman would become offended when you retrieved and attempted to return the section of a newspaper that she had dropped when preparing to depart, apparently mistaking what was intended as an act of politeness for a reprimand from a social inferior. So it appeared that in New York one had to choose the time, place, and person even when exercising one's Southern good manners.

On the other hand, it soon became clear that one could learn the subtleties of New York's racial manners only by being vulnerable and undiscriminating oneself; an attitude which the vast anonymity of the great metropolis encouraged. Here the claustrophobic provincialism which marked, say, Montgomery, Alabama, of that period, was absent, but one had to be on guard because reminders of the South could spring up from behind the most unlikely of façades.

Shopping for a work of T. S. Eliot's in a 59th Street bookstore, I struck up a conversation with a young City College student who turned out to share my literary interests, and in recounting an incident of minor embarrassment having to do with my misinterpretation of a poetic trope, I used the old cliché "And was my face red"—whereupon, between the utterance and the reality, the idea I intended to convey and my stereotype phrase, there fell the shadow of things I sought to forget.

"What do you mean by 'red,' he said, impaling me upon the points of his smirking stare, "what you *really* mean is 'ashes of roses'!"

And suddenly I was slapped into a conscious awareness of certain details of his presence that my eyes had registered but to which, in the context of our exchange, my brain had attached no special significance. Intent upon sharing his ideas of Eliot, I had seen only that which I wished to see, but now, out of the eyes of my past I saw that our differences of background and religion were imprinted upon his face no less indelibly than mine upon my own. And in my Southern-trained ear the echo of his trace of accent became amplified, the slight kink in his hair sprang into focus, and his nose evoked superimposed images of the Holy Land and Cyrano.

I didn't like it, but there it was—I had been hit in mid-flight; and so, brought down to earth, I joined in his laughter. But while he laughed in bright major chords I responded darkly in minor-sevenths and flatted-fifths, and I doubted that he was attuned to the deeper source of our inharmonic harmony. For how could he know that when a child in Oklahoma, I had played with members of his far-flung tribe and thus learned in friendly games of mutual insult the hoary formulae with which to make him squirm. But why bother? Out of some obscure need a stranger had chosen to define to his own advantage that which was at best a fleeting relationship. Perhaps because I had left an opening that was irresistible. Or perhaps he saw my interest in poetry as an invasion of his special turf, which had to be repelled with a reminder of my racial status. For what right had *I* to be interested in Eliot, even though the great poet had written of himself as having been "a small boy with a nigger drawl"?

Or was he implying that I was trying verbally to pass for white? But if so, wasn't that to confuse words with reality and a metaphor with the thing or condition it named? And didn't he realize that there might be as much of irony in one of his background embracing Eliot as he seemed to find in my doing so? And how take poetry seriously if he himself would limit the range of metaphor, that indispensable linguistic device for making unities of diversities?

That chance encounter left me a bit disenchanted, but also consciously aware of certain vague assumptions which I held concerning racial relations that I'd find in the North. I had hoped that in New York there would exist generally a type of understanding which obtained in the South between certain individual whites and Negroes. This was a type of Southern honor that did little to alter the general system of inequity, but it allowed individual whites to make exceptions in exerting the usual gestures of white supremacy. Such individuals refused to use racial epithets and tried, within the limitations of the system, to treat Negroes fairly. This was a saving grace and a balm to the aches and pains of the South's endless racial contention.

Thus I had assumed that in the North there would exist a general understanding between outsiders of whatever color or background, and that all would observe a truce or convention through which they would shun insults that focused on race, religion, or physical appearance; entities that were inherited and about which all were powerless to modify or change. (At that time I was unaware that there were whites who passed themselves off as being of other backgrounds.) And yet I realized that except for those rare Southern examples, there was no firm base for my expectations. For I knew that from the days of the minstrel shows to the musicals and movies then current, many non-Negro outsiders had reaped fame and fortune by assuming the sterotyped mask of blackness. I knew also that our forms of popular culture, from movies to comic strips, were a source of a national mythology in which Negroes were the chief scapegoats, and that the function of that mythology was to allow whites a more secure place (if only symbolically) in American society. Only years later would I learn that during periods of intense social unrest, even sensitive intellectuals who had themselves been victims of discrimination would find it irresistible to use their well-deserved elevation to the upper levels of their professions as platforms from which, in the name of the most abstract—and fashionable—of philosophical ideas, to reduce Negroes to stereotypes that were no less reductive and demeaning than those employed by the most ignorant and bigoted of white Southerners. Fortunately, that knowledge was still in the future, and so, doing unto another as I would have had him do unto me, I dismissed my chance acquaintance as an insecure individual, and not the representative of a group or general attitude. But he did serve as a warning that if I wished to communicate with New Yorkers, I must watch my metaphors, for here one man's cliché was another man's facile opportunity for victimage.

So I was learning that exploring New York was a journey without a map, Baedeker or Henry James, and that how one was received by the natives depended more upon how one presented oneself than upon any ironclad rule of exclusion. Here the portals to many places of interest were guarded by hired help, and if you approached with uncertain mien, you were likely to be turned away by anyone from doormen to waiters to ticket agents. However, if you acted as though you were in fact a New Yorker exercising a routine freedom, chances were that you'd be accepted. Which is to say that in many instances I found that my air and attitude could offset the inescapable fact of my color. For it seemed that in the hustle and bustle of that most theatrical of American cities, one was accepted on the basis of what one *appeared* to be. This involved risks to one's self-esteem, not to mention the discipline demanded by a constant state of wariness.

But W. B. Yeats had reminded us that "there is a relation between personal discipline and the theatrical sense [and that] if we cannot imagine ourselves as different from what we are and assume the second self, we cannot impose a discipline upon ourselves, though we may accept one from others." And he advised us that "active virtue, as distinct from the passive acceptance of a current code, is the wearing of a mask."

At the time I was unaware of Yeats's observation, but if I had been so fortunate, I would have applied it to my own situation by changing his "we" to "an Afro-American," his "what we are" to "what many whites assume an American Negro to be," and his "current code" to "prevailing racial attitudes." But with his contention that the assertion of a second self is to assume a mask, and that to do so is "the condition of an arduous full life," I would have agreed wholeheartedly. For in effect, I was attempting to act out a self-elected role and to improvise into being a "second self" that I strongly felt but vaguely visualized. And although I was finding life far from full, I was certainly finding it arduous.

For in Yeats's sense, "masking" is more than the adoption of a disguise. Rather, it is a playing upon possibility, a strategy through which the individual projects a self-elected identity and make of himself a "work of art." And in my case it was a means of discovering the dimensions and cost of Northern freedom. In his critical biography *Yeats: The Man & the Masks,* Richard Ellman notes that the great Irish poet was writing of himself, but his theory applies, nevertheless, to the problematic nature of American identity. For while all human societies are "dramatic"—at least to the extent that, as Kenneth Burke points out, the members of all societies "enact roles . . . change roles . . . participate . . . [and] develop modes of social appeal" —the semi-open structure of American society, with its many opportunities for individual self-transformation, intensifies the dramatic element by increasing the possibilities for both cooperation and conflict. It is a swiftly changing society in which traditional values are ever under attack, even as they are exploited by individuals and group alike. And with its upward—yes, and *downward*—mobility and its great geographical space, masking (which includes speech, and costume as well as pose and posture) serves the individual as a means for projecting that aspect of his social self which seems useful in a given situation.

Such a state of affairs encourages hope and confidence in

those who are not assigned and restricted to predesignated roles in the hierarchal drama of American society. Melville has great fun with the comic aspects of this situation in *The Confidence Man.* To an extent, and for an endless variety of motives—benign or malignant, competitive or cooperative, creative and/or destructive—the "American" is a self-confident man or woman who is engaged in projecting a second self and dealing with the second selves of others. The American creed of democratic equality encourages the belief in a second chance that is to be achieved by being born again—and not simply in the afterlife, but here and now, on earth. Change your name and increase your chances. Create by an act of immaculate self-conception an autobiography like that which transformed James Gatz into "Jay Gatsby." Alter the shape of your nose, tint of skin, or texture of hair. Change your sexual identity by dress or by surgery. "Get thee to boutique and barbershop and *Unisex* thyself," the ads exhort us—for anything is possible in pursuit of the second self. It sounds fantastic, but the second self's hope for a second chance has now been extended even beyond the limits of physical death, thanks to the ability of medical science to transplant hearts, lungs, and kidneys. Are you dissatisfied with your inherited self? Your social status? Then have a change of heart and associate with those of a different kidney!

> College boy, thy courage muster,
> Shave off that Fuzzy
> Cookie duster—
> Use Burma Shave!

So, to enjoy the wonders of New York, I assumed a mask which I conceived as that of a "New Yorker," and decided to leave it to those whites who might object to seek out the questioning Tuskegeian who was hidden behind the mask. But a famous poet had invited me to see *Tobacco Road,* and suddenly, there in the darkness of a Broadway theater, I was snatched back to rural Alabama, and before I realized what was happening, I had blown my cover.

Nor was it that the likes of Jeeter Lester and his family were new to me. As a Tuskegee student I had often seen them in Macon County, Alabama; but in that setting their capacity for racial violence would have been far more overwhelming than their comical wrong-headedness. Indeed, in look, gesture, and deed they had crowded me so continuously that I had been tempted to armor myself against their threat by denying them *their* humanity as they sought to deny me mine. And so in my mind I assigned them to a limbo beneath the threshold of basic humanity.

Which was one of the Southern Negroes' strategies for dealing with poor whites, and an attitude given expression in the child's jingle:

> My name is Ran,
> I work in the sand, but
> I'd rather be a *nigger*
> Than a poor white man . . .

But while such boasting brags—and there were others (*These white folks think they so fine/But their raggedy drawers/ Stink just like mine* is another)—provided a release of steam, they were not only childish but ultimately frustrating. For if such sentiments were addressed directly, their intended targets could prove dangerous. Thus the necessity for keeping one's negative opinions of whites within one's own group became a life-preserving discipline. One countered racial provocation by cloaking one's feelings in that psychologically inadequate equivalent of a plaster cast—or bulletproof vest—known as "cool." I had read Hemingway's definition, but for Negroes, "grace under pressure" was far less a gauge of courage than of good common sense. The provocative words of whites were intended to goad one *beyond* words and into the area of physical violence. But while sticks and stones broke bones, mere words could be dismissed by considering their source and keeping a cool eye on the odds arrayed against one. So when racial epithets flew, we reminded ourselves that our mission was not that of proving our courage to any mouthy white who sought to provoke us, but to stay alive and pursue our education. Coolness helped to keep our values warm, and racial hostility stoked our fires of inspiration. But even for students protected by a famous campus, this was an arduous discipline, and one which obviated any superstitious overevaluation of whiteness. Nevertheless, I tried, as I say, to avoid the class of whites from which Erskine Caldwell drew the characters of *Tobacco Road.*

For during the summer of 1933, while hoboing to Tuskegee, I had been hustled off a freight train by railroad detectives in the rail yards of Decatur, Alabama. This was at a time when the town and the surrounding countrysides were undergoing a siege of lynch-fever stirred up by the famous trial in which the Scottsboro boys were charged with the rape of two white girls on a freight train. I escaped unharmed, but the incident returned to mind whenever I went traveling. Therefore, I gave Jeeter Lester types a wide berth but found it impossible to avoid them entirely—because many were law-enforcement officers who served on the highway patrols with a violent zeal like that which Negro slave narratives ascribed to the "paterollers" who had guarded the roads during slavery. (As I say, Southern buses were haunted, and so, in a sense, were Southern roads and highways.) And that was especially true of a section of the route between Tuskegee and Columbus,

Georgia. I traveled it frequently, both as a member of a jazz orchestra and when on pleasure trips to Columbus. And it was on such travels that I was apt to relive my Decatur experience.

By a fateful circumstance of geography the forty-mile route passed through Phenix City, Alabama, then a brawling speed-trap of a town through which it was impossible to drive either slow enough or fast enough to satisfy the demands of its traffic policemen. No one, black or white, escaped their scrutiny, but since Tuskegee students were regarded as on their way to becoming "uppity educated nigras," we were especially vulnerable. The police lay in wait for us, clocked our speed by a standard known only to themselves, and used any excuse to delay and harass us. Usually they limited themselves to fines and verbal abuse, but I was told that the year before I arrived the police had committed an act that had caused great indignation on campus and become the inspiration of much bull-session yarn-spinning.

On that occasion, I was told, two Phenix City policemen had stopped a carload of Tuskegee students and learned during the course of routine questioning that one of the group, a very black-skinned young man, bore the surname of "Whyte"—and then, as one of my informants said, "It was shame on him!"

For when Whyte uttered his name the cops stared, exchanged looks of mock disbelief, and became red-faced with manic inspiration.

"Damn, boy," one of them said, "y'all been drinking?"

"No, sir," Whyte said.

"Well now, I don't know about that," the cop said, " 'cause you sho sound drunk to *me.*"

"No, sir," Whyte said. "Because I don't drink."

"You sho?"

"Yes, sir!"

So then the cop turns to his buddy and says, "What you think, Lonzo? Is he drunk, or am I mistaken?"

"Well now, if you want my opinion," the other cop said, "he's either drunk or something very serious is wrong with him. Yes, suh, something *seerious* is wrong with this boy."

"And why is that, Lonzo," the first cop said.

" 'Cause it stands to reason that there's no way in the *world* for a nigra as black as that to pretend that his name is 'White.' Not unless he's blind-staggers drunk or else plum out of his nappy-headed cotton-pickin' mind!"

"That's *my* exact opinion," the first cop said. "But anyway, lets us give 'im another chance. So now once agin, boy—what is your last name?"

"Officer, it's Whyte," Whyte said. "That's the truth and I'll swear to it."

So that's when the other cop, ol' Lonzo, *he* takes over. He frowns at Whyte and shakes his head like he's dealing with a *very* sad case. And naturally, he's a big potbellied mother who chews Brown Mule tobacco.

"Damn, boy," he says (in what proved to be a long-range prediction of then unimaginable things to come), "if we let you git away with a damn lie like that, next thing we know that ol' Ramblin' Wreck over at Georgia Tech'll have a goddamn nigra *engineer!* Now, you think about that and let's have that name agin!"

"But, Officer," Whyte said, "Whyte's the only last name I have."

And then, gentlemen, my informant, a sergeant in the ROTC and student of veterinary medicine, said, "the battle was *on*!" He then described how with simulated indignation the policemen forced Whyte to pronounce his name again and again while insisting that they simply couldn't believe that such a gross misnaming was possible—especially in the South—and gave a detailed account of the policemen's reactions.

"Man," he said, "they went after Whyte like he had insulted their mammas! And when he still wouldn't deny his name, they came down on him like he was responsible for all the fuckup [meaning the genetic untidiness and confusion of black and white nomenclature] of Southern history!"

"So then, man," another informant broke in, "those crackers got so damn disgusted with ol' Whyte that every time he said his name, the ignorant bastards tried to dot where they thought an 'i' should have been by pounding his head with their blackjacks. They did everything but shoot that cat!"

"That's right, cousin," someone else said, "they made him whisper his name and they made him shout it. They made him write it down on a pad and then they made him spell it out—and I mean out *loud!* And when he spelled it with a 'y' instead of an 'i' they swore he was lying and trying to be smart, and really went up side his head!"

"Yeah, man," my original informant said, "and when Whyte still wouldn't change his statement, they made him give the names of his mother and father, his granddaddys and grandmammas on both sides and their origins in slavery, present whereabouts, police records, and occupations—"

"That's right, cousin, and since ol' Whyte came from a very, *very* large family and the cops were putting all that pressure on him, the poor cat sounded like a country preacher scatting out the 'begats' from the Book of Genesis —Damn!"

And then it was back to Whyte's offensive surname, and the head-whipping sounded, in the words of another informant—a music major and notorious prevaricator—"like somebody beating out the *Anvil Chorus* on a coconut!"

"Yeah, cousin, but what really made the bastards mad was that ol' Whyte wouldn't let some crackers beat him out of his name!"

"Oh, yes, and you have to give it to him. That Whyte was a damn good man!"

Finally, tired of the hazing and defeated in their effort to make Whyte deny his heritage, the cops knocked him senseless and ordered his friends to place him in the car and get out of town . . .

Although obviously exaggerated in the telling, it was a nasty incident. However, my point is not its violence, but the contradiction between its ineffectiveness as intimidation while serving as a theme for a tall-tale improvisation. Thus was violence transcended with cruel but homeopathic laughter, and racial cruelty transformed by a traditional form of folk art. It did nothing to change the Phenix City police, and probably wouldn't have even if they heard the recitation. They continued to make life so uncertain that each time we reached Columbus and returned safely to Tuskegee, it was as though we'd passed through fire and emerged, like the mythical phoenix bird (after which, presumably, the town was named), from the flames. Still we continued to risk the danger, for such was our eagerness for the social life of Columbus—the pleasure of parties, dances, and picnics in the company of pretty girls—that we continued to run the gauntlet.

But it didn't cancel out the unpleasantness or humiliation. Thus, back on campus we were compelled to buffer the pain and negate the humiliation by making grotesque comedy out of the extremes to which whites would go to keep us in what they considered to be our "place." Once safe at Tuskegee, we'd become fairly hysterical as we recounted our adventures and laughed as much at ourselves as at the cops. We mocked their modes of speech and styles of intimidation, and teased one another as we parodied our various modes of feigning fear when telling them who we were and where we were headed. It was a wild, he-man, schoolboy silliness but the only way we knew for dealing with the inescapable conjunction of laughter and pain. My problem was that I couldn't completely dismiss such experiences with laughter. I brooded and tried to make sense of it beyond that provided by our ancestral wisdom. That a head with a few knots on it was preferable to a heart with bullets through it was obviously true. And if the philosopher's observation that absolute power corrupts absolutely was also true, then an absolute power based on mere whiteness made for a deification of madness. Depending on the circumstance, whiteness might well be a sign of evil, of a "motiveless malignancy" which was to be avoided as strange dogs in rabid weather.

But you were surrounded by whiteness, and it was far from secure in its power. It thrived on violence and sought endlessly for victims, and in its hunger to enforce racial discrimination, it was most indiscriminating as to its victims. It didn't care whether its victims were guilty or innocent, for guilt lay not in individual acts of wrong-doing but in non-whiteness, in Negro-ness. Whiteness was a form of manifest destiny which designated Negroes as its territory and challenge. Whiteness struck at signs, at coloration, hair texture, and speech idiom, and thus denied you individuality. How then avoid it, when history and geography brought it ever in juxtaposition with blackness? How escape it when it asserted itself in law, in the layout of towns, the inflections of voices, the nuances of manners, the quality of mercy, justice, and charity? When it raged at interracial sex, but then violated its own values in the manner of Senator Bilbo (the name means "shackle"), who was said to find sexual satisfaction only with Negro prostitutes? How escape it when it violated its own most sacred principles, both in spirit and in law, while converting the principles of democracy by which we sought to live into their opposites?

Considered soberly and without the consolation of laughter, it was mad, surreal, and further complicated by the fact that not all whites abhorred Negroes. The evil expressed itself most virulently in the mass and appeared to be regional, a condition of place, of climate, since most whites who supported the school were Northerners who appeared for a few days in spring and then departed. And since not even all white Southerners were hostile, you had ever to make fine distinctions between individuals just as you had to distinguish between the scenes and circumstances in which you encountered them. Your safety demanded a careful attention as to detail and mood of social scene, because you had to avoid even friendly whites when they were in the company of their fellows. Because it was in crowds that the hate, fear, and blood-madness took over. And when it did it could transform otherwise friendly whites into mindless members of mobs. Most of all, you must avoid them when women of their group were present. For when a Negro male came into view, the homeliest white woman became a goddess, a cult figure deified in the mystique of whiteness, a being from whom a shout or cry or expression of hand or eye could unleash a rage for human sacrifice. And when the ignorant, torch-bearing armies assembled by night, black men burned in the fire of white men's passions.

If all of this seems long ago and far away, it is worth remembering that the past, as William Faulkner warned, is never past. Nor are its social and political consequences guaranteed to be limited to a single geographical area. The past emerges no less in the themes and techniques of art than in the contentions of politics, and since art (and especially the art of the Depression period) is apt to be influenced by politics, it is necessary at this point to take a backward glance at my Tuskegee student's perception, admittedly immature and subjective, of Southern society as it influenced my reaction to *Tobacco Road.*

In the South of that day the bottom rung of the social ladder was reserved for that class of whites who were looked down upon as "poor white trash," and the area immediately beneath them and below the threshold of upward social mobility was assigned to Negroes, whether educated or ignorant, prosperous or poor. But although they were barely below the poor whites in economic status (and were sometimes better off), it was the Negroes who were designated the South's untouchable caste. As such they were perceived as barely controllable creatures of untamed instincts and a group against whom all whites were obligated to join in the effort required for keeping them within their assigned place. This mindless but widely held perception was given doctrinal credibility through oppressive laws and an endless rhetorical reiteration of anti-Negro stereotypes. Negroes were seen as ignorant, cowardly, thieving, lying, hypocritical and superstitious in their religious beliefs and practices, morally loose, drunken, filthy of personal habit, sexually animalistic, rude, crude, and disgusting in their public conduct, and aesthetically just plain unpleasant. And if a few were not, it was due to the presence of "white" blood, a violation of the Southern racial code which rendered mixed-bloods especially dangerous and repugnant.

In brief, Negroes were considered guilty of all the seven deadly sins except the sin of pride, and were seen as a sometimes comic but nevertheless threatening negative to the whites' idealized image of themselves. Most Negroes were characterized—in the jargon of sociology—by a "high visibility" of pigmentation which made the group easily distinguishable from other citizens and therefore easy to keep in line and politically powerless. That powerlessness was justified and reinforced by the stereotypes, which denied blacks individuality and allowed any Negro to be interchangeable with any other. Thus, as far as many whites were concerned, not only were blacks faceless, but that facelessness made the idea of mistaken identity meaningless, and the democratic assumption that Negro citizens should share the individual's recognized responsibility for the welfare of society was regarded as subversive.

In this denial of personality (sponsored by both law and custom) anti-Negro stereotypes served as an efficient and easily manipulated instrument of governance. Moreover, they prepared Negroes for the role of sacrificial scapegoat in the ritual drama of Southern society, and helped bind the poor whites to the middle and upper classes with whom they shared ethnic identity. Being uncomfortably close to the Negroes in economic status, the poor whites clung to the stereotypes as to a life raft in turbulent waters, and politicians were able to use their fear and antipathy toward blacks as a sure-fire source of power. Because not only were the stability of social order and the health of business seen as depending upon white dominance, but the sanctity of the *moral* order as well. For whether denied or admitted, in this area religion was in the service of politics.

Thus, by pitting the interests of the poor whites against those of the Negroes, Southern congressmen countered the South's Civil War defeat by using its carefully nurtured racial conflict as a means for amassing great political power in Washington. Being representatives of what were, in effect, one-party states, enabled them to advance to the chairmanship of powerful governmental committees, and through the political horse-trading which keeps the national government functioning, that power was used to foil the progress of Negroes in areas far from the geopolitical center of white supremacy. Here, however, it should be noted that Negroes owe much of their progress since the Second World War to Presidents who were of Southern background and heritage. People change, but as Faulkner has pointed out, "was" is never "was," it is "now," and in the South a concern with preserving the "wasness" of slavocracy was an obsession which found facile expression in word and in deed. Their memories of the War Between the States, of Reconstruction, and the difficult times that followed the Hayes-Tilden Compromise had long been mythologized both as a means for keeping Negroes powerless and for ensuring the loyalty of poor whites in keeping them so. Thus it is ironic that even though the condition of blacks became a national standard by which many whites, both North and South, measured their social advancement, Negroes themselves remained at the bottom of society and the most anti-Negro of whites remained with them. It was Booker T. Washington who had warned that it is impossible to keep another man in a ditch without remaining with him, but unfortunately, that advice came from a powerful Southern leader who was also an ex-slave.

More and more, through depression and war, America lived up to its claim of being the land of opportunity whose rewards were available to the individual through the assertion of a second self; but for many poor and unambitious Southern whites the challenge of such an assertion was far less inviting than clinging to the conviction that they by the mere fact of race, color, and tradition alone were superior to the black masses below them. And yet, in their own way, they were proud idealists to whom the South's racial arrangement was sacred beyond most benefits made possible by social change. Therefore, they continued to wrestle with the stereotype of Negro inferiority much as Brer Rabbit kept clinging to Tar Baby's stickiness. And they were so eager to maintain their grip on the status quo and to ignore its costs and contradictions that they willingly used anything, including physical violence, to do so. For in rationalizing their condition, they required victims, real or symbolic, and in the daily rituals which gave support to their cherished myth of white supremacy, anti-Negro stereotypes and epithets served as symbolic substitutes for that primitive blood-rite of human sacrifice to which they resorted in times of racial tension—but which, for a complexity of reasons, political, economic, and humane, were rejected by their more responsible leaders. So it was fortunate, both for Afro-Americans and for the nation as a whole, that the Southern rituals of race were usually confined to the realm of the symbolic. Anti-Negro stereotypes were the currency through which the myth of white supremacy was kept alive, while the awe-inspiring enactment of the myth took the form of a rite in which a human victim was sacrificed. It then became a ritual drama that was usually enacted in a preselected scene (such as a clearing in the woods or in the courthouse square) in an atmosphere of high excitement and led by a masked celebrant dressed in a garish costume who manipulated the numinous objects (lynch ropes, the American flag, shotgun, gasoline, and whiskey jugs) associated with the rite as he inspired and instructed the actors in their gory task. This was the anthropological meaning of lynching, a blood-rite that ended in the death of a scapegoat whose obliteration was seen as necessary to the restoration of social order. Thus it served to affirm white goals and was enacted to terrorize Negroes.

Normally, the individual dies his own death, but because lynch mobs are driven by a passionate need to destroy the distinction between the actual and the symbolic, its victim is forced to undergo death for all his group. Nor is he sacrificed to ensure its fertility or save its soul, but to fill its members with an unreasoning fear of whiteness.

For the lynch mob, blackness is a sign of satanic evil

given human form. It is the dark consubstantial shadow which symbolizes all that its opponents reject in social change and in democracy. And thus it does not matter if its sacrificial victim be guilty or innocent, because the lynch mob's object is to propitiate its insatiable god of whiteness, that myth-figure worshipped as the true source of all things bright and beautiful, by destroying the human attributes of its god's antagonist which they perceive as the power of blackness. In action, racial discrimination is as nondiscriminating as a car bomb detonated in a crowded public square—because both car bomb and lynch rope are savagely efficient ways of destroying distinctions between the members of a hated group while rendering quite meaningless any moral questioning that might arise regarding the method used. For the ultimate goal of lynchers is that of achieving ritual purification through destroying the lynchers' identification with the basic *humanity* of their victims. Hence their deafness to cries of pain, their stoniness before the sight and stench of burning flesh, their exhilarated and grotesque self-righteousness. And hence our horror at the idea of supposedly civilized men destroying—and in the name of their ideal conception of the human—an aspect of their own humanity. Yes, but for the group thus victimized, such sacrifices are the source of emotions that move far beyond the tragic conception of pity and terror and down into the abysmal levels of conflict and folly from which arise our famous American humor. Brother, the blackness of *Afro-American* "black humor" is not black, it is tragically human and finds its source and object in the notion of "whiteness" . . .

But let me not overstate beyond the point necessary for conveying an idea of my state of mind prior to my unanticipated stumble onto *Tobacco Road.* The threat, real or imagined, of being the subject of such victimization was offset by that hopeful attitude that is typical of youth and necessary for dealing with life everywhere. So while racial danger was always with me, I lived with it as with threats of natural disaster or acts of God. And just as Henry James felt it prudent to warn Americans against a "superstitious evaluation of Europe," Negro folklore with its array of survival strategies warned me against an overevaluation of white pretensions. And despite their dominance and low opinion of Negro intelligence, whites suspected the presence of profound reservations even when Negroes were far less assertive than they are today. This made for a constant struggle over the nature of reality, in which each group probed and sparred as they tried to determine the other's true motives and opinions. A poignant instance of such struggle appears in Faulkner's *The Sound and the Fury* when Quentin Compson gives Deacon, a raffish Negro mythomaniac who does odd jobs around Harvard, an important letter to be delivered to Quentin's roommate the following afternoon. But when Deacon notes that the envelope is sealed, he suspects that he is being sent on a fool's errand such as whites delighted in sending Negroes down South. This causes him to drop his Northern mask for that of an old inarticulate "darkey," a pose which reminds Quentin of a Negro retainer whom he'd known as a child. Deacon then asks if a joke is being played on him; which Quentin denies. But then, appealing for that flattering reassurance that Southern whites were accustomed to exacting from Negroes, he asks Deacon if any Southerner had ever played a joke on him. Deacon's reply, as was often true of such exchanges, is ambiguous.

"You're right," he says, "they're fine folks. But you cant live with them."

Then, looking through Deacon into his own hopeless despair, Quentin asks, "Did you ever try?"

But the answer is not forthcoming. For in a flash the transplanted black Southerner had retired behind one of the many trickster's masks which his second self had assumed upon coming north and agrees briskly to deliver the letter. Ironically, however, there *is* a fool's errand involved, but it isn't Deacon's. For the letter conveys Quentin's intention to drown himself. Thus Deacon, who has rejected the role assigned him by his native South, ends up playing not the traditional black fool but, all unknowingly, the death-messenger for a pathetic Southern aristocrat who is driven to self-destruction by the same prideful confusion of values from which, as Southerners, both suffered. Having tried to live in the South, both had come north dragging the past behind them; but while Deacon used his Southern craftiness to play upon life's possibilities, the past-haunted Quentin destroyed himself because he was unable to reconcile the mythical South he loved with that which had sent Deacon packing.

As Deacon said, many white Southerners were "fine folks," and that was the problem. Whites both hostile and friendly were part of my college scene, and thus a good part of my extracurricular education consisted in learning to live with them while retaining my self-esteem. Negro folklore taught the preservation of one's humanity by masking one's motives and emotions, just as it prepared one to be unsurprised at anything that whites might do, because a concern with race could negate all human bonds, including those of shared blood and experience.

So I tried to observe such ancestral wisdom as I awaited the day when I could leave the South. The catch here was that even the roads that led *away* from the South were also haunted; a circumstance which I should have learned, but did not, from numerous lyrics that were sung to the blues. And so, full of great expectations, I went north. And where uneducated Deacon assumed the mask of a former Harvard divinity student, I took on that of a sophisticated New Yorker.

* * *

In *Tobacco Road,* Erskine Caldwell appears to have taken a carefully screened assemblage of anti-Negro stereotypes and turned them against the very class in which they found their most fervent proponents—and what he did with them was most outrageous. Indeed, he turned things around in such a manner that it was as though Whyte, the Tuskegee victim of the Phenix City hazing, had read Mark Twain, George Washington Harris, Rabelais, Groucho Marx, and Voltaire, learned to write, and then, passing for "white" in order to achieve a more intimate knowledge of his characters, had proceeded to embody the most outrageous stereotypes in the Jeeter Lester family, in-laws, and friends. (Caldwell, I hasten to add, is a Georgia-born Anglo-Saxon.)

Nevertheless, Caldwell presents Jeeter Lester as an ignorant, impoverished, Depression-ruined poor white who urges Ellie May, his sixteen-year-old younger daughter, to seduce her older sister's husband so that he, Lester, may steal the equally impoverished young man's only food, a bag of turnips. The father of other mature children who now live in the city, he is a slothful farmer whose run-down farm is in such neglect that even the rats have abondoned the corncrib, and a criminally negligent son whose aged mother must forage for food in the woods, where, by the play's end, she dies alone and neglected. And yet Caldwell keeps Jeeter within the range of the human by having him be so utterly himself. He makes him a poor-white version of the "great sinner" on the order of Dostoevsky's elder Karamazov, and with a similar vitality and willfulness. He is a lecher who has fathered children by his neighbor's wife, and has incestuous inclinations toward one of his married daughters. But it is his stubborn refusal to bow before the economic and ecological developments that have rendered his type of farming no longer possible which gives the play its movement. Jeeter is a symbol of human willfulness reduced to its illogical essence.

Ada, Mrs. Lester, is an ineffectual wife and mother who has no control over either her husband or their children. Half starved and worn-out from childbearing, she exerts what physical and moral strength she has in trying to save Pearl, her pride and joy through a casual affair with a stranger, from the decay of Tobacco Road.

Pearl, whom Jeeter married off at the age of twelve, is the wife of Lov, a struggling young workman with whom she refuses either to sleep or talk—a situation utterly baffling for Lov, and annoying to Jeeter because it has become a subject for local Negro laughter.

Ellie May, the younger daughter, is harelipped, and so helplessly frustrated sexually that Jeeter tries to persuade Lov to exchange her for Pearl and take her away from Tobacco Road before, as he says, the Negroes get her. But if in Ellie May the Lester sex drive has gotten quite out of hand, in her brother Dude it is unawakened.

Dude, the adolescent son (who opens the play with a mindless bouncing of a ball against the house), is sadistic, disdainful of parental authority, and utterly disrespectful of life and death. And if Jeeter is a comic embodiment of selfish wrong-headedness, Dude (who takes more than his share of Jeeter's stolen turnips by physical force), is the embodiment of his father's character gone to violence. He is also the agent of his mother's death.

In brief, the Lester family is as seedy as the house in which they live. They have plunged through the fragile floor of civilized humanity, and even the religion which had once given a semblance of order to their lives had become as superstitious as that which the stereotypes attribute to Negroes.

That superstition is exploited by Sister Bessie Rice, a dowdy itinerant preacher of no known denomination who sees sin in even the most innocent of human actions and uses prayer as a magical incantation through which to manipulate her listener's residue of religious belief to her own advantage. She is a confidence woman who promises for small contributions to cure all ills through the magic of prayer.

Homely and gregarious in manner, Sister Bessie is a widow in search of a mate, both as husband and as a preaching partner with whom she can be more efficient in spreading her version of religion. Her unlikely choice toward this goal is teen-age Dude. But while Jeeter is quite agreeable to such a union of April and December, Dude is uninterested. Until, that is, Sister Bessie promises to use the money left by her deceased husband to purchase a new automobile. This does the trick. With Dude in tow, Sister Bessie buys first a marriage license and then the car; whereupon they speed back to the Lester farm. There Sister Bessie loses no time in performing her own marriage ceremony. And this accomplished, she rushes Dude to their wedding chamber—outside of which Jeeter stands on a chair in an effort to watch her initiate Dude into the sexual mysteries of wedlock.

As it turns out, however, Dude is less interested in connubial pleasure than in driving the new car—which, blowing its horn idiotically and speeding, he does, so recklessly that he runs into a loaded wagon and wrecks the car. Later he backs the car over his mother and kills her. Thus, not even the wedding of modern technology with sex and religion can restore Tobacco Road to a state of fertility. The sex instinct remained out of control, religious values corrupted, the laws guiding the relations between parents and children destroyed, and the words and rituals that once imposed religious and political ideals upon human conduct were used to justify greed, incest, sloth, and theft. In brief, the economic Depression, abetted by Jeeter's sloth and wrong-headedness, has deprived the family not only of its livelihood but denuded them of civilized humanity. Ultimately it was Ada's efforts to save Pearl from further humiliation and Jeeter's dogged will to survive the imbalance of nature and the bank's foreclosure on his farm that redeemed the family from a total fall into bestiality.

And yet, Caldwell's handling of such material does not produce a response of disgust and hopelessness in the audience. Instead it is swept by a wave of cathartic laughter which leaves it optimistic. Perhaps, as it has been noted in Cleanth Brooks, R.W.B. Lewis, and Robert Penn Warren's *American Literature: The Makers and the Making,* the Lesters' "lack of any burden of guilt and their ability to dispense with most of the contrivances of civilization gave a sense of release to a great many people."

I would add that during the Depression days of the play's great success, there was such great need for relief, both economic and spiritual, that the grotesque nature of its comedy was fully justified. Perhaps its viewers laughed, and then in retrospect grasped the interplay of social and economic forces upon which the play is focused, and trembled. Which, given Caldwell's anger over the despoilation of the South, must have been his intention.

According to Kenneth Burke, "Comedy should enable us to be observers of ourselves while acting. Its ultimate end would not be passiveness but maximum consciousness. [It should allow] one to 'transcend' himself by noting his own foibles . . . [and should] provide a rationale for locating the irrational and the non-rational."

To follow the action of a comedy is to react through its actors, and to identify either with them or with the values with which they struggle. For as David Daziel Duncan has written, "the difference between symbolic and social drama is the difference between imaginary and real obstacles, but to produce effects on audiences, symbolic drama must reflect the real obstacles of social drama. Conflict must be resolved in the symbolic realm by the expression of attitudes which make conformity possible. All such expression, like prayer, is an exhortation to the self and to others. It is a preparation for social action, an investment of the self with confidence and strength." Duncan is speaking of the drama of everyday life in which all successful stage plays are rooted, and when we consider the popularity of *Tobacco Road,* it suggests that during the Great Depression it was most successful in providing its viewers with a rationale for locating the irrational both in themselves and in their society.

The greater the stress within society the stronger the comic antidote required. And in this instance the stress imposed by the extreme dislocations of American society was so strong and chaotic that it called for a comedy of the grotesque. Jeeter Lester, the poor white as fool, was made to act the clown in order to save his audience's sanity. Here it is instructive to use the Southern Negroes' handling of stress for comparison. For since such stress was an enforced norm of their lives, Negroes struggled with the role assigned them for the same ends that Shakespeare juxtaposed the Fool with Lear—which was to maintain a measure of common sense before the extreme assertions of Lear's kingly pride. In the Lear-like drama of white supremacy Negroes were designated both clowns and fools, but they "fooled" by way of maintaining their own sense of rational order, no matter how they were perceived by whites. For it was far better to be looked down upon as "niggers" than to lose themselves in a world rendered surreal through an excess of racial pride. Their challenge was to endure while imposing their claims upon America's conscience and consciousness, just as they had imposed their style upon its culture. Forced to be wary observers, they recognized that American life is of a whole, and that what happens to blacks will accrue eventually, one way or another, to the nation as a whole. This is their dark-visioned version of the broader "American Joke." Like Faulkner, Caldwell appears to have recognized its existence, for in responding to the imbalance which was shaking American social hierarchy from its apex to its base, he placed the yokelike anti-Negro stereotypes upon the necks of whites, and thus his audience reacted with a shock of recognition. Caldwell was answering a deeply felt need, and it is interesting that it was during the period of *Tobacco Road's* record-breaking run that the Museum of Modern Art's presentation of its famous exhibit of Dadaist art was widely successful.

For me the shock of Caldwell's art began when Ellie May and Lov were swept up by a forbidden sexual attraction so strong that, uttering sounds of animal passion, they went floundering and skittering back-to-back across the stage in the startling action which father Jeeter, that randy Adam in an Eden gone to weed, named "horsing." For when the two went into their bizarre choreography of sexual "frustrabation" I was reduced to such helpless laughter that I distracted the entire balcony and embarrassed both myself and my host. It was a terrible moment, for before I could regain control, more attention was being directed toward me than at the action unfolding on the stage.

Then it was as though I had been stripped naked, kicked out of a low-flying plane onto an Alabama road, and ordered to laugh for my life. I laughed and laughed, bending and straightening in a virtual uncontrollable cloud-and-dam-burst of laughter, a self-immolation of laughter over which I had no control. And yet I was hypersensitive to what was happening around me, a fact which left me all the more embarrassed.

Seeing an expression of shocked disbelief on the face of my host, I imagined him saying, "Damn, if I'd known this would be his reaction I would have picked a theater with laughing-barrels!"

And suddenly, in addition to my soul-wracking agony of embarrassment, I was being devasted by an old in-group joke which played upon the themes of racial conflict, social freedom, and the blackness of Negro laughter; a joke whose setting was some small Southern town in which Negro freedom of expression was so restricted that its public square was marked by a series of huge whitewashed barrels labeled FOR COLORED, and into which any Negro who felt a laugh coming on was forced—*pro bono publico*—to thrust his boisterous head.

The joke was used by Tuskegee students, who considered themselves more sophisticated to kid freshmen from small Southern towns, but although I had heard it many times, it now flashed in my mind with implications that had hitherto escaped me. And as it played a counterpoint between my agony of laughter and the action taking place on the stage set of *Tobacco Road* below, it was as though Erskine Caldwell had snared me as an offstage instrument for extending the range of his outragous plotting—and I mean with a cacophony of minor thirds and flatted-fifths voiced fortissimo by braying gut-bucket brasses!

For now, in my hypersubjective state, viewers around me in the balcony were no longer following the action unfolding on the stage; they were getting to their feet to gawk at me. It was as though I had plunged into a nightmare in which my personality was split in twain, with the lucid side looking on in wonder while the manic side convulsed my body as though a drunken accordionist was using it to belt out the "Beer Barrel Polka." And while I wheezed and choked with laughter, my disgusted lucid self dramatized its cool detachment by noting that things were getting so out of control that Northern white folk in balcony and loge were now catching fire and beginning to howl and cheer the disgraceful loss of self-control being exhibited by a young Negro who had become deranged by the shock wave of comedy set in motion by a troupe of professional actors who were doing nothing more extraordinary than portraying the outrageous antics of a group of Southern whites who were totally imaginary; a young man who was so gross as to demonstrate his social unacceptability by violating a whole *encyclopedia* of codes that regulated proper conduct no less in the theater than in society at large.

In my distorted consciousness the theater was rapidly becoming the scene of a virtual orgy of disgraceful conduct, with everyone getting into the scene-stealing action. And so much so, that now the lucid side of me noted with despair that Jeeter Lester (played by Will Geer) and the other Lesters were now shading their eyes and peering open-mouthed toward the balcony—as if to say "What the hell's happening? Who's upstaging the stage and turning *Tobacco Road* upside down?" Or perhaps, in shock and dismay, they too were thinking of laughing-barrels.

For in the joke the barrels were considered a civic necessity and had been improvised as a means of protecting the sensibilities of whites from a pecular form of insanity suffered exclusively by Negroes, who in light of their social status and past condition of servitude were regarded as having absolutely *nothing* in their daily experience which could possibly inspire *rational* laughter. And yet Negroes continued—much as one side of me was doing—to laugh.

They laughed even when overcome by mirth while negotiating the public square, an area graced by its proud military statue, its Civil War cannon and pyramid of cannon balls, which was especially off-limits to all forms of Negro profanation. Thus, since any but the most inaudible Negro laughter was forbidden in public, Negroes who were wise —or at least fast on their feet—took off *posthaste* for a laughing-barrel. (Just as I, in my present predicament, would gladly have done.) For despite their eccentric risibility, the local Negroes bowed to public pressure and cooperated—at least to the extent that they were physically able.

But now as I continued to roar at the weird play-without-a play in which part of me was involved, my sober self marked the fact that the entire audience was being torn in twain. Most of the audience was white, but now many who occupied seats down in the orchestra section were beginning to protest the unscheduled disruption taking place above them. Leaping to their feet, they were shaking their fists at those in the balcony, and they in turn were shouting their disdain for those so lacking in an appreciation for the impromptu broadening of the expected comedy. And as they raged at one another in what was rapidly becoming a Grangerford-Shepherdson feud of expletives, I recalled a similar conflict which took place in the laughing-barrel town and cracked up again.

For there, too, certain citizens had assumed their democratic right of dissent to oppose the barrels as an *ipso jure* form of reverse discrimination. Why not, they argued, force Negroes to control themselves at their *own* expense, as did everyone else. An argument which fell on deaf ears, because it ignored the self-evident fact that Negro self-control was the very *last* thing in the world that they really wanted—whether in this or in any other area of Negro lives. Therefore, these passionate quodlibetarians and their objections to quotas were ignored because the great majority of the citizenry regarded their unique form of public accommodation as bestowing a dual blessing upon their town. And to an extent, that blessing included the Negroes. For not only did the laughing-barrels save many a black a sore behind (and the understaffed police force, energy sorely needed in other areas), they performed the far more important function of providing whites a means of saving face before the confounding, persistent, and embarrassing mystery of black laughter.

Unfortunately, it was generally agreed that the barrels were by no means an *elegant* solution of what whites regarded as a most grievous and inelegant problem. For after all, having to observe the posture of a Negro stuck halfway into a laughing-barrel (or rising and falling helplessly in a theater balcony) was far from an aesthetic experience. Nor was that all, for often when seen laughing with their heads stuck in a barrel and standing, as it were, upside down upon the turbulent air, Negroes appeared to be taken over by a form of schizophrenia which left them even more psychically frazzled than whites regarded them as being by nature.

But while the phenomenon was widely discussed, not even the wisest of whites could come up with a satisfactory explanation. All they knew was that when such an incident occurred, instead of sobering up, as any white man in a similar situation would have done, a Negro might well take off and laugh all the harder (as I in my barrelless state was doing). For it appeared that in addition to reacting to whatever ignorant, harebrained notion had set him off in the first place, the Negro was apt to double up with a second gale of laughter—and that triggered, apparently, by his own mental image of himself laughing at himself laughing upside down. It was, all whites agreed, another of the many Negro mysteries with which it was their lot to contend; and *whatever* its true cause, it was most disturbing to a white observer.

And especially on Market Day, a time when the public square teemed with whites and blacks seeking in their separate-but-equal fashions to combine business with pleasure while taking advantage of the square's holiday atmosphere. For on Market Days, thanks to the great influx of Negroes, the uproar from laughing-barrels could become so loud and raucous that it not only disturbed the serenity of the entire square, but shook up the whites' fierce faith in the stability of their most cherished traditions. For on such occasions the uproar from the laughing-barrels could become so contagious and irresistible that any whites who were so unfortunate as to be caught near the explosions of laughter would find themselves compelled to join in—and this included even such important figures as the mayor, lawyer, cotton broker, Baptist minister, and brewers of prime "white-lightning" whiskey. It was an appalling state of affairs, for despite their sternest resistance, even such distinguished whites literally cracked up and roared! And although it was recognized that it sprang from the *unnatural* and corrupting blackness of Negro laughter, it was a fact of Southern life, and thus it was that from time to time even the most dignified and tradition-bound whites found themselves joining in. (As, much to the discomfort of my somber balcony-trapped self, the whites around me were doing).

Nor did it help that many of the town's whites suspected that when a Negro had his head thrust into a laughing-barrel he became endowed with a strange form of extrasensory perception—or second sight—which allowed him to respond, and uproariously, to their unwilling participation. For it was clear that given a black laugher's own uncouth uproar, he could not possibly *hear* its infectious damage to them. And when such reversals occurred the whites assumed that in some mysterious fashion the Negro involved was not only laughing at *himself* laughing, but was also laughing at *them* laughing at his laughing against their own most determined wills. And if such was the truth, it suggested that somehow a Negro (and this meant *any* Negro) could become with a single hoot-and-cackle both the source and master of an outrageous and untenable situation. So it was viewed as a most aggravating problem, and, indeed, the most vicious of vicious circles ever to be imposed upon the long-suffering South by the white man's burden.

For since it was an undisputed fact that whites and blacks were of different species, it followed that they could by no means be expected to laugh at the same things. Therefore, when whites found themselves joining in with the coarse merriment issuing from the laughing-barrels, they suffered the double embarrassment of laughing against their own God-given nature while being unsure of exactly why, or at what, specifically, they were laughing. Which meant that somehow the Negro in the barrel had them *over* a barrel.

This, then, was the crux of the town's dilemma: efforts to control Negro laughter with laughing-barrels was as futile as attaining Christian grace by returning to the womb, because a Negro laughing in a laughing-barrel simply turned the world upside down and inside out. And in so doing, he *in*-verted (and thus *sub*-verted) tradition and thus the preordained and cherished scheme of Southern racial relationships was blasted asunder. Therefore, it was feared that if such unhappy instances of interracial laughter occurred with any frequency, it would create a crisis in which social order would be fatally undermined by something as unpolitical as a bunch of Negroes with their laughing heads stuck into the interiors of a batch of old whitewashed whiskey barrels.

The outrageous absurdity of this state of affairs was as vexing to the town as that in which I found myself as the old joke banged and shuddered through my memory. For despite the fact that the whites had done everything they could think of to control the blackness of Negro laughter, the Negroes continued to laugh. And the disapproval of the general public notwithstanding, they were even *bursting* barrels all over the public square, and thus adding to the high cost of maintaining public order. *And* since this was (in more ways than one!) at white expense, the whites were faced with a Hobson's choice between getting rid of the Negroes and suffering the economic loss of their labor, or living with the commotion in the laughing-barrels. (Yes, but they had at least a ghost of a choice, while by now it was as though I had been taken over by embattled Siamese twins who couldn't agree for disagreeing, and neither of whom could exit the scene, thanks to the detachment of one and the mirth-wracked state of the other.)

In the town, however, great argument raged on both sides of the question. All agreed that the laughing-barrels were an economic burden, but the proponents of the "Barrel Act," as it was known, justified their position with philosophical arguments to the effect that while it was true that the unique public facilities were costly, they served not only as a form of noise-pollution control, but the higher—and more spiritual—purpose of making it unnecessary for white folks to suffer the indignity of having to observe the confounding and degrading spectacle of a bunch of uncultivated Negroes knocking themselves out with a form of laughter that had no apparent motivation or discernible target . . .

What a terrible time and place to be ambushed by such an irreverent joke! By now my eyes were so full of tears that I could no longer see Hughes or anyone else, but at least the moisture had the effect of calming me down. Then, as the unruly world of *Tobacco Road* finally returned, my divided selves were made one again by a sense of catharsis. Yes, but at the expense of undergoing what a humiliating, body-wracking conflict of emotions! Embarrassment, self-anger, ethnic scorn, and at last a feeling of comic relief. And all because Erskine Caldwell compelled me to laugh at his symbolic, and therefore nonthreatening, Southern whites, and thus he shocked me into recognizing certain absurd aspects of our common humanity. Kenneth Burke would probably have said that I had been hit with a "perspective by incongruity," leading to a reversal of expectations in which the juxtaposition of past and present, comic Southland and quasi-illusory New York, had set up vibrations that routed my self-composure. It was as though I had plunged through the wacky mirrors of a fun house, to discover on the other side a weird distortion of perspective which made for a painful but redeeming rectification of vision. And in a flash, time was telescoped and the imaginary assumed the lineaments of past experiences through which Jeeter Lester's comic essence became a recognizable property of characters and events that I had known in the past.

Because, thanks to Governor "Alfalfa Bill" Murray's Jeeter Lesterish appeal to the bias of Oklahoma's farm vote, hadn't I seen the state capitol's grounds a-wave with grain "as high as an elephant's eye" (which proved to be a foreshadowing of events which led, years later, to the adoption of Rodgers and Hammerstein's "Oklahoma" as the state's official song)? And a bit later, hadn't I seen those same graciously landscaped grounds splattered with far more oil rigs than there were holes dug by Ty Ty in his futile search for gold in Caldwell's *God's Little Acre?* I had indeed, and the main difference was that the oil rigs produced oil; otherwise, Alfalfa Bill might have stepped out of a Caldwell novel. Thus I now recognized that there was much more of Jeeter Lester's outrageousness in my past than I had ever imagined, and quite a bit of it showed up on my side of the color line.

There were uneducated men whose attitudes and bearing ripped through the usual stereotypes like a Brahma bull goring the paper image displayed on Bull Durham Tobacco Company billboards. Their violence was usually directed against their own kind, but they were known to go after whites as well, and were no more respectful of what most people considered civilized conduct than Jeeter Lester. I had known the type in Oklahoma and admired a few for insisting upon being themselves. Often they were of vernacular folk culture but with active minds and were absolutely unrestrained in attacking any subject that caught their attention. Once while working as a barbershop shoeshine boy I had heard such a group engage in a long discussion of Mr. John D. Rockefeller Senior's relations with the women whom they assumed it natural for such a powerful man to have. They took it for granted that he had no less than a "stable full" and speculated as to how much he paid for their favors, and concluded that he rewarded them with trunks full of brand-new dimes.

Then they discussed the brands of brandy and whiskey which they assumed Mr. Rockefeller drank, and argued over the designs and costs of the silk underwear worn by his favorite fancy women, and then almost came to blows when estimating the number of "yard chillun" he had scattered around the country and abroad.

Poor old John D., he didn't know it, but they put him through the windmill of their fantasies with gusto. And what's more, he emerged enhanced in their sight as an even more exceptional man among such exceptional men as themselves—thanks to their having endowed him with a sexual potency and an utter disregard for genteel conduct that would have blown that gentleman's mind.

Before they were done they had the founder of Standard Oil shooting pool, playing strip poker, and engaging in a barbecue-eating contest with J. P. Morgan and Henry Ford—from which, naturally, he emerged the winner. Only when they put him through a Charleston contest with "Tickle-toes from Tulsa," a famous Negro dancer, did he fall below their exacting standards. Nevertheless he remained the mighty Rockefeller, though so magnified that he was far more "John Henry" than John Davidson. And in working him over, they created such an uproar of laughter that the owner had to ask them to leave the barbershop. But by that time, both to my bewilderment and to my delight, they had touched one of the most powerful men of the nation with the tarbrush of their comic imaginations, Afro-Americanized him, and claimed him as one of their very own.

It was amazing how consistently they sought (like Jeeter Lester) to make the world conform to the narrow compass of their own hopes and dreams. And there were still others who in pursuing their self-reliant wrong-headness had given me a glimpse of the "tragic."

For had not I seen a good part of my community, including teen-age boys, reduced to despair over the terrible death of a self-taught genius of an automobile mechanic, who after burning his fingers while working with the electrical system of a Model T Ford had cut out the offending flesh with his pocketknife—an act of ignorant pride which resulted in his death by lockjaw? In those days any boy who could lay hands on a coil from a Model T and the hand-cranked magneto from a discontinued telephone would rig it as a device for shocking his unsuspecting friends, but now to our dismay, death was revealed to be lurking within our rare electrical toys.

But even closer to my immediate experience, wasn't Ellie May's and Lov's "horsing" all over the stage of *Tobacco Road* embarrassingly symbolic of my own frustration as a healthy young man whose sexual outlet was limited (for the most part) to "belly-rubbing" with girls met casually at public dances? It was and it wasn't, depending upon my willingness to make or withhold a human identification. Actually, I had no choice but to identify, for Caldwell's art had seen to that.

Thus, for all its intentional outrageousness, the comedy of *Tobacco Road* was deeply rooted in the crazy-quilt life I knew. And Caldwell had me both coming and going, black side, white side, and straight down my improvised American middle. On one side of my mind I had thought of my life as being of a whole, segregated but in many ways superior to that of the Lesters. On the other side, I thought of the Lester type as being, in the Negro folk phrase, "a heap of whiteness gone to waste" and therefore a gross caricature of anything that was viable in the idea of white superiority. But now Caldwell had highlighted the warp and woof of my own ragtag American pattern. And so, laughing hysterically, I felt like the fat man whom I'd seen slip and fall on the icy sidewalk and who lay there laughing while passers-by looked on in bewilderment—until he got to his feet still laughing and punched the one man who had joined in his laughter square in the mouth. In my case, however, there was no one to punch, because I embodied both fat man and the passer-by who was so rash as to ignore Baudelaire's warning. Therefore I laughed and I trembled, and gained thereby a certain wisdom.

I couldn't have put it into words at the time, but by forcing me to see the comedy in Jeeter Lester's condition and allowing me to react to it in an interracial situation without the threat of physical violence, Caldwell told me something important about who I was. And by easing the conflict that I was having with my Southern experience (yes, and with my South-Southwestern identity), he helped initiate me into becoming, if not a "New Yorker," at least a more tolerant American. I suppose such preposterous comedy is an indispensable agency for dealing with American experience precisely because it allows for redeeming perspectives on our rampant incongruities. Given my background and yearnings, there was no question but that I needed such redemption, and for that I am eternally grateful to Erskine Caldwell—Southerner, American humorist, and mighty destroyer of laughing-barrels.

Remembering Richard Wright

Earlier today while considering my relationship with Richard Wright, I recalled Heraclitus' axiom "Geography is fate," and I was struck by the ironic fact that in this country, where Frederick Jackson Turner's theory of the frontier has been so influential in shaping our conception of American history, very little attention has been given to the role played by geography in shaping the fate of Afro-Americans.

For example, Wright was a Mississippian who migrated to Chicago and then to New York. I, by contrast, am an Oklahoman and by geographical origin a Southwesterner. Wright grew up in a part of what was the old Confederacy, while I grew up in a state which possesses no indigenous tradition of chattel slavery. Thus, while we both grew up in segregated societies, mine lacked many of the intensities of custom, tradition, and manners which "colored" the institutions of the Old South, and which were important in shaping Wright's point of view. Both of us were descendants of slaves, but since my civic, geographical, and political circumstances were different from those of Mississippi,

Wright and I were united by our connection with a past condition of servitude, and divided by geography and a difference of experience based thereupon. And yet it was that very difference of experience and background which had much to do with Wright's important impact upon my sensibilities.

And then there was New York. I met Wright there in 1937, and it was no accidental encounter. It came about because through my reading and working in the library at Tuskegee Institute, I'd become fascinated by the exciting developments that were taking place in modern literature. Somehow in my uninstructed reading of Eliot and Pound, I had recognized a relationship between modern poetry and jazz music, and this led me to wonder why I was not encountering similar devices in the work of Afro-American writers. Indeed, such reading and wondering prepared me not simply to *meet* Wright, but to seek him out. It led, in other words, to a personal quest. I insist upon the "seeking out" because, you see, I too have an ego and it is important to me that our meeting came about through my own initiative. For not only is it historically true, but it has something to do with my being privileged to be here on what I consider to be a very important moment in the history of our literature. Perhaps Richard Wright would have dismissed such a moment as impossible, even as late as 1957, but still, here we are, gathered in the hot summertime to pay him honor. *I* would not have been surprised, since it was my reading of one of Wright's poems in the *New Masses* which gave me a sense of his importance. I had arrived in New York on July 5, 1936—a date of no broad symbolic importance, but one highly significant to me because it made a meeting with Wright a possibility. For although the *New Masses* poem was not a masterpiece, I found in it traces of the modern poetic sensibility and technique that I had been seeking.

The morning after my arrival in New York, I encountered standing in the entrance of the Harlem YMCA two fateful figures. They were Langston Hughes, the poet, and Dr. Alain Locke, the then head of the philosophy department at Howard University. I had never seen Langston Hughes before, but regardless of what is said about the quality of education provided by the old Negro schools (ours was named for Frederick Douglass), we were taught what is now termed "Black History" and were kept abreast of current events pertaining to our people. Thus, as early as the sixth grade we were made aware of the poetry of Langston Hughes along with the work of the other Negro Renaissance writers. So I recognized Hughes from his photographs. But I recognized Dr. Locke because he had been at Tuskegee only a few weeks prior to my arrival in New York, having gone there to visit with Hazel Harrison, a teacher in the music department, and a very fine pianist who had been one of Ferruccio Busoni's prize pupils . . . Here I'm trying to provide a bit of historical background to give you an idea of the diverse cultural forces at play in the lives of Afro-Americans from the early 1920s to 1936.

Miss Harrison was a friend of Prokofiev, and possessed some of his scores at a time when few would have imagined that a Russian master's music was being made a part of the musical consciousness of an Afro-American college. And certainly not in such a college as Tuskegee—even though Tuskegee's musical tradition was actually quite rich and quite varied. But then, this is but another example of the contradictions of American culture which escape our attention because they are obscured by racism. And yet, thanks to Miss Harrison, I could, like any eager, young, celebrity-fascinated college junior, walk straight up to Dr. Locke and say, "Dr. Locke, do you remember me?" And to my delight he said, "Why, of course I do." He then introduced me to Langston Hughes and told Hughes of my interest in poetry.

Langston Hughes had with him copies of Malraux's *Man's Fate* and *The Days of Wrath*, and after a few moments' conversation he said, "Since you like to read so much, maybe you'd like to read these novels and then return them to their owner"—and so I did. And the returns were tremendous. This incident and this meeting later made it possible for me to ask Langston Hughes if he knew Richard Wright, "Yes, he said, "and it so happens that he's coming here from Chicago next week." And with his great generosity, and without telling me, Hughes wrote Richard Wright that there was a young Negro something-or-the-other in New York who wanted to meet him. The next thing I knew I received a postcard—which I still have—that said, "Dear Ralph Ellison, Langston Hughes tells me that you're interested in meeting me. I will be in New York . . . " on such and such a date in July . . . signed Richard Wright. Thus I was to meet Wright on the day after his arrival in New York in July of 1937.

At the time I still thought that I would return to Tuskegee to take my degree in music, but I was not to make it. I had come to New York to earn expenses for my senior year, but it was during the Depression and I was unable to make the money. Then, in talking with Wright, my plans and goals were altered; were, in fact, fatefully modified by Wright's.

Wright had come to New York for two purposes, one which was talked about openly, and the other quietly underplayed. The first was to become the editor of the magazine *New Challenge.* The other was to work in the Harlem Bureau of the Communist newspaper *The Daily Worker.* With Wright's presence in the *Worker*'s 135th Street office, my introduction to the craft of writing leaped ahead. For it was there that I read many of his unpublished stories and discussed his ideas concerning literature and culture.

Wright was quiet concerning his assignment to the

Worker's staff because he had left Chicago under a cloud. In 1936 he had been thrown out of the May Day parade—sacred to all Communists—for refusing to carry out some assignment. And the fact that he had been publicly humiliated by both white *and* black Communists had left him quite bitter. However, someone higher up in the hierarchy recognized his value and was able to persuade him to go to New York—which proved to be to my good fortune.

Being unemployed much of the time, I began to hang around the Harlem Bureau, not so much for the ideology being purveyed there—although I found it fascinating—but because of Wright and the manuscripts of a sheaf of novelettes (later published as *Uncle Tom's Children*) that lay in an open desk drawer. Of all those who visited the office, I was the only one who bothered to read those now-famous stories. Perhaps this was because his comrades looked upon Wright as an intruder. He was distrusted not only as an "intellectual" and thus a potential traitor, but as a possible "dark horse" in the race for Harlem party leadership; a "ringer" who had been sent from Chicago to cause them trouble. Wright had little sense of humor concerning their undisguised hostility, and this led, as would be expected, to touchy relationships. Despite his obvious organizational and journalistic abilities—the *Worker* featured his reportage—the members of the Communist rank and file sneered at his intellectuality, ridiculed his writings, and dismissed his concern with literature and culture as an affectation. In brief, they thought him too ambitious, and therefore a threat to their own ambitions as possible party functionaries.

Being a true outsider, I was amused by this comedy of misperception, for Wright seemed anything but a threat to their petty ambitions. Besides, I was absolutely intrigued by his talent and felt privileged to read his writings. I'd never met anyone who, lacking the fanfare of public recognition, could move me with the unpublished products of his fictional imagination. Of course, I read Wright's work uncritically, but there was no doubt in my mind that he was an exceptional writer. Even better, he was delighted to discuss the techniques, the ideological and philosophical implications of his writings, and this with one who'd never attempted to write anything beyond classroom assignments and a few poems. Evidently Wright wished to exchange ideas with someone of his own general background, and I was fortunate in being able to contribute more than curiosity to our discussion. For I had studied with creative musicians, both classical and jazz, and had been taught to approach the arts analytically. I had also read fairly widely on my own. But to encounter the possessor of such literary talent and have him make me his friend and confidant—that was indeed an exciting and inspiring experience.

Nor did it end with mere talk. As editor of *New Challenge,* Wright asked me to contribute a book review in its first issue. To one who had never attempted to write anything, this was the wildest of ideas. But still, pressed by his editorial needs, and sustained by his belief that an untapped supply of free-floating literary talent existed in the Negro community, Wright kept after me, and I wrote a review and he published it. But then he went even further by suggesting that I write a short story!

I said, "But I've never even tried to write a story . . . "

He said, "Look, you talk about these things, you've read a lot, and you've been around. Just put something down and let me see it . . . "

So I wrote a story, titled "Hymie's Bull," that was based upon experiences that I'd had a few years before when riding freight trains from Oklahoma to Alabama. I was dubious over the outcome, but to my delight Wright accepted the story and sent it to the printer.

Ah, but fate, as they say, was in the wings and *New Chal-*

lenge was not to appear again. I hasten to add that this was not a disaster created by my first attempt at fiction. Rather, it had to do with an aspect of Afro-American cultural history and involved certain lingering echoes of the Negro Renaissance, a movement which "ran out of gas" with the Crash of 1929. As the period ended, a number of figures important to the movement had died, and with the Great Depression upon them, those members of the white community who had sponsored the Renaissance were unable to continue. The money was no longer available, and so the movement languished. However, with the deepening of the Depression there came a significant development in the form of the federal projects for the arts that were organized by the Works Progress Administration. These projects were most important to the continuing development of Afro-American artists. For although a reaction to a national disaster, they provided—as have most national disasters—the possibility for a broader Afro-American freedom. This is a shocking thing to say, but it is also a very *blues,* or tragicomic, thing to say, and a fairly accurate description of the manner in which, for Negroes, a gift of freedom arrived wrapped in the guise of disaster. It is ironic, but no less true, that the most tragic incident of our history, the Civil War, was a disaster which ended American slavery.

Wright himself worked on both the Chicago and the New York Federal Writers' Project, and I could not have become a writer at the time I began had I not been able to earn my board and keep by doing research for the New York project. Through Wright's encouragement, I had become serious about writing, but before going on the project I sometimes slept in the public park below City College because I had neither job nor money. But my personal affairs aside, the WPA provided an important surge to Afro-American cultural activity. The result was not a "renaissance," but there was a resuscitation and transformation of that very vital artistic impulse that is abiding among Afro-Americans. Remember that our African forefathers originated in cultures wherein even the simple routines of daily living were highly ritualized and that even their cooking utensils were fashioned with forms of symbolism which resonated with overtones of godhead. And though modified, if not suppressed, by the experience of American slavery, that tradition of artistic expressiveness has infused the larger American culture. Afro-American cultural style is an abiding aspect of our culture, and the economic disaster which brought the WPA gave it an accelerated release and allowed many Negroes to achieve their identities as artists.

But now, back to Wright and *New Challenge. New Challenge* was organized by people active in the Negro Renaissance and whose outlook was in many ways at odds with Wright's. Thus, according to Wright, *New Challenge* ended publication because the two young women who were in charge before he came on the scene were afraid that his connection with the Communist party would lead to its being taken over. So rather than lose control, they got rid of Wright.

History has no vacuum. There are transformations, there are lesions, there are metamorphoses, and there are mysteries that cloak the clashing of individual wills and private interests. *New Challenge* faded, but Wright went on to publish *Uncle Tom's Children* and, shortly afterward, *Native Son.* When Richard Wright came to New York his talents as a writer were, to a large extent, already formed. Indeed, even before 1927, when he migrated to Chicago, he had published fiction in Robert S. Abbott's magazine *The Bronzeman.* So it isn't true, as has been said, that the Communist party "discovered" his talent. Wright was literary in an informed way even in Jackson, Mississippi. But what happened to him in Chicago resulted from his coming into contact with an organized political group which possessed a concept of social hierarchy that was a conscious negation of our racially biased social system. Thus, through his political affiliation Wright was able to identify his artistic ambitions with what was, for him, a totally new conception of social justice. In the discussions that took place in the Chicago John Reed Club he sharpened his conception of literary form and the relationship between fictional techniques and the world view of Marxism. And he came to see art and society in terms of an ideology that was concerned with power, and willing to forgo racial differences in order to take over the world. I realize that this is all rather abstract, but I am trying to suggest the tenor of our discussions. Fortunately, Wright's interest in literary theory was not limited to areas prescribed by the party line.

For instance, I was very curious as to how one could put Marx and Freud together. No real problem now, I suppose. But coming from where I did, it was puzzling. And I was to discover that it was also a problem for Communist intellectuals and for many of their opponents. Either Marx was raised up and Freud put down, or Freud raised up and Marx put down. So for me, all of this was pretty strange. But at least with Richard Wright, I could discuss such matters. This was very important for a young writer (and of course I became a young writer, for I soon realized that I wasn't going back to Tuskegee and to music). And since Wright had assured me that I possessed a certain talent, I decided that writing was the direction I would take. I don't know whether he was satisfied with my talent or not; I suspect not. This was interesting, for while I possessed more formal education, it was he who encouraged me and gave me a sense of direction. I'd like you to appreciate the irony of this development: Here was a young Afro-American who had gone only to grade school, but who had arrived in Chicago possessing a certain articulateness and an undeveloped talent for writing. He had no further formal education—although he was aware of the University of Chicago and came to associate with a number of its intellectuals—but he gave himself over to the complex reality of late 1927 Chicago and made it his own. Chicago, the city where after years of Southern Negro migration the great jazz was being played and reinvented, where the stockyards and railroads, and the steel mills of Gary, Indiana, were transforming a group of rural, agricultural Americans into city people and into a *lumpenproletariat,* a class over whom we now despair.

Wright found the scene challenging. He learned that in this country wherever one wanders, one must pay his dues to change and take advantage of possibility by asserting oneself. You'll recall my saying earlier that "geography is fate"; now let me say that one's fate is also determined by what one does and by what one does *not* do. Wright set out to come into a conscious possession of his experience as Negro, as political revolutionary, as writer, and as citizen of Chicago.

Somehow, in getting into the John Reed Club, Wright had learned the techniques of agitprop art—which he came later to despise—and before he went to Harlem he had been a contributing editor of the original *Partisan Review* and a founder of such magazines as *Anvil.* He had been poor in accepting discipline and had had his political troubles in the Communist party, but when I knew him he was not shrinking from the challenges of his existence. Nor complaining that he'd been " 'buked and scorned." Nor did he feel that he had handicaps that could not be overcome because of his identity as a Negro writer. Instead, he was striving to live consciously—at least artistically and intellectually—at the top of his times. Wright's spirit was such, and his sense of possibility was such, that even during the time when he was writing *Native Son* he was concerned with learning the stylistic and dialectical fine points found in the work of Steinbeck, of Hemingway, of Malraux, and of Thomas Mann; for these he viewed as his competitors. I warn you that this is only *my* interpretation, but it was as though Wright was thinking, "I have a finer sense, a more basic knowledge of American reality than Hemingway, or Steinbeck, or anybody else who is writing." He had the kind of confidence that jazzmen have, although I assure you that he knew very little about jazz and didn't even know how to dance. Which is to say that he didn't possess the full range of Afro-American culture. But having the confidence of his talent, having the sense (which he gained from Marxism) that he was living in a world in which he did not have to be confused by the mystifications of racism, Wright harnessed his revolutionary tendencies to a political program which he hoped would transform American society. Through his cultural and political activities in Chicago he made a dialectical leap into a sense of his broadest possibilities, as man and as artist. He was well aware of the forces ranked against him, but in his quiet way he was as arrogant in facing up to them as was Louis Armstrong in a fine blaring way.

To a young Oklahoman this attitude of Wright's was affirmative—and again, "geography is fate." For out there our people fought back. We seldom won more than moral victories, but we fought back—as can be seen from the many civil rights victories that were initiated there. And as can be heard in the Southwestern jazz and in the performances of the Jimmy Rushings, the Hot Lips Pages, the Count Basies, the Benny Motens, and Charlie Christians. We were an assertive people, and our mode of social assertion was artistic, mainly music, as well as political. But there was also the Negro church, wherein you heard the lingering accents of nineteenth-century rhetoric with its emphasis upon freedom and individual responsibility; a rhetorical style which gave us Lincoln, Harriet Tubman, Harriet

Beecher Stowe, and the other abolition-preaching Beechers. Which gave us Frederick Douglass and John Jasper and many other eloquent and heroic Negroes whose spirit still moves among us through the contributions they made to the flexibility, the music, and the idealism of the American language. Richard Wright was a possessor of that tradition. It is resonant in his fiction and it was a factor in his eager acceptance of social responsibility.

But now I should add that as far as Negroes in New York were concerned, Wright was for the most part friendless. Part of this was due to the fact that he kept to Communist circles and was intensely involved with writing and political activities. But as far as his rapid development as a writer is concerned, it would not have been possible but for the Chicago John Reed Club. This required an intellectual environment, and in Negro communities such were few and far between. Thus, given his talent and driving ambition, it was fortunate that he found the necessary associations among other young writers, many of whom were not Communists. Within such integrated groups he could question ideas, programs, theories. He could argue over philosophical interpretations of reality and say, if he chose, "Well, dammit, I'm black, and this concept of this program doesn't seem valid to me." This was most important for Wright, and since he affirmed many impulses which I felt and understood in my own way, it proved important to me. And no less important was his willingness to discuss problems encountered within the Communist party, and especially his difficulty in pursuing independent thought.

Because there, too, he was encountering a form of intellectual racism. It was not couched in the rhetoric of Negro inferiority *à l'americain,* but in the form of an insistance upon blind discipline and a constant pressure to follow unthinkingly a political "line." It was dramatized in the servile attitudes of certain black Communist functionaries who regarded Wright—with his eloquence and his tendency toward an independence of thought—as a dangerous figure who had to be kept under rigid control.

And of course, Wright's personality would not allow him to shun a battle. He fought back and was into all kinds of trouble. He had no interest in keeping silent as the price of his freedom of expression. Nor was he so dazzled by his freedom to participate in the councils of newspapers and magazines as to keep his mouth shut. Instead, he felt that his experience, insight, and talent were important to the party's correct assessment of American reality. Thus he fought to make his comrades understand that *they* didn't know a damn thing about the complexities of the South, whether black or white, and insisted that they could not possibly understand America's racial situation by approaching it through such facile slogans as "Black and White Unite and Fight." Not when the white workingman was doing us the greatest face-to-face damage, and when the unions were practicing policies of racial exclusion. In trying to get this across, in saying, as it were, "Your approach is too simple," Wright met all kinds of resistance, both ideological and personal. But at least he made the fight, and I bring it up here by way of offering you something of the background of emotional and intellectual conflict out of which *Native Son* was written.

I read most of *Native Son* as it came off the typewriter, and I didn't know what to think of it except that it was wonderful. I was not responding critically. After all, how many of you have had the unexpected privilege of reading a powerful novel as it was, literally, ripped off the typewriter? Such opportunities are rare, and being young, I was impressed beyond all critical words. And I am still impressed. I feel that *Native Son* was one of the major literary events in the history of American literature. And I can say this even though at this point I have certain reservations concerning its view of reality. Yet it continues to have a powerful effect, and it seems to me a mistake to say, as was said not long ago in *Life* magazine, that *Native Son* is a "neglected" novel. And here I should remind those of you who were too young to remember, that *Native Son* was such a popular work that the dust jacket of the Book-of-the-Month Club edition could consist of a collage made of accolades written by critics and reviewers from throughout the country. It was a financial as well as a critical success, and with its publication Wright became a famous man.

But its success was by no means to still his burning passion—not simply for justice, but to become the author of other compelling works of literature. His response to the reception of *12 Million Black Voices,* which is, I think, his most lyrical work, is an example. He was much bemused by the fact that this work could move his white readers to tears, and saw this as an evasion of the intended impact of his vision. Thus he began to talk over and over again of forging such hard, mechanical images and actions that no white reading them could afford the luxury of tears.

But here I must turn critic. For in *my* terms, Wright failed to grasp the function of artistically induced catharsis—which suggests that he failed also to understand the Afro-American custom of shouting in church (a form of ritual cartharsis), or its power to cleanse the mind and redeem and rededicate the individual to forms of ideal action. Perhaps he failed to understand—or he rejected—those moments of exultation wherein man's vision is quickened by the eloquence of an orchestra, an actor or orator or dancer, or by anyone using the arts of music or speech or symbolic gesture to create within us moments of high consciousness; moments wherein we grasp, in the instant, a knowledge of how transcendent and how abysmal and yet affirmative it can be to be human beings. Yet it is for such moments of inspired communication that the artist lives. The irony here is that Wright could evoke them, but felt, for ideological reasons, that tears were a betrayal of the struggle for freedom.

I disagreed with his analysis, for tears can induce as well as deter action. Nevertheless, it is imperative that I say that through his writings Richard Wright achieved, here in the social and racial chaos of the United States, a position of artistic equality. He insisted upon it. And not only in his own political party—with which he eventually broke—but internationally. He was never at peace. He was never at rest. The restlessness which sent our forefathers hurtling toward the West Coast, and which now has us climbing up all sorts of walls, was very much within him. In 1956, in Paris, when we were leaving the headquarters of the magazine *Presence Africaine* (and this is the first time I've revealed this and I hope he won't mind, since it might be meaningful to some scholar), he said to me, "Really, Ralph, after I broke with the Communist party I had nowhere else to go . . ." This was said in resigned explanation of his continued presence in Europe. And I think he was telling me that his dedication to communism had been so complete and his struggle so endless that he had had to change his scene, that he had had to find a new ground upon which to struggle. Because as long as he stayed within the framework of his political party, he had to struggle on two fronts: asserting on one the principles of equality and possibility (which the Communists stood for, or *pretended* to stand for), and on the other, insisting upon the fact *not* that it took a Negro to tell the truth about Afro-American experience, but that you had to at least get down into the mud and live with its basic realities to do so. And that you could not deal with its complexities simply from a theoretical perspective.

Black Boy was an attempt to depict some of those complexities.

So much of *Black Boy* (originally entitled *American Hunger*), is exaggerated, I think, precisely because Wright was trying to drive home, to dramatize—indeed, because of its many fictional techniques he could with justice have called it a "nonfiction" novel—the complexity of Negro American experience as he knew it and had lived it. The fictional techniques were not there in order to "con" anyone, but to drive home to Americans, black and white, something of the complexity and cost in human terms, in terms of the loss to literature and to art, and to the cause of freedom itself, imposed by racial discrimination; the cost, that is, of growing up in a society which operated on one side of its mind by the principle of equality while qualifying that principle severely according to the dictates of racism. Wright was thinking and fighting over these issues at close quarters—fighting with the Communists especially because he had thought that they offered a viable solution. Instead, he discovered that they were blind.

But now to more delightful relationships with Wright. He had as much curiosity about how writing is written as I had about how music is composed, and our curiosity concerning artistic creation became the basis of our friendship. Having studied music from the age of eight, and having studied harmony and symphonic form in our segregated school, I was also interested in how music related to the other arts. This, combined with my growing interest in literary creation, made my contact with Wright's enthusiasm an educational and spirit-freeing experience. Having read Pound and Eliot and Shaw and the criticism of Harriet Monroe and I. A. Richards—all available in Tuskegee's excellent little library—it was important that in Wright, I had discovered a Negro American writer who possessed a working knowledge of modern literature, its techniques and theories. My approach to literature was by no means racial, but Wright was not only available, he was eager to share his interests, and it gave me something of that sense of self-discovery and exaltation which is implicit in the Negro church and in good jazz. Indeed, I had found it in baseball and football games, and it turns up in almost any group activity of Afro-Americans when we're not really thinking about white folks and are simply being our own American selves.

I'm reminded of a discussion that another Tuskegeian and I were having with a group of white friends. The discussion had to do with our discovery of Hemingway (whom I discovered in a Negro barbershop), and Conrad (another writer I often discussed with Wright), and suddenly the Tuskegee graduate said to me, "Aren't you glad that we found those guys on our own at Tuskegee?"

Now, that was not Negro chauvinism, but a meaningful observation about the relationship between social scene and experience, and I concurred. Because I had had the same reaction when I first talked with Wright about fictional technique and we had gone on to discuss some of the complications and interconnections between culture and society that claimed our conscious attention despite the fact that we were segregated. The question reminded me of how wonderful it was to have read T. S. Eliot in the context of Tuskegee. The question was not raised to celebrate a then-segregated college in a violently segregated state, but to inform our white friends that racism aside, there are other important relationships between scenes, ideas, and experience. Scene and circumstance combined to give ideas resonance and compel a consciousness of perspective. What one reads becomes part of what one sees and feels. Thus it is impossible for me to reread certain passages from Joyce or Eliot or Sir Thomas Browne without seeing once again the deep magenta skies that descend upon the Tuskegee campus at dusk in summer. The scene, then, is always a part of personality, and scene and personality combine to give viability to ideas. Scene is thus always a part, the ground, of action—and especially of *conscious* action. Its associations and implicit conflicts provide the extra dimension which anchors poetry in reality and structures our efforts toward freedom.

Richard Wright was trying to add to our consciousness the dimension of being a black boy who grew up in Jackson, Mississippi (a scene that was not always so rugged, even for him, as he pictured it artistically), but a boy who grew up and who achieved through his reading a sense of what was possible out there in the wider world. A boy who grew up and achieved and accepted his own *individual* responsibility for seeing to it that America become conscious of itself. He insisted that it recognize the interconnections between its places and its personalities, its act and its ideals. This was the burden of Richard Wright and, as I see it, the driving passion of Richard Wright. It led to his triumphs as it led, inevitably, to some of his defeats. But one thing must be said of Richard Wright: In him we had for the first time a Negro American writer as randy, as courageous, and as irrepressible as Jack Johnson. And if you don't know who Jack Johnson was, I'll tell you that when I was a little boy that early heavyweight boxing champion was one of the most admired underground heroes. He was rejected by most whites and by many respectable Negroes, but he was nevertheless a hero among veterans of the Spanish-American War who rejoiced in the skill and élan with which Johnson set off the now-outrageous search for a "White Hope."

This suggests that we literary people should always keep a sharp eye on what's happening in the unintellectualized areas of our experience. Our peripheral vision had better be damned good. Because while baseball, basketball, and football players cannot really tell us how to write our books, they *do* demonstrate where much of the significant action is taking place. Often they are themselves cultural heroes who work powerful modification in American social attitudes. And they tell us in nonliterary terms much about the nature of possibility. They tell us about the cost of success, and much about the nonpolitical aspects of racial and national identity, about the changing nature of social hierarchy, and about the role which individual skill and excellence can play in creating social change.

In this country there were good Negro writers before Wright arrived on the scene—and my respects to all the good ones—but it seems to me that Richard Wright wanted more and dared more. He was sometimes too passionate, I think now as I offer you the memories of a middle-aged man. But at least Wright wanted and demanded as much as any novelist, any artist, should want: He wanted to be tested in terms of his talent, and not in terms of his race or his Mississippi upbringing. Rather, he had the feeling that his vision of American life, and his ability to project it eloquently, justified his being considered among the best of American writers. And in this crazy, mixed-up country, as is witnessed by this conference dedicated to his works and to his memory, it turns out that he was right.

—Lecture presented at the Institute for Afro-American Culture, University of Iowa, July 18, 1971

Homage to Duke Ellington on His Birthday

It is to marvel: the ageless and irrepressible Duke Ellington is seventy, and another piano player of note, President Richard M. Nixon, has ordered in his honor a state dinner to be served in the house where, years ago, Duke's father, then a butler, once instructed white guests from the provinces in the gentle art and manners proper to such places of elegance and power. It is good news in these times of general social upheaval that traces of the old American success story remain valid, for now where the parent labored the son is to be honored for his achievements. And perhaps it is inevitable that Duke Ellington should be shown the highest hospitality of the nation's First Family in its greatest house, and that through the courtesy of the chief of state all Americans may pay, symbolically, their respects to our greatest composer.

Perhaps it is also inevitable (and if not inevitable, certainly it is proper) that that which a Pulitzer Prize jury of a few years ago was too insecure, or shortsighted, to do, and that which our institutions dedicated to the recognition of artistic achievement have been too prejudiced, negligent, or concerned with European models and styles to do, is finally being done by Presidents. For it would seem that Ellington's greatness has been recognized by everyone except those charged with recognizing musical excellence at the highest levels—and even some of these have praised him privately while failing to grant him public honor.

Nevertheless, he is far from being a stranger to the White House, for during the occupancy of President and Mrs. Lyndon B. Johnson, Ellington became something of a regular guest there, and indeed, it was President Johnson who appointed him to the National Council on the Arts, thereby giving recognition to our most important indigenous art form in the person of its most outstanding creator. Certainly there is no better indication that those on the highest levels of governmental power have at last begun to recognize our arts and their creators as national treasures. Perhaps in Ellington's special case this is a proper and most fitting path to official national recognition, since for more than forty years his music has been not only superb entertainment but an important function of national morale. During the Depression whenever his theme song "East St. Louis Toodle-oo" came on the air, our morale was lifted by something inescapably hopeful in the sound. Its style was so triumphant and the moody melody so successful in capturing the times yet so expressive of the faith which would see us through them. And when the "Black and Tan Fantasy" was played we were reminded not only of how fleeting *all* human life must be, but with its blues-based tension between content and manner, it warned us not only to look at the darker side of life but also to remember the enduring necessity for humor, technical mastery, and creative excellence. It was immensely danceable and listenable music and ever so evocative of other troubled times and other triumphs over disaster. It was also most Negro American in its mocking interpolations from Chopin's B-flat minor piano concerto to which, as Barry Ulanov has reminded us, it was once popular to sing the gallows-humored words: "Where shall we all/Be/A hundred years/From now?"

And how many generations of Americans, white and black, wooed their wives and had the ceremonial moments of their high school and college days memorialized by Ellington's tunes? And to how many thousands has he brought definitions of what it should mean to be young and alive and American? Yes, and to how many has he given a sense of personal elegance and personal style? A sense of possibility? And who, seeing and hearing Ellington and his marvelous band, hasn't been moved to wonder at the mysterious, unanalyzed character of the Negro American—and at the white American's inescapable Negro-ness?

Even though few recognized it, such artists as Ellington and Louis Armstrong were the stewards of our vaunted American optimism and guardians against the creeping irrationality which ever plagues our form of society. They created great entertainment, but for them (ironically) and for us (unconsciously) their music was a rejection of that chaos and license which characterized the so-called jazz age associated with F. Scott Fitzgerald, and which has returned once more to haunt the nation. Place Ellington with Hemingway, they are both larger than life, both masters of that which is most enduring in the human enterprise: the power of man to define himself against the ravages of time through artistic style.

I remember Ellington from my high school days in Oklahoma City, first as a strangely familiar timbre of orchestral sounds issuing from phonograph records and radio. Familiar because beneath the stylized jungle sounds (the like of which no African jungle had ever heard) there sounded the blues, and strange because the mutes, toilet plungers, and derby hats with which I was acquainted as a musician had been given a stylized elegance and extension of effect unheard of even in the music of Louis Armstrong. It was as though Ellington had taken the traditional instruments of Negro American music and modified them, extended their range, enriched their tonal possibilities. We were studying the classics then, working at harmony and the forms of symphonic music. And while we affirmed the voice of jazz and the blues despite all criticism from our teachers because they spoke to a large extent of what we felt of the life we lived most intimately, it was not until the discovery of Ellington that we had any hint that jazz possessed possibilities of a range of expressiveness comparable to that of classical European music.

And then Ellington and the great orchestra came to town; came with their uniforms, their sophistication, their skills; their golden horns, their flights of controlled and disciplined fantasy; came with their art, their special sound; came with Ivy Anderson and Ethel Waters singing and dazzling the eye with their high-brown beauty and with the richness and bright feminine flair of their costumes, their promising manners. They were news from the great wide world, an example and a goal; and I wish that all those who write so knowledgeably of Negro boys having no masculine figures with whom to identify would consider the long national and international career of Ellington and his band, the thousands of one-night stands played in the black communities of this nation. Where in the white community, in *any* white community, could there have been found images, examples such as these? Who were so worldly, who so elegant, who so mockingly creative? Who so skilled at their given trade and who treated the social limitations placed in their paths with greater disdain?

Friends of mine were already collecting Ellington records, and the more mature jazzmen were studying, without benefit of formal institutions of learning, his enigmatic style. Indeed, during the thirties and forties, when most aspiring writers of fiction were learning from the style and example of Hemingway, many jazz composers, orchestrators, and arrangers were following the example of Ellington, attempting to make something new and uniquely their own out of the traditional elements of the blues and jazz. For us, Duke was a culture hero, a musical magician who worked his powers through his mastery of form, nuance, and style, a charismatic figure whose personality influenced even those who had no immediate concern with the art of jazz.

My mother, an Afro-American Methodist Episcopalian who shouted in church but who allowed me nevertheless to leave sunrise Christmas services to attend breakfast dances, once expressed the hope that when I'd completed my musical studies I'd have a band like Ellington's. I was pleased and puzzled at the time, but now I suspect that she recognized a certain religious element in Ellington's music—an element which has now blossomed forth in compositions of his own form of liturgical music. Either that, or she accepted the sound of dedication wherever she heard it and thus was willing to see Duke as an example of the mysterious way in which God showed His face in music.

I didn't meet Ellington at the time. I was but a young boy in the crowd that stood entranced around the bandstand at Slaughter's Hall. But a few years later, when I was a student in the music department at Tuskegee, I shook his hand, talked briefly with him of my studies and of my dreams. He was kind and generous even though harassed (there had been some trouble in travel and the band had arrived hours late, with the instruments misplaced and the musicians evil as only tired, black, Northern-based musicians could be in the absurdly segregated South of the 1930s), and those of us who talked with him were renewed in our determination to make our names in music.

A few years later, a stranger in Harlem, I lived at the YMCA and spent many a homesick afternoon playing Duke's records on the jukebox in Small's Paradise Bar, asking myself why I was in New York and finding reassurance in the music that although the way seemed cloudy (I had little money and would soon find it necessary to sleep in the park below City College), I should remain there and take my chances.

Later, I met Langston Hughes, who took me up to Sugar Hill to visit the Duke in his apartment. Much to my delight, the great musician remembered me, was still apologetic because of the lateness of the band's arrival at Tuskegee, and asked me what he could do to aid the music department. I suggested that we were sadly deficient in our library of classical scores and recordings, and he offered to make the school a gift of as extensive a library of recordings as was needed. It was an offer which I passed on to Tuskegee with great enthusiasm, but which, for some reason, perhaps because it had not come directly from Ellington himself or perhaps because several people in the department regarded jazz as an inferior form of music, was rejected. That his was a genuine gesture, I had no doubt, for at the time I was to see a further example of his generosity when Jimmie Lunceford's orchestra, then considered an Ellington rival, came on the radio. The other musicians present kidded Ellington about the challenge of Lunceford's group, to which he responded by listening intently until the number was finished and then commenting "Those boys are interesting. They are trying, they are really trying," without a trace of condescension but with that enigmatic Ellington smile. The brief comment and the smile were enough, the kidding stopped, for we had all been listening—and not for the first time—and we knew that Duke had little to fear from the challenge of Lunceford or anyone else.

Somewhere during his childhood a friend had nicknamed Edward Kennedy Ellington "Duke," and he had proceeded to create for himself a kingdom of sound and rhythm that has remained impregnable to the fluctuations of fad and novelty, even the passing on of key members of his band.

Jazz styles have come and gone and other composer-conductors have been given the title "King of Jazz" and Duke knew the reason why, as did the world—just as he knew the value of his own creation. But he never complained, he simply smiled and made music. Now the other kings have departed, while his work endures and his creativity continues.

When the Pulitzer Prize committee refused to give him a special award for music (a decision which led certain members of that committee to resign), Ellington remarked, "Fate is being kind to me. Fate doesn't want me to be too famous too young," a quip as mocking of our double standards, hypocrisies, and pretensions as the dancing of those slaves who, looking through the windows of a plantation manor house from the yard, imitated the steps so gravely performed by the masters within and then added to them their own special flair, burlesquing the white folks and then going on to force the steps into a choreography uniquely their own. The whites, looking out at the activity in the yard, thought that they were being flattered by imitation and were amused by the incongruity of tattered blacks dancing courtly steps, while missing completely the fact that before their eyes a European cultural form was becoming Americanized, undergoing a metamorphosis through the mocking activity of a people partially sprung from Africa. So, blissfully unaware, the whites laughed while the blacks danced out their mocking reply.

In a country which began demanding the projection of its own unique experience in literature as early as the 1820s, it was ironic that American composers were expected to master the traditions, conventions, and subleties of European music and to force their own American musical sense of life into the forms created by Europe's greatest composers. Thus the history of American classical music has been marked by a struggle to force American experience into European forms.

In other words, our most highly regarded musical standards remained those of the Europe from which the majority of Americans derived. Fortunately, however, not all Americans spring from Europe (or not only from Europe), and while these standards obtained, Negro American composers were not really held to them, since it seemed obvious that blacks had nothing to do with Europe—even though during slavery Negroes had made up comic verses about a dance to which "Miss Rose come in her mistress's clothes/But how she got them nobody knows/And long before the ball did meet/She was dancing Taglioni at the corner of the street . . ." Taglioni being a dancer who was the rage of Europe during the 1850s.

Be that as it may, the dominance of European standards did work a hardship on the Negro American composer because it meant that no matter how inventive he might become, his music would not be considered important—or even American— (1) because of his race and (2) because of the form, if he was a jazzman, in which he worked. Therefore, such a composer as Ellington was at odds with European music and its American representatives, just as he was at odds with the racial attitudes of the majority of the American population, and while primarily a creative composer, he was seen mainly in his role as entertainer. Doubtless this explains the withholding from Ellington of the nation's highest honors.

It isn't a matter of being protected, as he suggests, from being too famous too young—he is one of the world's most famous composers and recognized by the likes of Stravinsky, Stokowski, and Milhaud as one of the greatest moderns—but the fact that his creations are far too *American.* Then there is also the fact of Ellington's aura of mockery. Mockery speaks through his work and through his bearing. He is one of the most handsome of men, and to many his stage manners are so suave and gracious as to appear a put-on—which quite often they are. And his manner, like his work, serves to remind us of the inadequacies of our myths, our legends, our conduct, and our standards. However, Ellington's is a creative mockery in that it rises above itself to offer us something better, more creative and hopeful, than we've attained while seeking other standards.

During a period when groups of young English entertainers who based their creations upon the Negro American musical tradition have effected a questionable revolution of manners among American youths, perhaps it is time we paid our respects to a man who has spent his life reducing the violence and chaos of American life to artistic order. I have no idea where we shall all be a hundred years from now, but if there is a classical music in which the American experience has finally discovered the voice of its own complexity, it will owe much of its direction to the achievements of Edward Kennedy Ellington. For many years he has been telling us how marvelous, mad, violent, hopeful, nostalgic, and (perhaps) decent we are. He is one of the musical fathers of our country, and throughout all these years he has, as he tells us so mockingly, loved us madly. We are privileged to have lived during his time and to have known so great a man, so great a musician.

—From *The Sunday Star* (Washington, D.C.),
April 27, 1969

The Art of Romare Bearden

I regard the weakening of the importance given to objects as the capital transformation of Western art. In painting, it is clear that a painting of Picasso's is less and less a "canvas," and more and more the mark of some discovery, a stake left to indicate the place through which a restless genius has passed . . .

—André Malraux

This series of collages and projections by Romare Bearden represents a triumph of a special order. Springing from a dedicated painter's unending efforts to master the techniques of illusion and revelation which are so important to the craft of painting, they are also the result of Bearden's search for fresh methods to explore the plastic possibilities of Negro American experience. What is special about Bearden's achievement is, it seems to me, the manner in which he has made his dual explorations serve one another, the way in which his technique has been used to discover and transfigure its object. For in keeping with the special nature of his search and by the self-imposed "rules of the game," it was necessary that the methods arrived at be such as would allow him to express the tragic predicament of his people without violating his passionate dedication to art as a fundamental and transcendent agency for confronting and revealing the world.

To have done this successfully is not only to have added a dimension to the technical resourcefulness of art, but to have modified our way of experiencing reality. It is also to have had a most successful encounter with a troublesome social anachronism which, while finding its existence in areas lying beyond the special province of the artist, has nevertheless caused great confusion among many painters of Bearden's social background. I say *social,* for although Bearden is by self-affirmation no less than by public identification a Negro American, the quality of his *artistic* culture can by no means be conveyed by that term. Nor does it help to apply the designation "black" (even more amorphous for conveying a sense of cultural complexity), and since such terms tell us little about the unique individuality of the artist or anyone else, it is well to have them out in the open where they can cause the least confusion.

What, then, do I mean by anachronism? I refer to that imbalance in American society which leads to a distorted perception of social reality, to a stubborn blindness to the creative possibilities of cultural diversity, to the prevalence of negative myths, racial stereotypes, and dangerous illusions about art, humanity, and society. Arising from an initial failure of social justice, this anachronism divides social groups along lines that are no longer tenable while fostering hostility, anxiety, and fear; and in the area to which we now address ourselves it has had the damaging effect of alienating many Negro artists from the traditions, techniques, and theories indigenous to the arts through which they aspire to achieve themselves.

Thus, in the field of culture, where their freedom of self-definition is at a maximum and where the techniques of artistic self-expression are most abundantly available, they are so fascinated by the power of their anachronistic social imbalance as to limit their efforts to describing its manifold dimensions and its apparent invincibility against change. Indeed, they take it as a major theme and focus for their attention, they allow it to dominate their thinking about themselves, their people, their country, and their art.

And while many are convinced that simply to recognize social imbalance is enough to put it to riot, few achieve anything like artistic mastery, and most fail miserably through a single-minded effort to "tell it like it is."

Sadly, however, the problem for the plastic artist is not one of "telling" at all, but of *revealing* that which has been concealed by time, by custom, and by our trained incapacity to perceive the truth. Thus it is a matter of destroying moribund images of reality and creating the new. Further, for the true artist, working from the top of his times and out of a conscious concern with the most challenging possibilities of his form, the unassimilated and anachronistic—whether in the shape of motif, technique or image—is abhorrent, an evidence of conceptual and/or technical failure, of challenges unmet. And although he may ignore the anachronistic through a preoccupation with other pressing details, he can never be satisfied simply by placing it within a frame. For once there, it becomes the symbol of all that is not art and a mockery of his powers of creation. So at his best he struggles to banish the anachronistic element from his canvas by converting it into an element of style, a device of his personal vision.

For as Bearden demonstrated here so powerfully, it is of the true artist's nature and mode of action to dominate all the world and time through technique and vision. His mission is to bring a new visual order into the world, and through his art he seeks to reset society's clock by imposing upon it his own method of defining the times. The urge to do this determines the form and character of his social responsibility, it spurs his restless exploration for plastic possibilities, and it accounts to a large extent for his creative aggressiveness.

But it is here precisely that the aspiring Negro painter so often falters. Trained by the circumstances of his social predicament to a habit (no matter how reluctant) of accommodation, such an attitude toward the world seems quite quixotic. He is, he feels, only one man, and the conditions which thwart his freedom are of such enormous dimensions as to appear unconquerable by purely plastic means—even at the hands of the most highly trained, gifted, and arrogant artist.

"Turn Picasso into a Negro and *then* let me see how far he can go," he will tell you, because he feels an irremediable conflict between his identity as a member of an embattled social minority and his freedom as an artist. He cannot avoid—nor should he wish to avoid—his group identity, but he flounders before the question of how his group's experience might be given statement through the categories of a nonverbal form of art which has been consciously exploring its own unique possibilities for many decades before he appeared on the scene; a self-assertive and irreverent art which abandoned long ago the task of mere representation to photography and the role of storytelling to the masters of the comic strip and the cinema. Nor can he draw upon his folk tradition for a simple answer. For here, beginning with the Bible and proceeding all the way through the spirituals and blues, novel, poem, and the dance, Negro Americans have depended upon the element of narrative for both entertainment and group identification. Further, it has been those who have offered an answer to the question—ever crucial in the lives of a repressed minority—of who and what they are in the most simplified and graphic terms who have won their highest praise and admiration. And unfortunately, there seems to be (the African past notwithstanding) no specifically Negro American tradition of plastic design to offer him support.

How then, he asks himself, does even an artist steeped in the most advanced lore of his craft and most passionately concerned with solving the more advanced problems of painting as *painting* address himself to the perplexing question of bringing his art to bear upon the task (never so urgent as now) of defining Negro American identity, of pressing its claims for recognition and for justice? He feels, in brief, a near-unresolvable conflict between his urge to leave his mark upon the world through art and his ties to his group and its claims upon him.

Fortunately for them and for us, Romare Bearden has faced these questions for himself, and since he is an artist whose social consciousness is no less intense than his dedication to art, his example is of utmost importance for all who are concerned with grasping something of the complex interrelations between race, culture, and the individual artist as they exist in the United States. Bearden is aware that for Negro Americans these are times of eloquent protest and intense struggle, times of rejection and redefinition—but he also knows that all this does little to make the question of the relation of the Negro artist to painting any less difficult. And if the cries in the street are to find effective statement on canvas, they must undergo a metamorphosis. For in painting, Bearden has recently observed, there is little room for the lachrymose, for self-pity or raw complaint; and if they are to find a place in painting, this can only be accomplished by infusing them with the freshest sensibility of the times as it finds existence in the elements of painting.

During the late thirties when I first became aware of Bearden's work, he was painting scenes of the Depression in a style strongly influenced by the Mexican muralists. This work was powerful, the scenes grim and brooding, and through his depiction of unemployed workingmen in Harlem he was able, while evoking the Southern past, to move beyond the usual protest painting of that period to reveal something of the universal elements of an abiding human condition. By striving to depict the times, by reducing scene, character, and atmosphere to a style, he caught something of both the universality of Harlem life and the "harlemness" of the national human predicament.

I recall that later, under the dual influences of Hemingway and the poetic tragedy of Federico García Lorca, Bearden created a voluminous series of drawings and paintings inspired by Lorca's *Lament for Ignacio Sánchez Mejías.* He had become interested in myth and ritual as potent forms for ordering human experience, and it would seem that by stepping back from the immediacy of the Harlem experience—which he knew both from boyhood and as a social worker—he was freed to give expression to the essentially poetic side of his vision. The products of that period were marked by a palette which, in contrast with the somber colors of the earlier work and despite the tragic theme with its underlying allusions to Christian rite and mystery, was brightly sensual. And despite their having been consciously influenced by the compositional patterns of the Italian primitives, and the Dutch masters, these works were also resolutely abstract.

It was as though Bearden had decided that in order to possess his world *artistically,* he had to confront it *not* through propaganda or sentimentality, but through the finest techniques and traditions of painting. He sought to re-create his Harlem in the light of his painter's vision, and thus he avoided the defeats suffered by many of the aspiring painters of that period who seemed to have felt that they had only to reproduce, out of a mood of protest and despair, the scenes and surfaces of Harlem in order to win artistic mastery and accomplish social transfiguration.

It would seem that for many Negro painters even the *possibility* of translating Negro American experience into the modes and conventions of modern painting went unrecognized. This was, in part, the result of an agonizing fixation upon the racial mysteries and social realities dramatized by color, facial structure, and the texture of

Negro skin and hair. And again, many aspiring artists clung with protective compulsiveness to the myth of the Negro American's total alienation from the larger American culture—a culture which he helped to create in the areas of music and literature, and where in the area of painting he has appeared from the earliest days of the nation as a symbolic figure—and allowed the realities of their social and political situation to determine their conception of their role and freedom as artists.

To accept this form of the myth was to accept its twin variants, one of which holds that there is a pure mainstream of American culture which is "unpolluted" by any trace of Negro American style or idiom, and the other (propagated currently by the exponents of *Negritude*) which holds that Western art is basically racist, and thus anything more than a cursory knowledge of its techniques and history is to the Negro artist irrelevant. In other words, the Negro American who aspired to the title "Artist" was too often restricted by sociological notions of racial separatism, and these appear not only to have restricted his use of artistic freedom, but to have limited his curiosity as to the abundant resources made available to him by those restless and assertive agencies of the artistic imagination which we call technique and conscious culture.

Indeed, it has been said that these disturbing works of Bearden's (which literally erupted during a tranquil period of abstract painting) began quite innocently as a demonstration to a group of Negro painters. He was suggesting some of the possibilities through which commonplace materials could be forced to undergo a creative metamorphosis when manipulated by some of the nonrepresentational techniques available to the resourceful craftsman. The step from collage to projection followed naturally, since Bearden had used it during the early forties as a means of studying the works of such early masters as Giotto and de Hooch. That he went on to become fascinated with the possibilities lying in such "found" materials is both an important illustrative instance for younger painters and a source for our delight and wonder.

Bearden knows that regardless of the individual painter's personal history, taste, or point of view, he must, nevertheless, pay his materials the respect of approaching them through a highly conscious awareness of the resources and limitations of the form to which he has dedicated his creative energies. One suspects also that as an artist possessing a marked gift for pedagogy, he has sought here to reveal a world long hidden by the clichés of sociology and rendered cloudy by the distortions of newsprint and the false continuity imposed upon our conception of Negro life by television and much documentary photography. Therefore, as he delights us with the magic of design and teaches us the ambiguity of vision, Bearden insists that we *see* and that we see in depth and by the fresh light of the creative vision. Bearden knows that the true complexity of the slum dweller and the tenant farmer requires a release from the prison of our media-dulled perception and a reassembling in forms which would convey something of the depth and wonder of the Negro American's stubborn humanity.

Being aware that the true artist destroys the accepted world by way of revealing the unseen, and creating that which is new and uniquely his own, Bearden has used cubist techniques to his own ingenious effect. His mask-faced Harlemites and tenant farmers set in their mysteriously familiar but emphatically abstract scenes are nevertheless resonant of artistic and social history. Without compromising their integrity as elements in plastic compositions his figures are expressive of a complex reality lying beyond their frames. While functioning as integral elements of design, they serve simultaneously as signs and symbols of a humanity that has struggled to survive the decimating and fragmentizing effects of American social processes. Here faces which draw upon the abstract character of African sculpture for their composition are made to focus our attention upon the far from abstract reality of a people. Here abstract interiors are presented in which concrete life is acted out under repressive conditions. Here, too, the poetry of the blues is projected through synthetic forms which, visually, are in themselves tragicomic and eloquently poetic. A harsh poetry this, but poetry nevertheless; with the nostalgic imagery of the blues conceived as visual form, image, pattern, and symbol—including the familiar trains (evoking partings and reconciliations) and the conjure women (who appear in these works with the ubiquity of the witches who haunt the drawing of Goya) who evoke the abiding mystery of the enigmatic women who people the blues. And here, too, are renderings of those rituals of rebirth and dying, of baptism and sorcery which give ceremonial continuity to the Negro American community.

By imposing his vision upon scenes familiar to us all, Bearden reveals much of the universally human which they conceal. Through his creative assemblage he makes complex comments upon history, upon society, and upon the nature of art. Indeed, his Harlem becomes a place inhabited by people who have in fact been *resurrected,* re-created by art, a place composed of visual puns and artistic allusions and where the sacred and profane, reality and dream are ambiguously mingled. And resurrected with them in the guise of fragmented ancestral figures and forgotten gods (really masks of the instincts, hopes, emotions, aspirations and dreams) are those powers that now surge in our land with a potentially destructive force which springs from the very fact of their having for so long gone unrecognized, unseen.

Bearden doesn't impose these powers upon us by explicit comment, but his ability to make the unseen manifest allows us some insight into the forces which now clash and rage as Negro Americans seek self-definition in the slums of our cities. There is a beauty here, a harsh beauty that asserts itself out of the horrible fragmentation which Bearden's subjects and their environment have undergone. But, as I have said, there is no preaching; these forces have been brought to eye by formal art. These works take us from Harlem through the South of tenant farms and northward-bound trains to tribal Africa; our mode of conveyance consists of every device which has claimed Bearden's artistic attention, from the oversimplified and scanty images of Negroes that appear in our ads and photo-journalism, to the discoveries of the School of Paris and the Bauhaus. He has used the discoveries of Giotto and Pieter de Hooch no less than those of Juan Gris, Picasso, Schwitters, and Mondrian (who was no less fascinated by the visual possibilities of jazz than by the compositional rhythms of the early Dutch masters), and has discovered his own uses for the metaphysical richness of African sculptural forms. In brief, Bearden has used (and most playfully) all of his artistic knowledge and skill to create a curve of plastic vision which reveals to us something of the mysterious complexity of those who dwell in our urban slums. But his is the eye of a painter, not that of a sociologist, and here the elegant architectural details which exist in a setting of gracious but neglected streets and the buildings in which the hopeful and the hopeless live cheek by jowl, where failed human wrecks and the confidently expectant explorers of the frontiers of human possibility are crowded together as incongruously as the explosive details in a Bearden canvas—all this comes across plastically and with a freshness of impact that is impossible for sociological cliché or raw protest.

Where any number of painters have tried to project the "prose" of Harlem—a task performed more successfully by photographers—Bearden has concentrated upon releasing its poetry, its abiding rituals and ceremonies of affirmation—creating a surreal poetry compounded of vitality and powerlessness, destructive impulse, and the all-pervading and enduring faith in their own style of American humanity. Through his faith in the powers of art to reveal the unseen through the seen, his collages have transcended their immaculateness as plastic constructions. Or to put it another way, Bearden's meaning is identical with his method. His combination of technique is in itself eloquent of the sharp breaks, leaps in consciousness, distortions, paradoxes, reversals, telescoping of time, and surreal blending of styles, values, hopes, and dreams which characterize much of Negro American history. Through an act of creative will, he has blended strange visual harmonies out of the shrill, indigenous dichotomies of American life, and in doing so, reflected the irrepressible thrust of a people to endure and keep its intimate sense of its own identity.

Bearden seems to have told himself that in order to possess the meaning of his Southern childhood and Northern upbringing, that in order to keep his memories, dreams, and values whole, he would have to re-create them, humanize them by reducing them to artistic style. Thus, in the poetic sense, these works give plastic expression to a vision in which the socially grotesque conceals a tragic beauty, and they embody Bearden's interrogation of the empirical values of a society that mocks its own ideals through a blindness induced by its myth of race. All this, ironically, by a man who visually at least (he is light-skinned and perhaps more Russian than "black" in appearance) need never have been restricted to the social limitations imposed upon easily identified Negroes. Bearden's art is therefore not only an affirmation of his own freedom and responsibility as an individual and artist, it is an affirmation of the irrelevance of the notion of race as a limiting force in the arts. These are works of a man possessing a rare lucidity of vision.

—Introduction in catalogue "Romare Bearden: Paintings and Projections," for exhibition held at the Art Gallery of the State University of New York at Albany, November 25–December 22, 1968; reprinted in *The Massachusetts Review,* Winter 1977

Society, Morality, and the Novel

Surely it would be of more value for a novelist to write novels than to spend his energies discussing The Novel, for by carrying out his chosen task there he has the possibility of moving beyond the given level of either his talent or his cold perception of life's meaning—of "playing beyond his game," as it were, and thus achieving for himself and for his readers some new insight into the human predicament, some new facet of human possibility. By risking the unknown which appears whenever he follows the lead of his imagination as driven by his hopes and his fears, he has the chance of achieving the significantly new and thus becoming himself a part of that which he achieves. While on the other hand, theorizing about the form, function, and *raison d'être* of the novel leads him straightway into the fields of social and aesthetic criticism, the domain of specialists. Here he is held in by rules which are alien to his obsessive need to play with the fires of chaos and to rearrange reality to the patterns of his imagination. For while it is the drive of the critic to create systems of thought, it is that of the novelist to re-create reality in the forms which his personal vision assumes as it plays and struggles with the vividly illusory "eidetic-like" imagery left in the mind's eye by the process of social change. Life for him is a game of hide-and-seek in which he is eternally the sometimes delighted but more often frustrated "it."

Critics are, on the whole, more "adult" types. They share a liking for order and have little patience with dashing about trying to pin down the multiple illusions projected by life with arbitrary ones of one's arrogant own; it is their function to dispense with that annoying characteristic of life with the bright pure light of their methods. The novelist must take chances or die, while the critic would make it unnecessary to do so. Critics would give you the formula that would make the achievement of a major fiction as certain as making a pre-mixed apple pie. They analyze, they classify, they man the lines of continuity linking up present developments with past achievements of the form; and with their specialized knowledge, they compose the novelists' most sensitively aware audience—or so we have long been accustomed to regarding them. Presently we shall take a closer look at just how contemporary fiction criticism mediates between the American novelist and the American reader, but here let us simply observe that novelists have, for the most part, been content to keep out of the critics' domain. They either confine those critical formulations necessary to the clarification of their own artistic purposes to their notebooks, or they have used them to give substance to occasional book reviews. Most often they have merely played them out by ear as they went about composing specific works of fiction. And for good reason.

Actually, the best way for a novelist to discuss the problem of The Novel is in the form of *a specific novel,* for whenever fictional technique makes conjunction with an image of reality, each is mutually transformed. Every serious novel is, beyond its immediate thematic preoccupations, a discussion of the craft, a conquest of the form, and a conflict with its difficulties; a pursuit of its felicities and beauty. To engage in this by way of getting at specific aspects of experience is enough to do, and difficult enough to do, to keep the novelists busy; but today, with some of our more important critics handing down the death sentence of the form (for in their solemn "The novel is dead," there sounds a Platonist "*Let* it be dead"), or when they boast left-handedly in print of their loss of interest in contemporary novels, the novelist is feinted into a position of defending his craft. If he is to pay the critics the serious attention which certainly a few of them deserve, and if he is at all interested in winning those readers who would listen to the critics, he is moved to attempt some broad public formulation of his personal approach to his craft. One writes because one wishes to be read on one's own terms; thus, since the critics dismiss the novel as moribund, a bit of explicit communication between the novelist and his prospective readers is most in order. He must prepare to play Antony to the novel's Caesar, for truly an act of assassination has been commissioned. Nor is this all, for a question of personal dignity and rationality is raised. For if the critics are correct, and some are so persuaded, how then does the novelist justify, even to himself, his passionate involvement with a literary form which is dead? Why does he pour his energies into a form that dooms his best efforts to dust even before the effort of the imagination takes place, and upon what does he base his faith?

But first an attempt at definition, which inasmuch as such definition represents the general assumptions out of which I personally approach the abstract form, it will make up for what it lacks in precision with its validity as autobiography.

Let us begin by mentioning a characteristic of the novel which seems so obvious that it is seldom mentioned, and which as a consequence tends to make most discussions of the form irritatingly abstract: By its nature it seeks to communicate a vision of experience. Therefore, whatever else it achieves artistically, it is basically a form of communication. When successful in communicating its vision of experience, that magic thing occurs between the world of the novel and the reader—and indeed, between reader and reader in their mutual solitude—which we know as communion. For, as with all the fictive arts, the novel's medium of communication consists in a "familiar" experience occurring among a particular people, within a particular society or nation (and the novel is bound up with the notion of nationhood), and it achieves its universality, if at all, through accumulating images of reality and arranging them in patterns of universal significance. It is not, like poetry, concerned primarily with words, but with action depicted in words; and it operates by amplifying and giving resonance to a specific complex of experience until, through the eloquence of its statement, that specific part of life speaks metaphorically for the whole.

The novel can communicate with us only by appealing to that which we "know," through actual experience or through literature, to be the way things occur. "Yes, this is how it is," we tell ourselves when the fictive illusion works its spell; or we say, "Yes, but such and such is left out." Thus, between the novelist and his most receptive reader (really a most necessary collaborator who must participate in bringing the fiction into life), there must exist a body of shared assumptions—concerning reality and necessity, possibility and freedom, personality and value—along with a body of feelings, both rational and irrational, which arise from the particular circumstances of their mutual society. Even the technical means through which this collaboration is brought about depends upon the reader's acceptance of a set of artistic conventions, those "once upon a time" devices which announce the telling of a tale and which introduce a mood of receptiveness in the reader and through which alone the novelist is able to bring his fiction alive. Even surrealism depended for its effects upon those who were initiated into its conventions and who shared its assumptions concerning art and value. It is by appealing to our sense of experience and playing upon our shared assumptions that the novelist is able to reveal to us that which we do not know—that is, the unfamiliar within the familiar—and affirm that which we assume to be truth and to reveal to us his own hard-won vision of truth.

In this sense the novel is rhetorical. For whatever else it tries to do, it must do so by persuading us to accept the novelist's projection of an experience which, on some level or mixtures of levels, we have shared with him, and through which we become empathetically involved in the illusory and plotted depiction of life which we identify as fictional art. We repay the novelist in terms of our admiration to the extent that he intensifies our sense of the real—or, conversely, *to the extent that he justifies our desire to evade certain aspects of reality which we find unpleasant beyond the point of confrontation.* In the beginning was not only the word but the contradiction of the word; sometimes we approach life out of a tragic sense of necessity, and again with its denial. In this lies the novel's flexibility and its ability to transcend the bounds of class and nation, its endless possibilities of mutation. It is rooted in man's most permanent feelings and it brings into full vision the processes of his current social forms. This is almost enough in itself to keep the novelist at his task, for in it lies the possibility of affirmation and personal definition.

As an art form the novel is obsessed by the relationship between illusion and reality as revealed in duration, in process. "All poetry," writes Malraux, "implies the destruction of the relationship between things that seems obvious to us in favor of particular relationships imposed by the poet."

Thus the novel seeks to take the surface "facts" of experience and arrange them in such ways that for a magic moment reality comes into sharp and significant focus. And I believe that the primary social function of the novel (the function from which it takes its form and which brought it into being) is that of seizing from the flux and flow of our daily lives those abiding patterns of experience which, through their repetition and consequences in our affairs, help to form our sense of reality and from which emerge our sense of humanity and our conception of human value.

More than any other literary form, the novel is obsessed with the impact of change upon personality. It was no mere historical accident that the novel came into prominence during the eighteenth century or that it became fully conscious of itself as an art form during the nineteenth. Its appearance marked the fulfillment of a social need that arose out of the accelerated process of historical change. Before the eighteenth century, when man was relatively at home in what seemed to be a stable and well-ordered world (and if not well-ordered, stable nevertheless), there was little need for this change-obsessed literary form. Nor was there literacy enough, nor was the individual, tied as he was to an order imposed by religion and kingship, isolated enough. Nor was individual self-consciousness sufficiently widespread. Human beings were agreed both as to what constituted reality and as to what were the limits of human possibility; and social change—one of our key words to the understanding of the novel—was by no means the problem it became during the nineteenth and twentieth centuries; nor is it accidental that it was during the nineteenth that the novel revealed itself as the most flexible art form for dealing with social change. When the middle class broke the bounds of the feudal synthesis and took its fustian stance, such a literary form was needed, and the novel was the answer. And it is here that the novel assumed the role which makes it so useful today: it thrives on change and social turbulence.

Vaguely, at first, an awareness had grown in men's minds that social reality had cut loose from its traditional base and that new possibilities of experience and new forms of personality had been born into the awfully expanded world. Old class lines were being liquidated and new lines were being formed and broken and re-formed; new types of men were arising mysteriously out of a whirling social reality which revealed itself protean in its ability to change its appearance and its alignments rapidly, ruthless in its impiety toward old images of order, toward traditional modes of behavior. This is of course to telescope many things; there were several phases of the novel and many variations on the form—from the picaresque to the more stable and refined novel of manners, from the sociology-obsessed novel to the Flaubertian "art" novel—nevertheless, the form attempted to deal with the disparate experiences which society now threw up, and it tried to synthesize these disparate elements. Often quite consciously, and by way of being sheer narrative entertainment, it created new values and affirmed those values which endured specific social changes; and it rejected those acts and ideals which threatened middle-class society.

Perhaps the novel evolved in order to deal with man's growing awareness that behind the façade of social organization, manners, customs, myths, rituals, religions of the post-Christian era, lies chaos. Man knows, despite the certainties which it is the psychological function of his social institutions to give him, that he did not create the universe and that the universe is not at all concerned with human values. Man knows even in this day of marvelous technology and the tenuous subjugation of the atom, that nature can crush him, and that at the boundaries of human order the arts and the instruments of technology are hardly more than magic objects which serve to aid us in our ceaseless quest for certainty. We cannot live, as someone has said, in the contemplation of chaos, but neither can we live without an awareness of chaos, and the means through which we achieve that awareness, and through which we assert our humanity most significantly against it, is great art. And in our time the most articulate art form for defining ourselves and for asserting our humanity is the novel. Certainly it is our most rational art form for dealing with the irrational.

In the nineteenth century, during the moment of greatest middle-class stability—a stability found actually only at the center and there only relatively, in England and not in the colonies; in Paris rather than in Africa, for there the baser instincts, the violence and greed could destroy and exploit non-European societies in the name of humanism and culture, beauty and liberty, fraternity and equality while protecting the humanity of those at home—the novel reached its first high point of formal self-consciousness. Appropriated by the middle class (for such art forms are the creation of total civilizations, not of a single class), it was characterized by an expansiveness which reflected a class of people who had learned to live with the tempo of change and to absorb the effects of change into its frame of existence. And it marked the course of its development and charted the health of its ideals. Perhaps we admire the nineteenth-century European novel today, in our time of frantic uncertainty, because we find it vibrant and alive and confidently able to confront good and evil in all their contradictory entanglement. In it was implicit the tragic realization that the treasure of possibility is always to be found in the cave of chaos, guarded by the demons of destruction. It is Abel Magwitch, the jailbird, who makes Pip's dream of a gentleman's life a reality in *Great Expectations;* just as it was the existence of human slavery and colonial exploitation which made possible many of the brighter achievements of modern civilization. And just as the muted insincerities and snobberies of Jane Austen's characters are but highly refined versions of those major insincerities and snobberies, connected with the exercise of power, which have led in our time to the steady crumbling of the empire upon which genteel English society has rested. In that moment of genteel stability, however, those who were most willfully aware of their destiny viewed freedom not simply in terms of necessity but in terms of possibility, and they were willing to take the risks necessary to attain their goals. It was the novel which could communicate their awareness of this sense of possibility along with its cost, and it was the novel which could, on the other hand, reconstruct an image of experience which would make it unnecessary for one to be aware of the true reality upon which society rested. Men, it is said, can stand reality in small doses only, and the novel, sometimes consciously, sometimes not, measured out that dosage.

This was the dark side of the novel's ability to forge images which would strengthen man's will to say No to chaos and affirm him in his task of humanizing himself and the world. It would, even while "entertaining" him, help create that fragile state of human certainty and stability (or the illusion of it at least, for perhaps illusion is all we ever have) and communion which is sometimes called love, brotherhood, democracy, sometimes simply the good life! And it could limit those who would share that life and justify our rejection of their humanity, and while condemning snobbery, could yet condone it, for society was admittedly hieratic and closed to pressure from below.

Enough of general definition; if the novel had not existed at the time the United States started becoming conscious of itself as a nation—a process still, fortunately, for ourselves and the world, unachieved—it would have been necessary for Americans to invent it. For in no other country was change such a given factor of existence; in no other country were the class lines so fluid and change so swift and continuous *and intentional.* In no other country were men so conscious of having defined their social aims or so committed to working toward making that definition a reality. Indeed, a conscious awareness of values describes the condition of the American experiment, and very often much of our energy goes into finding ways of losing that consciousness. In the beginning was not only the word, but its contradiction.

I would be on dangerous ground if I tried to trace too closely a connection between documents of state and literature, since in literature universality is an accepted aim; yet the novel is an art of the specific, and for my own working orientation that connection exists in the United States beyond all questions of cultural chauvinism. Certainly this is evident in our great nineteenth-century novels. The moral imperatives of American life that are implicit in the Declaration of Independence, the Constitution, and the Bill of Rights were a part of both the individual consciousness and the conscience of those writers who created what we consider our classic novels—Hawthorne, Melville, James, and Twain; and for all the hooky-playing attitude of the twenties or the political rebelliousness of the thirties, and the reluctance of contemporary writers to deal explicitly with politics, they still are. They are in fact the baffle against which Mr. Lionel Trilling's "hum and buzz of implication" (his understandably vague definition of manners in the novel) sound. These documents form the ground of assumptions upon which our social values rest; they inform our language and our conduct with public meaning, and they provide the broadest frame of reference for our most private dramas. One might deliberately overemphasize and say that most prose fiction in the United States—even the most banal bedroom farce, or the most rarefied, stylized, and understated comedy of manners—is basically "about" the values and cost of living in a democracy. Being an American, wrote Henry James, is a complex fate, but perhaps far more troublesome than the necessity of guarding against superstitious overevaluation of Europe is the problem of dealing with the explicitness of the omnipresent American ideal. For out of the consciously experimental and revolutionary origins of the country has grown the obsession with defining the American experience; first in order to distinguish it from that of Europe and now to determine our uniqueness as a civilization and our proper historical role among the nations. The impetus was twofold, the need to achieve national self-consciousness being, from the beginning, a political goal springing from our rejection of European social forms; and along with this was the pressure of our broad cultural diversification brought about by the open character of the society, the waves of immigration and the rapid expansion, horizontally along the frontier and then vertically through the processes of urbanization and industrialization. Out of this came our most urgent problem of identity, and who and what is American are still perplexing questions even today. Many definitions are offered, in naturalistic art, in *Life* picture portfolios of the American woman, in government photographs of American workers (in which one seldom sees a Negro), in the racial and aesthetic types of movie queens, in works of sociology, in attempts to depict aspects of the American experience in novels—but few are acceptable without qualification, not even during wartime. All Americans are in this sense members of minority groups, even the Anglo-Saxons, whose image has from the beginning dominated all the rest—and one meaning of the social friction in American life is the struggle of each racial, cultural, and religious group to have its own contribution to the national image recognized and accepted. The novelist can bemoan this pressure, for it can be oppressive, but he cannot escape it; and indeed, in our time, it might be his road to a meaningful relationship to the community. "Who," asks Constance Rourke in her *American Humor,* "ever heard of a significant English novel called *The Englishman,* or an excellent French novel called *Le Français?* The simple aggressive stress belonged to an imagination perennially engaged by the problem of the national type. . . ."

Moreover, this national need gives us a clue to one of the enduring functions of the American novel, which is that of defining the national type as it evolves in the turbulence of change, and of giving the American experience, as it unfolds in its diverse parts and regions, imaginative integration and moral continuity. Thus it is bound up with our problem of nationhood. During the nineteenth century it was clearly recognized by those writers who speak meaningfully to us today, and it comes through novels which in their own times went, like *Moby-Dick,* unread. *Moby-Dick, The Adventures of Huckleberry Finn, The Bostonians,* and so on, are all "regional" novels, and each simultaneously projects an image of a specific phase of American life, and each is concerned with the moral predicament of the nation. For all the optimism of the early years, there was in this literature no easy affirmation, and for all its involvement with a common set of political and social assumptions, there was, as the list makes plain, no lack of variety of theme. It has been observed that modern American fiction is the only body of literature which is not the work of intellectuals, yet from the beginning our novelists have been consciously concerned with the form, technique, and content of the novel, not excluding ideas. What the observer (a Frenchman) missed was that the major ideas of our society were so alive in the minds of every reader that they could be stated implicitly in the contours of the form. For it is all grounded in a body of the most abstract and explicitly stated conceptions of human society and one which in the form of the great documents of state constitutes a body of assumptions about human possibility which is shared by all Americans—even those who resist most violently any attempt to embody them in social action.

Indeed, these assumptions have been questioned and resisted from the very beginning, for man cannot simply say, "Let us have liberty and justice and equality for all," and have it; and a democracy more than any other system is always pregnant with its contradiction. The contradiction was to erupt in the Civil War, an event which has had a profound effect upon the direction of our fiction and which continues to influence our thinking about the novel far more than we bother to recognize. For it marked an interruption of our moral continuity, and the form of our novels changed as a result.

As Henry James wrote in his study of Hawthorne:

> The subsidence of that great convulsion has left a different tone from the tone it found, and one may say that the Civil War marks an era in the history of the American mind. It introduced into the national consciousness a certain sense of proportion and relation, of the world being a more complicated place than it had hitherto seemed, the future more treacherous, success more difficult. At the rate at which things are going, it is obvious that good Americans will be more numerous than ever; but the good American, in days to come, will be a more critical person than his complacent and confident grandfather. He has eaten of the tree of knowledge. He will not, I think, be a sceptic, and still less, of course, a cynic; but he will be, without discredit to his well-known capacity for action, an observer. He will remember that the ways of the Lord are inscrutable, and that this is a world in which everything happens; and eventualities, as the

late Emperor of the French used to say, will not find him intellectually unprepared.

Actually, the good American fell quite a bit short of James's prediction, and he made far less of his traumatic fraternal conflict than might have been expected. And if it did not make him skeptical (and how could he have been really, with all the material progress released after the war with which to affirm his optimism?), it did make him evasive and given to compromise on basic principles. As a result, we have the interruption of moral continuity symbolized in the failure of Reconstruction and the Hayes-Tilden Compromise, and now in the 1950s, at a time when our world leadership has become an indisputable and perplexing fact, we have been forced to return to problems, in the form of the current desegregation issue, which should have been faced up to years ago. What is more, the event of World War I found the good American hardly less innocent than he had been fifty-three years before; only now, instead of such critical and morally affirmative novels as *Huckleberry Finn, The Gilded Age,* or *The Bostonians* (in which James depicts the decay of moral values among those who had been leaders in the struggle for abolition) or *Moby-Dick* or *The Confidence-Man,* we had literature which came out of the individual writer's private need to express a national mood of glamorized social irresponsibility. Certainly the attitude of moral evasion expressed in the failure of Reconstruction and the materialism of the Gilded Age prepared for the mood of glamorized social irresponsibility voiced in the fiction of the twenties, and it created a special problem between the American novelist and his audience.

Being committed to optimism, serious novels have always been troublesome to Americans, precisely because of their involvement with our problem of identity. If they depict too much of reality, they frighten us by giving us a picture of society frozen at a point so far from our optimistic ideal (for in depiction there is a freezing as well as a discovery and release of possibility) that we feel compelled to deny it. Yet if they leave out too much, we cannot take them seriously for very long, even though we might buy them in hundreds of thousands of copies. As readers we wait for definition, and even now in this so-called age of conformity we wish to discover some transcendent meaning in at least some of the turbulence which whirls through our lives, and which during a period of highest prosperity makes it necessary for all the media of communication to set up an incessant "hard sell" incantation to reassure us that all is well, all meaningful, the very best state of affairs; that things confer happiness, beauty, and grace; and that fertility is a smiling face in a magazine ad.

Another way of putting it is that we are a people who, while desiring identity, have been reluctant to pay the cost of its achievement. We have been reluctant since we first suspected that we are fated to live up to our sacred commitments or die, and the Civil War was the form of that fateful knowledge. Thus we approach serious novels with distrust until the moment comes when the passage of time makes it possible for us to ignore their moral cutting edge. In the nineteenth century serious fiction was fairly easily disposed of—it was given to children, especially to boys; and then only after being purged of those matters that were less likely to disturb the juvenile than his parents. *Huckleberry Finn* was banned from libraries, *Moby-Dick* went unread, and those who understood James were very few. It was as though the older generation was saying, "These are problems which you are likely to encounter when you come of age; we are too busy making progress to give them our attention"; but when the younger generation was grown up, so much had happened in the swift change, and they had been joined by so many new arrivals, that they forgot both the nature of the problem and its historical source. By the twenties the relationship between the serious novel and themselves as readers had undergone a remarkable change, and if they had lost little of the simplicity of James's earlier good American, they were now full of doubts as to the possibility of the ideal and they had begun to resent it much as they resented the necessity of participating in the war.

And so with the novel; where before it had affirmed the sacred assumptions, now, as in the Caporetto scene in *A Farewell to Arms,* it denied the very words in which the ideals were set down. The nineteenth-century novelist had stood within society even as he criticized its behavior, and now the novelist thought of himself as alienated. Yet, ironically, men like Fitzgerald and Hemingway were actually more celebrated than any American writer since Mark Twain. America, for all her shocks and traumas, has been an extremely lucky country, and Time, as with the little boy in Dylan Thomas's poem, has let her be "golden in the mercy of his means," allowing her a generosity of mistakes and laxities and a childlike ability to forget her falls from grace, wealth and movement and a ruddy strength of people and national resources and a ceaseless stream of wonderful toys with which to excite her imagination and to keep her unaware of Time's ambiguousness—and her luck was extended to her writers of the twenties.

After the clangor and pain of the war and its booming echo in the expansion and hysterical faddism of the twenties, the moral irresponsibility had become so chronic that one would have expected the writers either to depict it critically or to become silent, but instead they had the luck to give at least part of their attention to the so-called revolution of the word, which was offered as a literary equivalent of that distraction from the realities of the moral situation provided by the material prosperity of the boom. Nor was it simply a matter of luck. For all their pose of alienation, the writers of the twenties worked hard, found images that were simple enough to project those feelings of impotence and moral irresponsibility that were typical of the times, and make them romantically attractive. The brave lonely man, broken by war and betrayed by politicians—who had lost faith in everything except the basic processes of existence and his own physical strength; who could no longer believe in the old American creed; who traveled to Pamplona and Paris; who drank too much and who made love compulsively and was romantically unhappy (but who yet had the money to indulge in his escape)—became the dominant image of the American. And so gripping was this image that some critics look back today and actually confuse the image with the reality of the times.

By the twenties, in other words, the novel, which in the hands of our greatest writers had been a superb moral instrument, became morally diffident and much of its energy was turned upon itself in the form of technical experimentation. Which is not to deny that a writer like Hemingway has profound moral seriousness, or to imply that technique is ever void of moral implications, but to say that here the personal despair which gave the technique its resonance became a means of helping other Americans to avoid those aspects of reality which they no longer had the will to face. This is the tragedy implicit in Hemingway's morality of craftsmanship, the attempt to make a highly personal morality the informing motive of an art form which by its very nature is extremely social and, despite its pose, deeply rooted in the assumption it denied. For as I read Hemingway today I find that he affirms the old American values by the eloquence of his denial; makes his moral point by stating explicitly that he does not believe in morality; achieves his eloquence through denying eloquence; and is most moral when he denies the validity of a national morality which the nation has not bothered to live up to since the Civil War. The confusion—for both Hemingway's imitators and his readers—lay in the understatement, and here the basic American assumptions exerted their power. For although it is seldom mentioned, Hemingway is as obsessed with the Civil War and its aftermath as any Southern writer, and the fact turns up constantly in his work. The children of the good Americans of the 1880s had forgotten the historical problems which made Hemingway's understatement fully meaningful—even though it was here exactly that the ideas which were said to be absent were most present and powerful. But many readers, unhappy with the compact we'd made with history, took the novelist's point of view as authority to go on a binge of hooky-playing, as an assurance that there were no new lessons to learn and the old ones were invalid anyway. And this with the Depression only a few years away.

Yet so fascinating were the images of the twenties, and so deep and irrational the feelings which they made articulate, that thirty years later critics who readily admit the superficiality of most novels written during the thirties (for they tried to be responsible by avoiding complexity), and who reject most contemporary fiction even when written to their formulas, insist that we measure ourselves by the triumphs of the twenties. They tell us again and again of the Lost Generation novelists, and their names (with Faulkner's recently added) clang in our ears like gongs in evidence of our failure and our doom. They, we are told, did that which we cannot hope to do, and if this fails to discourage us, the nineteenth-century novel of manners is held before us as final evidence of our futility and the novel's point of highest glory and swift decline.

Not that we disagree absolutely with any of this, but we must reply to these charges. Thank God that we can't do what the Lost Generation novelists did, because as good as it was, it was not good enough or broad enough to speak for today. And thank God again that the nineteenth-century European novel of manners is dead, for it has little value in dealing with our world of chaos and catastrophe. We have lived a different life and we have seen it with different eyes. Nor are we innocent of the world's new complexity or given to false pieties, easy hopes, or facile rejections; nor are we unaware of the weakness implicit in our tremendous strength or of the possibilities of strength in our apparent weaknesses, for the iron-weight of tragic awareness has descended upon us. Ours is a task which, whether recognized or not, was defined for us to a large extent by that which the novels of the twenties failed to confront, and implicit in their triumphs and follies were our complexity and our travail.

Indeed, so much has been written about the triumphs of the twenties that we either forget its failures or forgive them; which would be well if the critics would only leave it at that. But the contemporary novelist cannot afford to forget the failures, even if he makes no accusations, and the intentions of such a novelist as Saul Bellow can be properly understood only in light of that failure. After two well-written, neatly constructed novels which paid their respects to the standards of the twenties, Bellow's major work to date is *The Adventures of Augie March,* which at first glance looks like the work of a completely different man. It is characterized by a big conception of human possibility and a quality of wonder arising out of the mysteriousness of a reality which keeps its secret despite the documentation of the social scientists, and it is informed by a knowledge of chaos which would have left the novelists of the twenties discouraged. Certainly it confronts large areas of American reality which simply didn't get into the novels of the twenties.

I would go further here and say that neither the American fiction of the twenties nor that of the fifties can be understood outside the perspective provided by the nineteenth century. Edmund Wilson seems to suggest this by his current reexamination of the Civil War and post-Reconstruction periods, and certainly the younger writers who came through the Depression and who shared the social and political preoccupations of the thirties feel this, even though they've bothered little to write about it. Yet it is one of the goals of the current serious novel to create precisely that moral perspective. Here perhaps is one of our most serious failures, for not only has the drift of our internal social affairs brought this period and its unsolved moral problems back into the national consciousness; world events have revealed their broad relevance to areas far beyond our national borders. In other words, the events which wracked the United States during the Civil War period and again during the twenties were the archetype of events which are now sweeping all societies, and our failure to confront them when they arose (for perhaps they could not have been *solved*) has proved not only an impediment to our leadership among the nations but a hindrance to our achievement of national identity.

Perhaps the attitude of those novelists who matured during the forties has been too quietly aloof, our absorption in craft problems too concentrated, and our dependence upon the perceptiveness of critics too trusting. Perhaps we who disdain the easy pose are far more alienated than the writers of the Lost Generation, for we have assumed an understanding on the part of both reader and critic which is at best rare, and we fail to say very much that is explicit about our intentions or points of view.

By contrast the writers of the twenties did a brilliant job of publicizing their own efforts. During the time when *Ulysses* and *Finnegans Wake* were being written, both were being eagerly discussed in several languages and in several countries. Because Joyce (no member of the Lost Generation but the most "difficult" novelist of the period) was not only writing his books; he was, with the help of magazine editors, friends, and critics, just as busily establishing the convention by which he wished his novels read. Whatever his success in absenting himself from his novels as omniscient author—a technical problem already solved by Conrad and James—in his correspondence he did anything but pare his nails; he was far too busy telling those who tell the readers how to read just what the godlike author was about. Clearly it is no accident that more people have read about how his books should be read than have read them. And for all of the legend of Hemingway's nonintellectuality, and the aesthetic ideas spun in metaphors from the sports, he has nevertheless written so much and so significantly about writing that two younger writers are busy making a volume of his observations. One needs but mention the examples of Eliot, Gertrude Stein, Ezra Pound, and Henry James before them.

Looked at coldly, the notion of a Lost Generation was a literary conceit of such major proportions that today it seems like a swindle. The alienation of these writers had something of the character of putting on a mask in Macy's window at high noon and pretending that no one knows who you are. They had not only the comfort of being in the well-advertised advance guard; they were widely read and their characters' way of life was imitated to the extent that several generations of young people stylized their speech and attitudes to the pattern of Fitzgerald's and Hemingway's fiction. While "Papa" Hemingway (who *is* the "father" of many writers who today sneer at him) was so alienated that a song, "Pul-eeze, Mr. Hemingway," could find popularity. With *Esquire* carrying their work to readers in most of the barbershops throughout the country, these writers were lost in a crowd of admirers, of whom I was one.

For all the personal despair which informed it and the

hard work which brought it into being, the emphasis on technique gave something of a crossword-puzzle-fad aspect to the literature of the twenties, and very often the question of the Sphinx was lost in the conundrums. Without doubt, major questions went unanswered. Yet, happily, its concentration upon the problems of craft made it impossible for us to ignore the fact that literature, to the extent that it is art, is *artificial.* Each of us must learn to read and to understand the devices through which fiction achieves its illusion of reality. Thanks to their popularizers and the generations of critics who followed, we know how to read their books extremely well—especially in terms of those matters which preoccupied them—and the level of craft consciousness is so high in the United States that today by keeping to formula and the neat theme (neat because smoothed down and polished since Flaubert's time) the writer may turn out readable, smoothly fashioned novels which evoke a response much like that we extend those miniaturists who work in ivory. The phrases are neatly done, there is a great economy of means (because so little of substance) and tightness of structure, great texture and facile sensibility; and anyone who has had a course in modern literature or who has read a little criticism has the satisfaction of knowing just how each image and metaphor operates, who the hero's literary ancestors were, just how Joyce, James, Freud, Marx, Sartre, Camus, Unamuno, Kierkegaard, and Fitzgerald, Hemingway, and Lionel Trilling, came into it. There is, in this writing, no excess of emotion (if any at all) or shrillness of tone; no vulgarity or uncertainties of taste; nor are there any patterns of action that would violate the assumptions concerning life or art that are held by the most timid middle-class reader. The writer may, if he likes, play the turns of the whole corpus of genteel nineteenth- and twentieth-century fiction, especially the European, and never exhaust himself in the process of translating these well-polished themes and situations into American backgrounds, and utilizing along the way all the latest verbal techniques approved by the critics.

Despite their skill, however, these novels are not widely read, and the reader who looks here for some acknowledgment of the turbulence he feels around him would be better satisfied by a set of comic books. He thus turns to "fact" books for "scientific" consolation because the orientation in reality which the novel should afford him is not forthcoming, and the critics, appalled by the stillborn children which they have called forth, look backward to those highly dubious Edens of the nineteenth century and of the Lost Generation, and pronounce the novel dead. If so, perhaps they have helped to dig its grave.

For if the nineteenth-century way with troublesome novels was to turn them over to the children, we in our time, being more sophisticated and literate, turn them over to the critics, who proceed to reduce the annoying elements to a minimum. And more deplorable is that fact that once the critics have spoken, the story is likely to appear in subsequent editions with the troublesome, the difficult, material edited out—as happened to one of the most sublime stories in the language—really an extremely foreshortened novel—Faulkner's "The Bear." Perhaps the test of a work's becoming a classic in the United States depends upon the extent to which it can withstand this process of conscious reduction. Perhaps what I am saying is that since the novel is a moral instrument possessing for us an integrative function, our typical American reaction to it is to evade as much of its moral truth as possible; perhaps out of an effort to postpone completing that identity which we are compelled nonetheless to seek. But as to the critics' role in this process, I am struck that while their reductions are made on aesthetic grounds, it turns out that what they consider expendable is usually the heart of the fiction. And here, out of fairness I must include novelists like James and Hemingway who, by way of defining their own aesthetic positions, have contributed to some of the current confusion.

Let us take Henry James on Hawthorne, Hemingway on *The Adventures of Huckleberry Finn,* and Malcolm Cowley on Faulkner's "The Bear"—these three, because each has been quite influential in shaping our ideas of American fiction and how it should be read, and because at least two have been offered as guides for the younger novelists who have come upon the scene since the thirties. Each of the texts constitutes a definition of American fiction; each has been most helpful in giving us orientation; and today all three have become quite mischievous in adding to the current confusion over the role, the character, and the condition of the contemporary novel. Indeed, it is as though a set of familiar and useful touchstones had become inflated and transformed into a set of wandering rocks which threatens to crush us.

Each of the texts which I shall quote is so familiar that there would be no need to quote them except for the fact that each has achieved its importance by virtue of its being a statement by reduction of either a perceptive critical observation or the meaning of an important novel. So that in order to determine where we are and how we arrived at some of our current convictions concerning the novel, it is useful to take a look at exactly what was discarded from the originals.

Mr. Trilling has almost alone been responsible for making a single statement of Henry James more prominent in our thinking than all the complex aesthetic ideas spelled out in the prefaces and the essays. In developing his theory of the novel of manners, he paraphrases James's catalogue of those items of civilization which were missing from Hawthorne's America, itself an extension of a list which Hawthorne had himself made in the preface to his novel *Transformation (The Marble Faun):*

> No author, without a trial, can conceive of the difficulty of writing a romance about a country where there is no shadow, no antiquity, no mystery, no picturesque and gloomy wrong, nor anything but a commonplace prosperity, in broad and simple daylight, as is happily the case with my dear native land.

This is Mr. Hawthorne, and while admiring what he made of his position one must observe that in this world one finds that which one has the eyes to see. Certainly there was gloomy wrong enough both in the crime against the Indians and in the Peculiar Institution which was shortly to throw the country into conflict; there was enough mystery in Abraham Lincoln's emergence, then in process, still to excite us with wonder; and in that prosperity and "broad and simple daylight" enough evil was brewing to confound us even today. But let us see what James made of this quote, for it is upon James that Mr. Trilling bases much of his argument:

> The perusal of Hawthorne's American Note-Books operates as a practical commentary upon this somewhat ominous text. It does so at least to my own mind; it would be too much perhaps to say that the effect would be the same for the usual English reader. An American reads between the lines—he completes the suggestions—he constructs a picture. I think I am not guilty of any gross injustice in saying that the picture he constructs from Hawthorne's American diaries, though by no means without charms of its own, is not, on the whole, an interesting one. It is characterized by an extraordinary blankness—a curious paleness of colour and paucity of detail. Hawthorne, as I have said, has a large and healthy appetite for detail, and one is therefore the more struck with

the lightness of the diet to which his observation was condemned. For myself, as I turn the pages of his journals, I seem to see the image of the crude and simple society in which he lived. I use these epithets, of course, not invidiously, but descriptively; if one desires to enter as closely as possible into Hawthorne's situation, one must endeavour to reproduce his circumstances. We are struck with the large number of elements that were absent from them, and the coldness, the thinness, the blankness, to repeat my epithet, present themselves so vividly that our foremost feeling is that of compassion for a romancer looking for subjects in such a field. It takes so many things, as Hawthorne must have felt later in life, when he made the acquaintance of the denser, richer, warmer European spectacle—it takes such an accumulation of history and custom, such a complexity of manners and types, to form a fund of suggestion for a novelist. If Hawthorne had been a young Englishman, or a young Frenchman of the same degree of genius, the same cast of mind, the same habits, his consciousness of the world around him would have been a very different affair; however obscure, however reserved, his own personal life, his sense of the life of his fellow-mortals would have been almost infinitely more various. The negative side of the spectacle on which Hawthorne looked out, in his contemplative saunterings and reveries, might, indeed [And it is here that Mr. Trilling's much repeated paraphrase begins], with a little ingenuity, be made almost ludicrous; one might enumerate the items of high civilization, as it exists in other countries, which are absent from the texture of American life, until it should become a wonder to know what was left. No State, in the European sense of the word, and indeed barely a specific national name. No sovereign, no court, no personal loyalty, no aristocracy, no church, no clergy, no army, no diplomatic service, no country gentlemen, no palaces, nor castles, nor manors, nor old country-houses, nor parsonages, nor thatched cottages, nor ivied ruins; no cathedrals, nor abbeys, nor little Norman churches; no great Universities nor public

> schools—no Oxford, nor Eton, nor Harrow; no literature, no novels, no museums, no pictures, no political society, no sporting class—no Epsom nor Ascot! Some such list as that might be drawn up of the absent things in American life—especially in the American life of forty years ago, the effect of which, upon an English or a French imagination, would probably as a general thing be appalling. The natural remark, in the almost lurid light of such an indictment, would be that if these things are left out, everything is left out. [And it is here that Mr. Trilling leaves us.] The American knows that a good deal remains; what it is that remains—that is his secret, his joke, as one may say. It would be cruel, in this terrible denudation, to deny him the consolation of his natural gift, that "American humour" of which of late years we have heard so much.

"That is," says Mr. Trilling, "no sufficiency of means for the display of a variety of manners, no opportunity for the novelist to do his job of searching out reality, not enough complication of appearance to make the job interesting." Mr. Trilling states in the same essay that while we have had great novels in America, they "diverge from [the novel's] classic intention . . . the investigation of the problem of reality beginning in the social field."

All this is admittedly a damaging list—of reasons why American novelists cannot write French or English novels of manners. And when I read the much quoted passage in context (one of Mr. Trilling's disciples has deduced from it that personality exists in the United States only in New England and in the South) it struck me as amusing that Mr. Trilling missed the point that these lacks were seen as appalling for the French or English imagination—for it seems obvious that in that time neither Frenchmen nor Englishmen were going to try to write American novels (though things are different today), that James was addressing his remarks to Europeans and that all the energy that has been wasted in bemoaning the fact that American society is not English or French society could have stopped right there.

James's remarks on Hawthorne are justified to the extent that the perspective he was creating helped him to establish his own point of departure; it is to the insistence that his observations be binding upon other writers that I object. Nor can I overlook the fact that James was basing his remarks on the thinness of Hawthorne's notebooks—which, compared with James's, were thin indeed. Yet just when, one might ask without too much irreverence, did a writer's quality—James's prolific notebooks notwithstanding—depend upon the kind of notebooks he kept? Did anyone ever see Shakespeare's notebooks? And would anyone who read Dostoevsky's *A Writer's Diary* without an acquaintance with the novels suspect that it was the journal of one of the greatest novelists of all time?

For me the most surprising aspect of Mr. Trilling's paraphrase is that he says nothing at all concerning what James calls the "American joke"—a matter which, as a novelist, intrigues me no end. I take it that James's reference to American humor was nothing more than condescension and that he did not mean it in the sense that it was used by Miss Constance Rourke, who saw American humor as having the function of defining and consolidating the diverse elements—racial, cultural, and otherwise—which go into the American character; a business to which James made a profound contribution, even when irritated by what he considered the thinness of American experience. One wonders what the state of novel criticism would be today if Mr. Trilling had turned his critical talent to an examination of the American joke. Perhaps *this* has been the objective of the American novel all along, even the Jamesian novel, and perhaps this is its road to health even today.

But now another touchstone: "All modern American literature comes from one book by Mark Twain called *Huckleberry Finn* . . . it's the best book we've had. All American writing comes from that." So wrote Ernest Hemingway in *Green Hills of Africa* in a much-quoted statement. It is significant that here again we have a statement by reduction which, although it helped Hemingway to create his own position, has helped us ignore what seems to me to be the very heart of *Huckleberry Finn.* He tells us in the same context that we should stop reading at the point where Jim is stolen from Huck and Tom Sawyer because from that point on it is cheating. And here we have something different from the first example and perhaps, in light of Hemingway's great influence upon American fiction, more important. In order to define his own position (or perhaps to justify it, since the statement comes some ten years after he caught the public's imagination) Hemingway found it necessary to reduce the meaning of *Huckleberry Finn* to the proportions of his own philosophical position. Far more meaningful to him than the moral vision and sense of language which summoned them into being were the techniques through which Twain gave it expression. And so with the critics who usually quote Hemingway's remarks with the most important phrase in his statement omitted. For when he goes on to advise us that we should stop reading *Huckleberry Finn* at that point where Jim is stolen from Huck and Tom Sawyer, he reveals either a blindness to the moral point of the novel or his own inability to believe in the moral necessity which makes Huck know that he must *at least make the attempt* to get Jim free; to "steal" him free, is the term by which Twain reveals Huck's full awareness of the ambiguousness of his position, and through which he roots the problem in American social reality and draws upon the contradiction between democratic idealism and the existence of slavery. Nevertheless, it is exactly that part of the action which represents the formal externalization of Huck-Twain's moral position; and if one may speak of ritual here, it is in this part of the action that the fundamental American commitment, the myth, is made manifest. Without this attempt *Huckleberry Finn* becomes the simple boy's book that many would rather it be, a fantasy born of pure delight and not really serious at all.

Yet Hemingway is a most serious author and in this statement he not only tells us more about himself than about Twain or American fiction, he expresses the basic difference in points of view between nineteenth- and twentieth-century writers. Thus not only did *Huckleberry Finn* lose some of its meaning; many of those whom it might have helped to some sense of the moral and historical continuity of American life were advised, in effect, that such continuity was nonexistent. But it is useless to quarrel with history, and as one who is committed to the craft I can even admit that Hemingway's art justifies what he made of Twain's. But what are we to say of the critics who circulate his statement as though it were the word of God? What of their responsibility to the reader?

One can easily agree with Hemingway as to the importance of *Huckleberry Finn* in the continuity of the American novel while rejecting his dismissal of its ethical intention, for we have in William Faulkner a twentieth-century writer who not only continues, in his own way, the technical direction outlined by Mark Twain, but also, despite Lionel Trilling's dismissal of him as "being limited to a provincial scene," continues the moral commitment which was at the heart of Twain's fiction.

Just as experimental and technically "difficult" as Hemingway and, perhaps, as Joyce, Faulkner missed the broad publicity accorded their experimentation; not only because his more important works were published somewhat later, but because there is no doubt that he is involved both as a Southerner and as an artist with those issues which most white Americans have evaded since the Civil War. It was not until about 1946 that Faulkner began to win the attention of Americans generally, and a great aid in this was the Viking Portable, edited by Malcolm Cowley. By this time several of the most important novels were out of print, and one cannot overstress the service rendered by Cowley and the publisher in issuing their collection with Cowley's introduction and commentary. Through it many Americans not only made their first contact with a great writer, but were introduced to a superb imaginative account of what so much of the conflict in American life is all about. Thus my reason for mentioning Cowley's reduction of the meaning of Faulkner's "The Bear" is not to detract from the importance of the Portable, but further to illustrate the reduction of the moral intention of American prose fiction by way of making it easier for the reader.

> "The Bear" [writes Mr. Cowley] is the longest of Faulkner's stories and in many ways the best. It is divided into five parts. If you want to read simply a hunting story, and one of the greatest in the language, you should confine yourself to the first three parts and the last, which are written in Faulkner's simplest style. The long fourth part is harder to read and deals with more complicated matters. In it Faulkner carries to an extreme his effort toward putting the whole world into one sentence, between one capital letter and one period. . . . In all this section of "The Bear" the reader may have difficulty in fitting the subjects to the predicates and in disentangling the subordinate clauses; and yet, if he perseveres, he will discover one of Faulkner's most impressive themes: the belief in Isaac McCaslin's heart that the land itself had been cursed by slavery, and that the only way for him to escape the curse was to relinquish the land.

But not only does this fourth section (which takes up thirty-four of the 136 pages) contain this theme; it is in fact the dislocated beginning of the story and the time-present in which the bear hunt is evoked out of the memory of the hero, who at the age of twenty-one confronts his cousin with his decision to give up the land. Although it has recently been included in a volume of hunting stories with the fourth section missing, "The Bear" is not about a bear hunt at all, but about a young American's hunt for moral identity. Significantly, it is the centerpiece of a volume which takes its title from the Negro spiritual "Go Down, Moses," and its main concern is with the problem of American freedom as faced by a specific white Southerner in relation to his individual heritage. Here, in *Go Down, Moses,* Faulkner comes most passionately to grips with the moral implications of slavery, the American land, progress and materialism, tradition and moral identity—all major themes of the American novel. And it is in the fourth section—not really difficult once it is grasped that it is a remembered dialogue with the "he saids" left out—where Isaac and his cousin McCaslin argue out the issues between them (McCaslin basing his arguments on tradition and history and Isaac on a form of Christian humanism) that Faulkner makes his most extended effort to define the specific form of the American Negro's humanity and to get at the human values which were lost by both North and South during the Civil War. Even more important, it is here that Isaac McCaslin demonstrates one way in which the individual American can assert his freedom from the bonds of history, tradition, and things, and thus achieve moral identity. Whether we accept Isaac McCaslin's solution or not, the problem is nevertheless basic to democratic man—as it was to Ahab and as it was to Huck Finn.

Nor do I wish to oversimplify Mr. Cowley's problem; if serious fiction is to be made available to those to whom it is addressed—those who, as Ike McCaslin puts it, "have nothing else to read with but the heart"—the critic must interpret for them, and in the process of making literature available to all the levels of a democratic society, some loss of quality, some blunting of impact, seems inevitable. Nevertheless the critic has some responsibility in seeing that the reader does not evade the crucial part of a fiction simply because of its difficulty. For sometimes the difficulty is the mark of the writer's deepest commitment to life and to his art. To water down his work is not only to mock the agony and the joy which go into his creation but to rob the reader of that transcendence which, despite his tendency to evade the tragic aspects of reality, he seeks in literature. The intent of criticism is frustrated, the fiction reduced to mere entertainment, and the reader is encouraged to evade self-scrutiny. In the leveling process to which all things are subjected in a democracy, one must depend always upon the *individual's* ability to rise out of the mass and achieve the possibility implicit in the society. One must depend upon his ability, whoever he is and from whatever class and racial group, to attain the finest perception of human value, to become as consciously aware of life, say, as any of Henry James's "super-subtle fry." Certainly the novelist must make some such assumption if he is to allow himself range in which to work toward the finest possibilities of his talent and his form without a frustrating sense of alienation.

Which tells us something of why the novelists keep writing despite the current attempts to legislate the novel a quiet death. It also gives us a hint as to why a number of the younger novelists are not at all hindered by the attempt to reduce the novel to only one of its possible forms; yes, and why the picaresque, many-leveled novel, swarming with characters and with varied types and levels of experience, has appeared among us. Though we love the classics, some of us have little interest in what Mr. Trilling calls the "novel of manners," and I don't believe that a society hot in the process of defining itself can for long find its image in so limited a form. Surely the novel is more than he would have it be, and if it isn't, then we must make it so.

One of the comic aspects of the current controversy over what a novel should be is the implicit assumption, held by Cooper, James, and Hawthorne, as well as several contemporary critics, that society was created mainly so that novelists could write about it. It is felt that society should be of such shape that the novelist can settle it neatly into prefabricated molds with the least spilling of rude life over the sides. The notion started when the forest was still being cleared, and it is understandable that a certain type of writer would have liked to deal with fine cabinetry instead of crude logs. Still, minds that were philosophically and politically most advanced and sophisticated conceived this society, but even they had nonetheless to deal with raw and rapidly moving materials. And so in the beginning did the American novel, and so today. We are not so crude now as during James's time but we have even less stability and there is no longer a stable England to which to withdraw for perspective. World War I, the Depression, World War II and Korea, the Cold War, the threat of the atom, our discovery of the reality of treason, and now Egypt and Hungary make us aware that reality, which during Dickens's time seemed fairly stable, has broken loose from its old historical base, and the Age of Anxiety is truly more than a poetic conceit. Closed societies are now the flimsiest of illusions, for all the outsiders are demanding in.

In fact, there is no stability anywhere and there will not be for many years to come, and progress now insistently asserts its tragic side; the evil now stares out of the bright sunlight. New groups will ceaselessly emerge, class lines will continue to waver and break and re-form; great wealth there will be and a broader distribution of that wealth, and a broader distribution of ideas along with it. But the problem of what to do with the increased leisure which wealth makes possible will continue to plague us—as will the problem of deciding just what constitutes a truly human way of life. The fundamental problems of the American situation will repeat themselves again and again and will be faced more or less by peoples throughout the world: Where shall we draw the line upon our own freedom in a world in which culture, tradition, and even history have been shaken up? At how fast a pace should we move toward social ideals? What is worth having and what worth holding? Where and in what pattern of conduct does true value, at a given moment, lie? These questions will continue to press upon us even if the dream of world peace is achieved, for they are questions built into the core of modern experience.

For the novelist the existence of these questions creates a basic problem of rhetoric. How does one in the novel (the novel which is a work of art and not a disguised piece of sociology) persuade the American reader to identify that which is basic in man beyond all differences of class, race, wealth, or formal education? How does one not only make the illiterate and inarticulate eloquent enough so that the educated and more favorably situated will recognize wisdom and honor and charity, heroism and capacity for love when found in humble speech and dress? And conversely, how does one persuade readers with the least knowledge of literature to recognize the broader values implicit in their lives? How, in a word, do we affirm that which *is* stable in human life beyond and despite all processes of social change? How give the reader that which we do have in abundance, all the countless untold and wonderful variations on the themes of identity and freedom and necessity, love and death, and with all the mystery of personality undergoing its endless metamorphosis?

Here are questions which cannot be answered by criticism; they call for the novel, many novels; and as long as there are writers willing to accept the challenge of reducing the reality in which they exist to living form, there will be readers interested in their answers, and we need have no fear that the novel is moribund.

—From *The Living Novel,* Macmillan, Inc., 1957

"A Very Stern Discipline"

Interviewers: *Do you think that one of the faults of the Negro writer is that he is unable to come to terms with the human condition—particularly that of the Negro in America?*

Ellison: Here I don't like to speak generally. The conception of the human condition varies for each and every writer just as it does for each and every individual. Each must live within the isolation of his own senses, dreams, and memories; each must die his own death. For the writer the problem is to project his own conception eloquently and artistically. Like all good artists, he stakes his talent against the world. But if a Negro writer is going to listen to sociologists—as too many of us do—who tell us that Negro life is thus and so in keeping with certain sociological theories, he is in trouble because he will have abandoned his task before he begins. If he accepts the clichés to the effect that the Negro family is usually a broken fam-

This interview (given in 1965), which the author has revised from the original tapes, was conducted by three young Negro writers: James Thompson, Lennox Raphael, and Steve Cannon.

ily, that it is matriarchal in form and that the mother dominates and castrates the males, if he believes that Negro males are having all of these alleged troubles with their sexuality, or that Harlem is a "Negro ghetto"—which means, to paraphrase one of our writers, "piss in the halls and blood on the stairs"—well, he'll never see the people of whom he wishes to write. He'll never learn to use his own eyes and his own heart, and he'll never master the art of fiction.

I don't deny that these sociological formulas are drawn from life, but I do deny that they define the complexity of Harlem. They only abstract it and reduce it to proportions which the sociologists can manage. I simply don't recognize Harlem in them. And I certainly don't recognize the people of Harlem whom I know. Which is by no means to deny the ruggedness of life there, nor the hardship, the poverty, the sordidness, the filth. But there is something else in Harlem, something subjective, willful, and complexly and compellingly human. It is that "something else" that challenges the sociologists who ignore it, and the society which would deny its existence. It is that "something else" which makes for our strength, which makes for our endurance and our promise. This is the proper subject for the Negro American writer. Hell, he doesn't have to spend all the tedious time required to write novels simply to repeat what the sociologists and certain white intellectuals are broadcasting like a zoo full of parrots—*and* getting much more money for it than most Negro writers will ever see. If he does this, he'll not only go begging, but worse, he'll lie to his people, discourage their interest in literature, and emasculate his own talent.

This is tricky terrain, because today the sociologists are up to their necks in politics and have access to millions of governmental dollars, which, I'm afraid, have been secured at the cost of propagating an image of the Negro condition that is apt to destroy our human conception of ourselves just at the moment when we are becoming politically free. Those who buy this image are surely in trouble, no matter the money it brings.

One of the saddest sights currently to be seen is that provided by one of our most "angry" Negro writers, who has allowed himself to be enslaved by his acceptance of negative sociological data. He rants and raves against society, but he's actually one of the safest Negroes on the scene. Because he challenges nothing, he can only shout " 'taint" to some abstract white " 'tis," countering lies with lies. The human condition? He thinks that white folks have ruled Negroes out of it.

A few years ago there was a drunk who collected newspapers from the shops along Broadway between 145th and 153rd streets. He was a Negro who had fought the wine for a long time and who when drunk was capable of a metaphysical defiance. His favorite pastime was to take a stand near a stoplight and accost white people who stopped for the traffic signal with shouts of "Why don't you go back downtown! I want all you white motherfuckers—mens *and* womens—to go on back downtown!" Our hate-mongering fellow writer reminds me very much of this man, for he is about as effective and no less obscene. Yes, we do have a terrible time in dealing with the human condition.

One critic has said that the Jewish writer went through a similar period. I think he was trying to say that the Negro writer would very soon get over this and become the major strength in American literature.

I hope he's right, but I wouldn't want to make a prediction. I think, however, that the parallel is much too facile. Jewish writers are more familiar with literature as a medium of expression. Their history provides for a close identification with writers who were, and are, Jewish even when they wrote or write in languages other than Yiddish or Hebrew; and this even when that identification rests simply on a shared religious tradition and hardly on any other cultural ground whatsoever. It reminds me of our attempts to claim Pushkin and Dumas as Negroes.

By contrast, neither Negro American expression nor religion has been primarily literary. We are by no means, as is said of the Jews, "people of the Book"—not that I see this as a matter for regret. For we have a wider freedom of selection. We took much from the ancient Hebrews and we do share, through Christianity, the values embodied in the literature of much of the world. But our expression has been oral as against "literary." And when it comes to the question of identifying those writers who have shaped American literature—the framers of the Declaration, the Constitution, and Lincoln excepted—we tend to project racial categories into the areas of artistic technique, form, insight; areas where race has no proper place. We seem to forget that one can identify with what a writer has written, with its form, its manner, techniques, while *rejecting* the writer's beliefs, his prejudices, philosophy, values.

The Jewish American writers have, on the other hand, identified with Eliot, Pound, Hemingway, and Joyce *as writers* while questioning and even rejecting their various attitudes toward the Jews, toward religion, politics, and many other matters. They have taken possession of that which they could use from such writers and converted it to express their own personal and group sense of reality; they have used it to express their own definitions of the American experience. But we Negro writers seem seldom to have grasped this process of acculturation. Too often we've been in such haste to express our anger and our pain as to allow the single tree of race to obscure our view of the magic forest of art.

If Negro writers ever become the mainstay of American literature, it will be because they have learned their craft and used the intensity, emotional and political, of their group experience to express a greater area of American experience than the writers of other groups. What the Jewish American writer had to learn before he could find his place was the American-ness of his experience. He had to see himself as American and project his Jewish experience as an experience unfolding within this pluralistic society. When this was done, it was possible to project this variant of the American experience as a metaphor for the whole.

However, I don't believe that any one group can speak for the whole experience—which isn't, perhaps, desirable. They can only reduce it to metaphor, and no one has yet forged a metaphor rich enough to reduce American diversity to form. Certainly the current group of Jewish writers —among whom there are several I admire—do not speak adequately for me or for Negroes generally. But during the thirties Jewish writing, although more skillful, was as provincial as most Negro American writing is today. That's the way it was, and we don't solve problems of history by running away from them. And what I mean by provincial is an inability to see beyond the confines, the constrictions, placed upon Jewish life by its religious and cultural differences with the larger society; by its being basically the experience of an immigrant people who were, by and large, far less cultured than their more representative members.

It took long years of living in this country, long years of being a unique part of American society and discovering that they were not *forced* to live on the Lower East Side, of discovering that there *was* a place for the Jews in this society which did not depend upon their losing their group identity. They discovered that they possessed something precious to bring to the broader American culture, on the lowest as well as on the highest levels of human activity, and that it would have a creative impact far beyond the Jewish community. Many had not only to learn the language but, more wonderful, they had to discover that the Jewish American idiom would lend a whole new dimension to the American language.

How do the situations of the Negro and Jewish writers differ?

I think that Negro Americans as *writers* run into certain problems which the Jews don't have. One is that our lives, since slavery, have been described mainly in terms of our political, economic, and social conditions as measured by outside norms, seldom in terms of our *own* sense of life or our *own* unique American experience. Nobody bothered to ask Negroes how they felt about their own lives. Southern whites used to tell the joke about the white employer who said to a Negro worker, "You're a good hand and I appreciate you. You make my business go much better. *But* although you work well every day, I can never get you to work on Saturday night, even if I offer to pay you overtime. Why is this?" Of course, you know the answer: "If you could just be a Negro one Saturday night, you'd never want to be a white man again." Now, this is a rather facile joke, and a white Southern joke on Negroes; nevertheless, it does indicate an awareness that there is an internality to Negro American life, that it possesses its own attractions and its own mystery.

Now, the pathetic element in the history of Negro American writing is that it started out by reflecting the styles popular at the time, styles uninterested in the human complexity of Negroes. These were the styles of dialect humor transfused into literature from the *white* stereotype of the Negro minstrel tradition. This was Paul Laurence Dunbar and Charles Waddell Chestnutt. It helped them get published but it got in the way of their subject matter and their goal of depicting Negro personality. And let's face it, these were times when white publishers and the white reading public wished to encounter only certain types of Negroes in poetry and fiction.

Even so, it was not a Negro writer who created the most memorable character in this tradition but Mark Twain, whose "Nigger Jim" is, I think, one of the important characters in our literature. Nevertheless, Jim is flawed by his relationship to the minstrel tradition. Twain's drawing of Jim reflected the popular culture of the 1880s, just as the Negro characters you get in much of current fiction are influenced by the stereotypes presented by the movies and by sociology—those even more powerful media of popular culture.

The Negro writers who appeared during the 1920s wished to protest discrimination; some wished to show off their high regard for respectability; they wished to express their new awareness of the African background, and, as Americans trying to win a place as writers, they were drawn to the going style of literary decadence represented by Carl Van Vechten's work. This was an extremely ironic development for a group whose written literature was still in its infancy—as incongruous as the notion of a decadent baby. More ironic, this was a time when Eliot, Pound, Hemingway, and Stein were really tearing American literature apart and reshaping its values and its styles in the "revolution of the word." We always picked the moribund style. We took to dialect at a time when *Benito Cereno, Moby-Dick,* and *Leaves of Grass* were at hand to point a more viable direction for a people whose demands were revolutionary, and whose humanity had been badly distorted by the accepted styles.

During the 1930s we were drawn, for more understandable reasons, to the theories of proletarian literature. So during the twenties we had wanted to be fashionable, and this ensured, even more effectively than the approaching

Depression, the failure of the "New Negro" movement. We fell into that old trap by which the segregated segregate themselves by trying to turn whatever the whites said against us into its opposite. If they said Negroes love fried chicken (and why shouldn't we?), we replied, "We *hate* fried chicken." If they said Negroes have no normal family life, we replied, "We have a staider, more refined, more puritanical family life than you." If they said that Negroes love pork chops, we replied, "We despise them!" With few exceptions, our energies as writers have too often been focused upon outside definitions of reality, and we've used literature for racial polemics rather than as an agency through which we might define experience as we ourselves have seen and felt it. These are negative charges, I know, but they seem true to me.

Indeed, it's very difficult, even today, for younger Negro writers to come along and overcome these negative tendencies. Far too often they have been taught to think in Jim Crow terms: "I can do thus and so—not because human beings express themselves in these ways, but because such and such a *Negro* dared to do so." And if no other Negro has involved himself in the activity in question, then we tend to draw back and doubt that we might do very well even as pioneers. And so the younger writer comes along and tries to write on the models of other Negro writers rather than on the best writers regardless of race, class, or what have you—completely ignoring the fact that all other writers try to pattern themselves on the achievements of the greatest writers, regardless of who the hell they were.

This is how the Jim Crow experience has gotten into our attitudes and set us back. We have been exiled in our own land and, as for our efforts at writing, we have been little better than silent because we have not been cunning. I find this rather astounding, because I feel that Negro American folklore is very powerful, wonderful, and universal. And it became so by expressing a people who were assertive, eclectic, and irreverent before all the oral and written literature that came within its grasp. It took what it needed to express its sense of life and rejected what it couldn't use.

But what we've achieved in folklore has seldom been achieved in the novel, the short story, or poetry. In the folklore we tell what Negro experience really is. We back away from the chaos of experience and from ourselves, and we depict the humor as well as the horror of our living. We project Negro life in a metaphysical perspective and we have seen it with a complexity of vision that seldom gets into our writing. One reason for this lies in the poor teaching common to our schools and colleges, but the main failure lies, I think, in our simpleminded attempt to reduce fiction to a mere protest.

I notice that you mentioned, quite some time ago, that you learned a lot of skill under Richard Wright. Do you find that he gauged his craft to the great writers of the world?

He certainly tried to do so. He was constantly reading the great masters, just as he read the philosophers, the political theorists, the social and literary critics. He did not limit himself in the manner that many Negro writers currently limit themselves. And he encouraged other writers—who usually rebuffed him—to become conscious craftsmen, to plunge into the world of conscious literature and take their chances unafraid. He felt this to be one of the few areas in which Negroes could be as free and as equal as their minds and talents would allow. And like a good Negro athlete, he believed in his ability to compete. In 1940 he was well aware that *Native Son* was being published at a time when *The Grapes of Wrath* and *For Whom the Bell Tolls* would be his main competition. Nevertheless, he looked toward publication day nervously but eagerly. He wished to be among the most advanced artists and was willing to run the risk required.

Earlier you referred to the minstrel as a stereotype. Is it possible to treat such stereotypes as Sambo, or even Stepin Fetchit, as archetypes or motives instead of using them in the usual format?

Well, in fiction stereotypes partake of archetypes. And to the extent that stereotypes point to something basically human, they overlap. And yes, in literary form stereotypes function, as do other forms of characterization, as motives. But the point is that they act as *imposed* motives which treat reality and character arbitrarily. Thus, to redeem them as you suggest, the writer is challenged to reveal the archetypical truth hidden within the stereotype. Here archetypes are embodiments of abiding patterns of human existence which underlie racial, cultural, and religious differences. They are, in their basic humanity, timeless and raceless; while stereotypes are malicious reductions of human complexity which seize upon such characteristics as color, the shape of a nose, an accent, hair texture, and convert them into emblems which render it unnecessary for the prejudiced individual to confront the humanity of those upon whom the stereotype has been imposed.

So in answer to your question as to whether it is possible to use such stereotypes as Sambo and Stepin Fetchit, I'd say that it depends upon the writer's vision. If I should use such stereotypes in fiction, I'd have to reveal their archetypical aspects because my own awareness *of,* and identification *with,* the human complexity which they deny would compel me to transform them into something more recognizably human. To do less would be to reveal a brutalization of my own sense of human personality.

On the other hand, let's take Faulkner. When Lucas Beauchamp first appears in Faulkner's work he appears as a stereotype, but as he was developed throughout the successive novels, he became one of Faulkner's highest representatives of human quality. Or again, when Ned in the last book, *The Reivers,* is seen superficially he appears to be the usual head-scratching, eye-rolling Negro stereotype. But beneath this mask, Ned is a version of John, the archetypical Negro slave of Negro folklore, who always outwits and outtalks his master. Ned masterminds the action of the novel, and in so doing he is revealed as Faulkner's own persona. He is the artist disguised as Negro rogue and schemer.

This suggests that attempts to approach stereotypes strictly in racial terms is, for the Negro writer, very, very dangerous. We must first question what they conceal, otherwise we place ourselves in the position of rejecting the basic truth concealed in the stereotype along with its obvious falsehood. Truth is much too precious for that.

On the stage of Town Hall a few days before the 1964 Democratic Convention, a group from the Mississippi Freedom Democratic party talked of their experiences. To the facile eye one of the men who talked there might well have been mistaken for the Sambo stereotype. He was Southern, rural; his speech was heavily idiomatic, his tempo slow. A number of his surface characteristics seemed to support the stereotype. But had you accepted him as an incarnation of Sambo, you would have missed a very courageous man—a man who understood only too well that his activities in aiding and protecting the young Northern students working in the Freedom Movement placed his life in constant contact with death, but who continued to act. Now, I'm not going to reject that man because some misinformed person, some prejudiced person, sees him as the embodiment of Uncle Tom, or Sambo. What's inside you, brother; what's your heart like? What are your real values? What human qualities are hidden beneath your idiom?

Do you think the reason for this is that Negroes in the U.S. are caught, if they allow themselves to be, in a bind? Do you think that the Negro writer then is forced, sometimes, to go away to gain a perspective? Or can he transcend his situation by remaining in it?

Well, again, I would say that the individual must do that which is necessary for him individually. However, I would also say that it is not objectively necessary to go away. He might solve his problem by leaving the Village or by leaving Harlem. Harlem has always been a difficult place for Negroes to gain perspective on the national experience, because it has sponsored a false sense of freedom. It has also sponsored a false sense of superiority regarding Negroes who live elsewhere. I remember getting into an argument during World War II with a fellow who insisted that Southern Negroes had no knowledge of boxing or baseball. This came from refusing to use his eyes around New York.

One frees oneself, as a writer, by actually going in and trying to get the shape of experience *from the writer's perspective.* I see no other way. But this, unfortunately, requires a writer's type of memory—which is strongly emotional and associative—and a certain amount of technique. You must pay the Negro community the respect of trying to see it through the enrichening perspectives provided by great literature—using your own intelligence to make up for the differences in economy, in class background, in education, in conscious culture, in manners and in attitude toward values. Human beings are basically the same and differ mainly in life-style. Here revelation is called for, not argument.

How do you mean "argument"?

I mean that it's futile to argue our humanity with those who willfully refuse to recognize it, when art can reveal on its own terms more truth while providing pleasure, insight, and, for Negro readers at least, affirmation and a sense of direction. We must assert our own sense of values, beginning with the given and the irrevocable, with the question of heroism and slavery.

Contrary to some, I feel that our experience as a people involves a great deal of heroism. From one perspective, slavery was horrible and brutalizing. It is said that "Those Africans were enslaved, they died in the 'middle passage,' they were abused, their families were separated, they were whipped, they were raped, ravaged, and emasculated." And the Negro writer is tempted to agree. "Yes! God damn it, wasn't that a horrible thing!" And he sometimes agrees to the next step, which holds that slaves had very little humanity because slavery destroyed it for them and their descendants. That's what the Stanley M. Elkins "Sambo" argument implies. But despite the historical past and the injustices of the present, there is from *my* perspective something further to say. I have to *affirm* my forefathers and I *must* affirm my parents or be reduced in my own mind to a white man's inadequate—even if unprejudiced—conception of human complexity. Yes, and I must affirm those unknown people who sacrificed for me. I'm speaking of those Negro Americans who never knew that a Ralph Ellison might exist, but who by living their own lives and refusing to be destroyed by social injustice and white supremacy, real or illusory, made it possible for me to live my own life with meaning. I am forced to look at these people and upon the history of life in the United States and conclude that there is another reality behind the appearance of reality which they would force upon us as truth.

Any people who could endure all of that brutalization and keep together, who could undergo such dismemberment and resuscitate itself, and endure until it could take the initiative in achieving its own freedom is obviously more than the sum of its brutalization. Seen in this perspective, theirs has been one of the great human experiences and one of the great triumphs of the human spirit in modern times. In fact, in the history of the world.

Some might say to your argument that you are expressing your own hopes and aspirations for Negroes, rather than reporting historical reality.

But hope and aspiration are indeed important aspects of the reality of Negro American history, no less than that of others. Besides, it's one of our roles as writers to remind ourselves of such matters, just as it is to make assertions tempered by the things of the spirit. It might sound arrogant to say so, but writers, poets, help create or reveal hidden realities by asserting their existence. Otherwise they might as well become social scientists.

I do not find it a strain to point to the heroic component of our experience, for these seem to me truths which we have long lived by but which we must now recognize consciously. And I am not denying the negative things which have happened to us and which continue to happen, but I am compelled to reject all condescending, narrowly paternalistic interpretations of Negro American life and personality from whatever quarters they come, whether white or Negro. Such interpretations would take the negative details of our existence and make them the whole of our life and personality. But literature teaches us that mankind has always defined itself *against* the negatives thrown it by both society and the universe. It is human will, human hope, and human effort which make the difference. Let's not forget that the great tragedies not only treat of negative matters, of violence, brutalities, defeats, but they treat them within a context of man's will to act, to challenge reality and to snatch triumph from the teeth of destruction.

You said it's unnecessary for one to leave the country to get a perspective. We notice in some of your older writings that after having come back from Rome, you sat up in New Hampshire and wrote Invisible Man.

No, I started *Invisible Man*—that novel about a man characterized by what the sociologists term "high visibility"—in Vermont, during the few months before the war came to an end. I was cooking on merchant ships at the time and had been given shore leave, so I accepted the invitation of a friend and went up there. I had no idea that I was going to start a book. But maybe I should add this: it isn't *where* you are that's important, but what you seek to depict, and most important of all is perspective. And the main perspective through which a writer looks at experience is that provided by literature—just as the perspective through which a physician looks at the human body is the discipline of medicine; an accumulation of techniques, insights, instruments, and processes which have been slowly developed over long periods of time. So when I look at my material I'm not looking at it simply through the concepts of sociology—and I do know something about sociology. I look at it through literature; English, French, Spanish, Russian—especially nineteenth-century Russian literature. And Irish literature, Joyce and Yeats, and through the international literature of the twenties. And through the perspective of folklore. When I listen to a folk story I'm looking for what it conceals as well as what it states. I read it with the same fullness of attention I bring to *Finnegans Wake* or *The Sound and the Fury* because I'm eager to discover what it has to say to me personally.

Living abroad is very necessary for those Negro writers who feel that they've been too cramped here and who wish to discover how it feels to live free of racial restrictions. This is valid. I should also say this: I came to New York from Tuskegee with the intention of going back to finish college. I came up to work. I didn't earn the money, so I stayed. But while I lived at the Harlem YMCA, I did *not* come to New York to live in Harlem—even though I thought of Harlem as a very romantic place. I'm pointing to an attitude of mind; I was not exchanging Southern segregation for Northern segregation, but seeking a wider world of opportunity. And, most of all, the excitement and impersonality of a great city. I wanted room in which to discover who I was.

So one of the first things I had to do was to enter places from which I was afraid I might be rejected. I had to confront my own fears of the unknown. I told myself, "Well, I might be hurt, but I won't dodge until they throw a punch." Over and over again I found that it was just this attitude (which finally became unselfconsciously nondefensive) which made the difference between my being accepted or rejected, and this during a time when many places practiced discrimination.

This requires submitting oneself to personal ordeals, especially if one grew up in the South and Southwest. Nor is this because you are afraid of white people so much as a matter of not wishing to be rebuffed. You don't wish to be upset when you're going to see a play by having a racial hassle on your hands. This distaste is very human. I've had a white Mississippian stop me on the streets of Rome asking if he would be admitted to a certain place which had caught his eye. I said, with a certain pleasurable irony, "Sure, go ahead; just tell them you're a friend of mine."

What do you consider the Negro writer's responsibility to American literature as a whole?

The writer, *any* American writer, becomes basically responsible for the health of American literature the moment he starts writing seriously. And this regardless of his race or religious background. This is no arbitrary matter. Just as there is implicit in the act of voting the responsibility of helping to govern, there is implicit in the act of writing a responsibility for the quality of the American language—its accuracy, its vividness, its simplicity, its expressiveness—and responsibility for preserving and extending the quality of the literature.

How do you regard President Johnson's statement that "art is not a political weapon"? He made it at the White House in 1965.

I don't think you've got it complete; let's read it. He said, "Your art is not a political weapon, yet much of what you do is profoundly political, for you seek out the common pleasures and visions, the terrors and cruelties of man's day on this planet. And I would hope you would help dissolve the barriers of hatred and ignorance which are the source of so much of our pain and danger."

You think that he is far ahead of many people?

He is far ahead of most of the intellectuals—especially those Northern liberals who have become, in the name of the highest motives, the new apologists for segregation. Some of the *Commentary* writers, for instance. Let's put it this way. President Johnson's speech at Howard University spelled out the meaning of full integration for Negroes in a way that no one, no President, not Lincoln nor Roosevelt, no matter how much we love and respect them, has ever done before. There was no hedging in it, no escape clauses.

About Robert Lowell's refusal in 1965 to participate in the White House Art Festival, was this justly done, or do you think that he was engaged too much in politics? Do you think it was necessary?

I do not think it was necessary. When Lowell wrote to the President—and it was a skillfully written letter—he stated his motives of conscience, his fear that his presence would commit him to the President's foreign policy. In other words, he feared the potency of his own presence in such a setting, a potency which would seem to rest in his person rather than in the poetry for which we praise him and consider him great. But he didn't stop there, the letter got to the press, and once this happened, it became a political act, a political gesture.

I think this was unfortunate. The President wasn't telling Lowell how to write his poetry, and I don't think he's in any position to tell the President how to run the government. Had I been running the Festival, I'd simply have had an actor read from Lowell's poetry—with his permission, of course—for then not only would we have had the best of Lowell, but the question of his feelings concerning foreign policy wouldn't have come up.

Actually, no one was questioned as to his attitudes, political or otherwise—except by Dwight Macdonald. It wasn't that kind of occasion. Any and every opinion was represented there. Millard Lampell, who had been picketing the White House, had part of his play presented, and his background is no secret. So it was not in itself a political occasion, and all of the hullabaloo was beside the point. I was very much amazed, having gone through the political madness that marked the intellectual experience of the thirties, to see so many of our leading American intellectuals, poets, novelists—free creative minds—once again running in a herd. One may take a personal position concerning a public issue that is much broader than his personal morality, and the others make a herd of free creative minds! Some of my best friends are mixed up in it—which leaves me all the more amazed.

Speaking of herd activity, do you think that writers, generally, band together for the added stimulation or appreciation that they need? Or do you think that it is a lack, on their part, of a certain kind of intelligence?

It depends upon their reason for coming together. I think it very important for writers to come together during the early stages of their careers, especially during the stage when they are learning their techniques, when they are struggling for that initial fund of knowledge upon which they form their tastes and upon which artistic choices are made. And it's good for artists to get together to eat and drink—for social activities. But when they get together in some sort of political effort, it usually turns out that they are being manipulated by a person or group of persons who are not particularly interested in art.

In other words, are you denying what happened to you in the thirties, during the New Masses *experience?*

No, I don't deny that at all; instead, I speak out of that experience. But what happened to me during the thirties was part of a great swell of events which I plunged into when I came to town an undergraduate musician, and through which I gradually transformed myself into a writer. The stimulus that existed in New York during the thirties was by no means limited to art; it was also connected with politics, it was part of the *esprit de corps* developed in the country after we had endured the Depression for a few years. It had to do with my discovering New York and the unfamiliar areas of the society newly available to me. It had to do with working on the New York Writers Project and getting to know white friends, and being around Richard Wright and around the *New Masses* and the League of American Writers crowd.

But, if you'll note—and the record is public—I never

wrote the official type of fiction. I wrote what might be called propaganda—having to do with the Negro struggle—but my fiction was always trying to be something else; something different even from Wright's fiction. I never accepted the ideology which the *New Masses* attempted to impose on writers. They hated Dostoevsky, but I was studying Dostoevsky. They felt that Henry James was a decadent, some sort of snob who had nothing to teach a writer from the lower classes—I was studying James. I was also reading Marx, Gorki, Sholokhov, and Isaac Babel. I was reading everything, including the Bible. Most of all, I was reading Malraux. I thought so much of that little Modern Library edition of *Man's Fate* that I had it bound in leather. This is where I was really living at the time. So perhaps it is the writers whose work has most impact upon us that are important, not those with whom we congregate publicly. Anyway, I think style is more important than political ideologies.

Do you see, then, a parallel between the thirties and the sixties, with this new resurgence of young Negro writers, with this turning toward Africa and, shall we say again, the resurgence of a particular kind of provincialism in New Negro writing?

I think that we should be very careful in drawing parallels. This is a period of affluence as against the poverty of the Depression. True, during that period a lot of Negroes had the opportunity to work in WPA at clerical jobs and so on, so that for us the Depression represented in many ways a lunge forward. We were beneficiaries of the government's efforts toward national recovery. Thanks to the national chaos, we found new places for ourselves. Today our lunges forward are facilitated by laws designed precisely to correct our condition as a group—by laws which start at the very top and which have the Supreme Court, the Executive branch, and Congress behind them. This is quite different from the thirties.

As to Africa, I think it probably true that more of the present crop of writers are concerned with Africa than was true during that period. In fact, quite a number who were concerned with communism are now fervid black nationalists. Oddly enough, however, their way of writing hasn't changed significantly. Of course, I might not know what I'm talking about, but there seem to be fewer Negro writers around who seem publishable at the moment. Surely there are fewer than the more favorable circumstances of today warrant.

Some people think that you should play a larger part in civil rights . . . This is similar to Sartre's rebuttal to Camus in Situations, *this idea of "engagement."*

Well, I'm no Camus and they're no Sartres. But literature draws upon much deeper and much more slowly changing centers of the human personality than does politics. It draws mainly from literature itself, and upon the human experience which has abided long enough to have become organized and given significance through literature. I think that revolutionary political movements move much too rapidly to be treated as the subjects for literature in themselves. When Malraux drew upon revolution as the settings for his novels, he drew for his real themes upon much deeper levels of his characters' consciousness than their concern with Marxism; and it is to these deeper concerns, to the realm of tragedy, that they turned when facing death. Besides, political movements arise and extend themselves, achieve themselves, through fostering myths which interpret their actions and their goals. And if you tell the truth about a politician, you're always going to encounter contradiction and barefaced lies—especially when you're dealing with left-wing politicians.

If I were to write an account of the swings and twitches of the U. S. Communist line during the thirties and forties, it would be a very revealing account, but I wouldn't attempt to do this in terms of fiction. It would have to be done in terms of political science, reportage. You would have to look up their positions, chart their moves, look at the directives handed down by the communist International—whatever the overall body was called. And you would be in a muck and a mire of dead and futile activity—much of which had little to do with their ultimate goals or with American reality. They fostered the myth that communism was twentieth-century Americanism, but to be a twentieth-century American meant, in their thinking, that you had to be more Russian than American and less Negro than either. That's how they lost the Negroes. The Communists recognized no plurality of interests and were really responding to the necessities of Soviet foreign policy, and when the war came, Negroes got caught and were made expedient in the shifting of policy. Just as Negroes who fool around with them today are going to get caught in the next turn of the screw.

Do you think there is too much pressure on the Negro writer to play the role of politician, instead of mastering his craft and acting as a professional writer?

Yes, and if he doesn't resist such pressure, he's in a bad way. Because someone is always going to tell you that you can't write, and then they tell you *what* to write.

Among the first things the Negro writer has to resist is being told that he'll find it difficult to make a buck. I waded through tons of that. But I decided that I would make sacrifices, go without clothing and other necessities, in order to buy books, in order to be in New York where I could talk to certain creative people and where I could observe this or that phenomenon. Resisting these warnings is most important. And if you deflect this particular pressure, there will always be people who will tell you that you have no talent. We understand the psychological dynamics of it—Booker T. Washington gave it the "crabs in a basket" metaphor: if a Negro threatens to succeed in a field outside the usual areas of Negro professionals, others feel challenged. It's a protective reaction, a heritage from slavery. We feel "Well, my God, he has the nerve to do that—I don't have the nerve to do that; what does he think he's doing, endangering the whole group?" Nevertheless the writer must endure the agony imposed by this group pessimism.

Why do you think this exists?

Because our sense of security and our sense of who we are depends upon our feeling that we can account for each and every member of the group. And to this way of thinking, any assertion of individuality is dangerous. I'm reminded of a woman whom I met at a party. We were discussing Negro life and I uttered opinions indicating an approach unfamiliar to her. Her indignant response was "How do you come talking like that? I never even heard of you!" In her opinion I had no right to express ideas which hadn't been certified by her particular social group. Naturally, she thought of herself as a member of a Negro elite and in the position to know what each and every Negro thought and should think. This is a minority-group phenomenon, and I won't nail it to Negroes because it happens in the Jewish community as well.

In the interview that you had in Robert Penn Warren's Who Speaks for the Negro? *he addressed a question to you that has something to do with Negroes being culturally deprived, and you answered that many of the white students whom you'd taught were also culturally deprived. They were culturally deprived, you said, because while they might have understood many things intellectually, they were emotionally unprepared to deal with them. But the Negro was being prepared emotionally, whether intellectually or not, from the moment he was placed in the crib. Would you expand that a bit?*

I think you've touched *the* important area that gets lost when we hold such discussions. I get damn tired of critics writing of me as though I don't know how hard it is to be a Negro American. My point is that it isn't *only* hard, that there are many, many good things about it.

But they don't want you to say that. This is especially true of some of our Jewish critics. They get quite upset when I say: *I like this particular aspect of Negro life and would not surrender it. What I want is something else to go along with it.* And when I get the other things, I'm not going to try to invade the group life of anybody else. And of course they don't like the idea that I reject many of the aspects of life which they regard highly. But you know, white people can get terribly disturbed at the idea that Negroes are not simply being restricted from many areas of our national life, but that they are also judging certain aspects of our culture and rejecting their values. That's where assumptions of white superiority, conscious or unconscious, make for blindness and naïveté. For in fact we've rejected many of their values from the days before there were Jim Crow laws.

Only a narrowly sociological explanation of society could lead to the belief that we Negroes are what we are simply because whites would refuse us the right of choice through racial discrimination. Frequently Negroes are able to pay for commodities available in the stores, but we reject them as a matter of taste—not economics. There is no *de facto* Jim Crow in many areas of New York, but we don't frequent them, not because we think we won't be welcome—indeed, many Negroes go to places precisely because they are unfairly and illegally rejected—but because they simply don't interest us. All this *we* know to be true.

Negro Americans had to learn to live under pressure—otherwise we'd have been wiped out, or in the position of the Indians, set on a reservation and rendered powerless by the opposing forces. Fortunately, our fate was different. We were forced into segregation, but within that situation we were able to live close to the larger society and to abstract from that society enough combinations of values—including religion and hope and art—which allowed us to endure and impose our own idea of what the world should be and of what man should be, and of what American society should be. I'm not speaking of power here, but of vision, of values and dreams. Yes, and of will.

What is missing today is a corps of artists and intellectuals who would evaluate Negro American experience from the inside, and out of a broad knowledge of how people of other cultures live, deal with experience, and give significance to their experience. We do too little of this. Rather, we depend upon outsiders—mainly sociologists—to interpret our lives for us. It doesn't seem to occur to us that our interpreters might well be not so much prejudiced as ignorant, insensitive, and arrogant. It doesn't occur to us that they might be of shallow personal culture, or innocent of the complexities of actual living.

It's ironic that we act this way, because over and over again when we find bunches of Negroes enjoying themselves, when they're feeling good and in a mood of communion, they sit around and marvel at what a damnably marvelous human being, what a confounding human type the Negro American really is. This is the underlying significance of so many of our bull sessions. We exchange accounts of what happened to someone whom the group once knew. "You know what that so-and-so did," we say; and then his story is told. His crimes, his loves, his outrages, his adventures, his transformations, his moments of courage, his heroism, buffooneries, defeats, and triumphs are recited, with each participant joining in. And this catalogue soon becomes a brag, a very exciting chant celebrating the metamorphosis which this individual in question underwent within the limited circumstances available to us.

This is wonderful stuff; in the process the individual is enlarged. It's as though a transparent overlay of archetypal myth is being placed over the life of an individual, and through him we see ourselves. This, of course, is what literature does with life; these verbal jam sessions are indeed a form of folk literature and they help us to define our own experience.

But when we Negro Americans start "*writing,*" we lose this wonderful capacity for abstracting and enlarging life. Instead we ask, "How do we fit into the sociological terminology? Gunnar Myrdal said this experience means thus and so. And Dr. Kenneth Clark, or Dr. E. Franklin Frazier, says the same thing . . ." And we try to fit our experience into their concepts. Well, whenever I hear a Negro intellectual describing Negro life and personality with a catalogue of negative definitions, my first question is: How did you escape, is it that you were born exceptional and superior? If I cannot look at the most brutalized Negro on the street, even when he irritates me and makes me want to bash his head in because he's goofing off, I must still say within myself, "Well, that's you too, Ellison." And I'm not talking about guilt, but of an identification which goes beyond race.

You have said that Hemingway tells us much more about how Negroes feel than all the writings done by those people mixed up in the Negro Renaissance.

What I meant was this: Hemingway's writing of the twenties and the thirties—even of the forties—evoked certain basic, deeply felt moods and attitudes within his characters which closely approximated certain basic attitudes held by many Negroes in regard to their position in American society, and in regard to their sense of the human predicament. And he did this not only because he was a greater writer than the participants in the Negro Renaissance, but because he possessed a truer sense of what the valid areas of perplexity were and a more accurate sense of how to get life into literature. He recognized that the so-called "Jazz Age" was a phony, while most Negro writers jumped on that illusory bandwagon when they, of all people, should have known better.

I was also referring to Hemingway's characters' attitude toward society, to their morality, their code of technical excellence, to their stoicism, their courage or "grace under pressure," to their skepticism as to the validity of political rhetoric and all those abstractions in the name of which our society was supposed to be governed, but which Hemingway found highly questionable when measured against our actual conduct. Theirs was an attitude springing from an awareness that they lived outside the values of the larger society, and *I* feel that their attitudes came close to the way Negroes felt about the way the Constitution and the Bill of Rights were applied to us.

Further, I believe that Hemingway, in depicting the attitudes of athletes, expatriates, bullfighters, traumatized soldiers, and impotent idealists, told us quite a lot about what was happening to that most representative group of Negro Americans, the jazz musicians—who also lived by an extreme code of withdrawal, technical and artistic excellence, rejection of the values of respectable society. They replaced the abstract and much-betrayed ideals of that society with the more physical values of eating, drinking, copulating, loyalty to friends, and dedication to the discipline and values of their art.

Now, I say all this while fully aware that Hemingway seldom depicted Negroes, and that when he did they were seldom the types we prefer to encounter in fiction. But to see what I mean, one has only to look upon the world of Hemingway's fiction as offering a valid metaphor not only for the predicament of young whites, but as a metaphor for the post-World War I period generally. Seen in this inclusive light, he tells us a hell of a lot about the way Negroes were feeling and acting.

At any rate, this is how I use literature to come to an understanding of our situation. It doesn't have to be, thank God, *about* Negroes in order to give us insights into our own predicament. You do not, to my way of thinking, assume that a writer can treat of his times, if he writes well, *without* revealing a larger segment of life than that of the specific milieu which engaged his attention; for it must if it is to be valid go beyond and touch the reality of other groups and individuals. Faulkner tells us a great deal about many different groups who were not his immediate concern because he wrote so truthfully. If you would find the imaginative equivalents of certain civil rights figures in American writing, Rosa Parks and James Meredith, say, you don't go to most fiction by Negroes, but to Faulkner.

You have said that you don't accept any theory which implies that culture is transmitted through the genes. What, then, is your reaction to the concept of "negritude"?

To me it represents the reverse of that racism with which prejudiced whites approach Negroes. As a theory of art, it implies precisely that culture is transmitted through the genes. It is a blood theory.

There are members of my family who are very black people, and there are some who are very white—which means that I am very much Negro, very much Negro American, and quite representative of that racial type with its mixture of African, European, and indigenous American blood. This is a biological fact; but recognizing this, and loving my family, and recognizing that I'm bound to them by blood and family tradition is by no means to agree with the proponents of negritude. Because even while I affirm our common bloodline, I recognize that we are bound less by blood than by our cultural and political circumstances.

Further, I don't believe that my form of expression springs from Africa, although it might be easier for me as an artist if it did, because then, perhaps, a massive transfusion of pure Nigerian blood would transform me into a great sculptor. I've been reading the classics of European and American literature since childhood, was born to the American tongue and to the language of the Bible and the Constitution; these, for better or worse, shaped my thought and attitudes and pointed the direction of my talent long before I became a conscious writer. I also inherited a group style originated by a "black" people, but it is Negro American, not African. And it was taught to me by Negroes or copied by me from those among whom I lived most intimately.

All this is similar to the notion that Negroes have a corner on soul. *Well, we don't.*

You're right, and anyone who listens to a Beethoven quartet or symphony and can't hear *soul* is in trouble.

Maybe they can hear the sound of blackness, but they're deaf to *soul.*

Richard Wright was called a white man.

I've had something like that happen. When I was teaching at Bard College a young Negro girl approached one of my white colleagues and said, "Is this Mr. Ellison a Negro?" Now, I can't understand that; it sounds as if she was putting him on. Because there I was facing classes with my big African nose, teaching American literature and highlighting the frame so that they could become aware of the Negro experience in it—and she wants to know whether I'm Negro! I suppose the social patterns are changing faster than we can grasp.

Recently we had a woman from the South who helped my wife with the house but who goofed off so frequently that she was fired. We liked her and really wanted her to stay, but she simply wouldn't do her work. My friend Albert Murray told me I shouldn't be puzzled over the outcome. "You know how we can be sometimes," Al said. "She saw the books and the furniture and paintings, so she knew you were some kind of white man. You couldn't possibly be a Negro. And so she figured she could get away with a little boondoggling on general principles, because she'd probably been getting away with a lot of stuff with Northern whites. But what she didn't stop to notice was that you're a *Southern* white man . . ."

So you see, here culture and race and a preconception of how Negroes are supposed to live—a question of taste—had come together and caused a comic confusion. Such jokes as Al Murray's are meaningful because in America culture is always cutting across racial characteristics and social designations. Therefore, if a Negro doesn't exhibit certain attitudes, or if he reveals a familiarity with aspects of the culture, or possesses qualities of personal taste which the observer has failed to note among Negroes, then such confusions in perception are apt to occur.

But the basic cause is, I think, that we are all members of a highly pluralistic society. We possess two cultures—both American—and many aspects of the broader American culture are available to Negroes who possess the curiosity and taste—if not the money—to cultivate them. It is often overlooked, especially in our current state of accelerated mobility, that it is becoming increasingly necessary for Negroes themselves to *learn* who they are *as Negroes.* Cultural influences have always outflanked racial discrimination—*wherever and whenever there were Negroes receptive to them, even in slavery times.* I read the books which were to free me for my work as a writer while studying at Tuskegee Institute, Macon County, Alabama, during a time when most of the books weren't even taught. Back in 1937, I knew a Negro who swept the floors at Wright Field in Dayton, Ohio, who was nevertheless designing planes and entering his designs in contests. He was working as a porter, but his mind, his ambitions, and his attitudes were those of an engineer. He wasn't waiting for society to change, he was changing it by himself.

What advice would you give to a young person of eighteen who was setting out to be a writer?

My first advice would be to make up his mind to the possibility that he might have to go through a period of depriving himself in order to write. I'd remind him that he was entering into a very stern discipline, and that he should be quite certain that he really wanted to do this to the extent of arranging his whole life so that he could get it done. He should regard writing very much as a young physician is required to regard his period of training. Next, I'd advise him to read everything, all the good books he can manage, especially those in the literary form in which he desires to become creative. Because books contain the culture of the chosen form and because one learns from the achievements of other writers. Here is contained the knowledge which he must have at his fingertips as he projects his own vision. And because without it, no matter how sensitive, intelligent, or passionate he is, he will be incomplete.

Beyond that, he shouldn't take the easy escape of involving himself exclusively in *talking* about writing, or carrying picket signs, or sitting-in as a substitute activity. Because while he might become the best picket in the world, or the best sitter-inner, his writing will remain where he left it.

Finally, he should avoid the notion that writers require no education. Very often Hemingway and Faulkner are summoned up to support this argument, because they didn't finish college. What is overlooked is that these were very gifted, very brilliant men. And very well-read men of great intellectual capacity. So no matter how you acquire an education, you must have it. You must know your society, and know it beyond your own neighborhood or region. You must know its manners and its ideals and its conduct. And you should know something of what's happening in the sciences, in religion, in government, and in the other arts.

I suppose what I'm saying is that he should have a working model of the society and of the national characteristics present within his mind. The problem of enriching that model and keeping it up-to-date is one of the greatest challenges to the Negro writer, who is, by definition, cut off from firsthand contact with large areas of the society—especially from those centers where power is translated into ideas and into manners and into values. Nevertheless, this can be an advantage, because in this country no writer should take anything for granted, but must use his imagination to question and penetrate the façade of things. Indeed, the integration of American society on the level of the imagination is one of his basic tasks. It is one way in which he is able to possess his world and, in his writings, help shape the values of large segments of the society which otherwise would not admit his existence, much less his right to participate or to judge.

—From *Harper's Magazine,* March 1967

The Novel as a Function of American Democracy

I am a writer who writes very slowly; because of this, I am often tempted to convince myself that I should spend a lot of time theorizing about what the novel is. One fact I am sure about, the writing of novels is the damnedest thing that I ever got into, and I've been into some damnable things. Nevertheless, there is a certain sincerity in my choice of the title for this address; you will note, however, that I do not say that all novels have a nonartistic function or that they owe something to American democracy. But I do happen to feel that in this country the novel, a particular art form to which I am giving my life, found a function which it did not have in any of the nations where it was developed by artists who made it resound so effectively with their eloquence.

As you know, the emergence of the novel occurred at a time when the stability of social class lines was being shaken (please don't let my use of the term "class lines" upset you). Although the conception of freedom existed before the eighteenth century, it was revitalized during that century of many wars and revolutions; societies began to change; new classes to emerge; new values were established. Traditional forms were modified; the conception of kingship gave way to the conception of democracy and individualism. Change was everywhere.

One of the aesthetic results of this change was the emergence of a literary form which could project the shiftings of society with a facility and an intimacy that had not existed before, either in the theater or in romantic poetry. This form was much concerned with the emergence of new personality types, with what was happening to tradition, as individuals began to explore the nature of possibility which had been brought about for them through the crack-ups of the old society. The writers themselves were challenged into taking all the traditional forms—oral storytelling, the ballad, poetry, drama—and exploiting them in this new medium of the novel. All of this was very necessary, because people no longer knew exactly who they were. They knew that they were doing things; they knew that there were changes; they knew that they were tied up with the old values, that they sometimes wore the old clothing. But inside they felt different; they felt the need to test themselves against the new possibilities because it was *possible* to test themselves. If Robinson Crusoe wanted to go to a desert isle, he took with him certain techniques, certain values, from whence he came; these he adapted to the new environment, to the people whom he found on his isle. Such a plot proved exciting, for it projected for the reader a sense of reality, a sense of what was immanent, a sense of what was possible for himself.

By the middle of the nineteenth century the novel had become a recognized art form which had absorbed all of the unstructured techniques of narrative, whether oral or literary, that had preceded it. And in the hands of such novelists as Dostoevsky, Flaubert, Melville, it had become a literary form which, along with its powers to entertain, was capable of deadly serious psychological and philosophical explorations of the human predicament.

As I see it, the novel has always been tied up with the idea of nationhood. What are we? Who are we? What has the experience of the particular group been? How did it become this way? What is it that stopped us from attaining the ideal? In Russian literature, particularly, we can see this very clearly as we follow the work of Pushkin, who wrote knowingly of the superfluous individual, the dilettante, the man of great sensitivity and great possibilities who could not find his way in a society that had been unable to break away from the stagnation of life inherent to that period of Russian history.

In reading Pushkin and Gogol, Dostoevsky and Tolstoy, one can see the drawing out, the investigation, of what the idea of the superfluous individual amid the stagnated society had to suggest to men who came later and who chose the novel as a means of exploring reality. It is the very nature of this exploration which attracts me to the novel, and which causes me to take it very, very seriously. I can say this without any reference to my personal abilities, which are limited. The novel is a form which deals with change in human personality and human society, bringing to the surface those values, those patterns of conduct, those dilemmas, psychological and technological, which abide within the human predicament. It can abstract, from the flow and fury of existence, these patterns, which are abiding, and re-create them in the forms of artistic models that can be controlled and imbued with the personal values of the writer, down even to the last punctuation mark. In other words, the novel is a way of possessing life, of slowing it down, and of giving it the writer's own sense of values in a delicately and subtly structured way. All this, of course, is not simply a matter of entertaining, but is a way of confronting reality, confronting the nature of the soul and the nature of society. As a form, the novel permits a writer to survive the consequences of encountering the chaos he must reckon with when he attempts to deal with the basic truths of human existence.

In turning now to the American novel, I wish to emphasize that the American nation is based upon revolution, dedicated to change through basic conceptions stated in the Bill of Rights and the Constitution. It is dedicated also to the ideal of an *open* society, a society in which a great land mass allowed peoples to move about, to change their identities if they would, to advance themselves, to achieve results based on their own talents and techniques. With such a society, it seems only natural that the novel existed to be exploited by certain personality types who found their existence within the United States. What I am trying to describe is the relationship between the form in which I work and the society as I see it. Of course, the first writers of any stature in the United States were not novelists; they were essayists and preachers and philosophers and poets. When I think of the meaning of the essays of Ralph Waldo Emerson, now dismissed as being a little too much on the optimistic side, I remind myself that there was a need for his optimism. Some voice had to be raised to remind Americans that they were not Europeans. Emerson's essays fulfilled a need, precisely because Americans existed in a society and in a country which was not very tightly structured and in which no one, at that time especially, could set a limit upon individual possibility, certainly not at the level of the imagination.

Such limits might have been set on the slaves; but even so, there was always some slave who was confounding to the general conception. So the Emersons and the Whitmans and the Thoreaus reminded us that the stance of secession had its own value. They told us that this stance was an obligation for us, not only as Americans but as members of a civilization, actors in a long, continued action which started before history and which, through some miracle, produced on this land, after bloody assaults, the condition in which, we hoped, human society could make a leap forward. Someone had to tell us that the price we pay for progress is terrible, but that we cannot afford to close our eyes and stop.

These early writers enjoined us to experience nature and society to the hilt. They asked us to interrogate ourselves, to interrogate nature and the universe by way of realizing ourselves, by way of paying our debt to history. The Whitmans were necessary to point out to us that this was a lyrical, as well as a rugged, experience. There is nothing like having a harsh reality nudging you along, to make you feel that there is some virtue in song. I am not suggesting, by the way, that life is best for the poet or the novelist when it is harshest. What I am saying is that when we are closest to the tragic realities of human existence, we have a deeper appreciation for song, for the lyric mode. Be that as it may, let me remind you that almost as early as the great European nations produced great novelists, this country also produced a few great novelists and some great poets. But as remarkable as this is, it must be remembered that we are a continuation of a European civilization, not a thing in ourselves, although our variations upon the theme, our amplification of the themes, are unique.

The Melvilles and Hawthornes, however, were a part of our early nineteenth century; by midcentury this country had reached a certain crisis, implicit in our approach to the new possibility of freedom, a crisis so profound that we fought a civil war, one of the bloodiest in history. It was then that America produced Henry James, Mark Twain, and Stephen Crane. By the time I began to write, Henry

James was considered a snob, an upper-class expatriate who, in New York and around Boston, had fallen into some sort of decadent hothouse in which his head became much too large for his body. His sensibility was considered too delicate to interest anyone who was a real man concerned with the things of this world as they existed. It was forgotten, however, that James came on the scene at a time when the abolitionists were coming in and out of his father's house, that he was part of a period in which there was great intellectual ferment, religious ferment, civil rights ferment. Few critics recalled that in that war James lost one of his older brothers, who had been a member of Colonel Shaw's Massachusetts regiment of free slaves. It was also forgotten that James's second published story, "The Story of a Year," was based on an incident which occurred in the Civil War. But what does all of this have to do with Henry James? He was, on first glance, a novelist highly conscious of the form of the novel as an artistic unity; one of the first writers, European or American, to rationalize, or to attempt to rationalize, an aesthetic of the novel. He was a writer with a great and subtle awareness of how the novel differed from all other forms of narrative and drama and other forms of storytelling; one who knew how the characters function; who knew how they related, one to another; who knew that they had to function as an organic form.

Thematically, James knew much more. He recognized—as demonstrated in his novel *The Bostonians*—that in his time the United States had reached a moment of crisis, and, in fact, that he was writing during a new period in the life of the nation, when the lyrical belief in the possibilities of the Constitution and the broadness of the land was no longer so meaningful. Mindful that hundreds and thousands of men had died in the Civil War, James knew for his own time what Emerson knew for his. Emerson constantly reminded Americans that they had to discover the new possibilities of the new land. What James realized was that the old enduring evil of the human predicament had raised its face, revealing itself within this land. This evil could no longer be confronted in the name of religion, in the name of kingship or of aristocracy—although James was himself an aristocrat. James recognized that each and every individual who lived within the society had to possess, and to be concerned with, the most subtle type of moral consciousness. He was as aware of the labyrinth in which Americans walk as was Emerson. Yet neither man liked the other, perhaps because they were approaching the same reality from different positions and through different disciplines. Today, not too many people read James, although he is by no means an ignored writer. For me one minor test of this is the fact that I don't know of many Negro youngsters who are named Henry James Jones. There were, and are, a number who are named Waldo. I happen to be one of them. Amusing as this is, it reveals something of how the insight and values of literature get past the usual barriers in society and seep below the expected levels. I shall speak more of that later.

Another major writer of this midcentury period was Stephen Crane. Younger than James, Crane nonetheless lived during his lifetime, a young man from upstate New York, born into a Methodist family, well known for its preachers. At twenty-nine, this young man, who had never experienced warfare, wrote one of our classics, *The Red Badge of Courage,* a very unique book about the Civil War, one which was praised, at first, precisely because the writer was too young to have experienced warfare. Indeed, it is a very unique book about any war. What was missed, of course, was the fact that Crane used the Civil War as a *metaphor* for the human condition in the United States. Here is a book about a war in which you see no close-ups of generals. Whenever officers are involved, whenever they come on the scene, we feel that the camera in the motion picture has been withdrawn about the length of a football field. You can never quite get up to the brass. You get very, very close to the dead, even to seeing the ants crawling out of their eye sockets, and you get the fury and panic of deadly action —but most important, you penetrate very deeply into the mind of an uninstructed American who had no idea what the war was about, an American for whom the encounter was almost totally personal until, of course, he broke and ran and found himself in the false position of pretending that he was a hero when he knew within his soul that he was a coward.

Having no conception of the overall strategy of battle, he was the dismembered little man, caught up in a great social action. Here was the other side, you see, of the early American conception that every man was a king, every man a philosopher, every American the possessor of insight into the complexity of things, of every American standing right at the tip point of history. No. For Crane, the American was a man who tested himself in terms of his personal courage, his moral courage, his ability and willingness to tell himself the truth about himself. *The Red Badge of Courage* offered its readers a metaphor for their own feelings regarding their relationship to their society. Its significance lay not in the fact that the young man who wrote it had never seen war, but in its articulation for its readers of a sense of loss, a loss of faith and direction, after the great crisis of the Civil War. It is this same sense of loss which James celebrates in his novel *The Bostonians,* a portrait not of courageous people who had fought for abolition while living their lives with quivering nerves and searching intellect, but a portrait instead of a people who had lost their sense of direction and who were floundering in many, many ways. Even the theme of homosexuality, in this instance, female homosexuality, was introduced—not to shock the reader but to indicate how profound was the disintegration of moral tone in the Boston of that day.

Another book which states the moral predicament of its times, metaphorically, is *Huckleberry Finn.* Written by a white Southerner who had been freed of certain narrow prejudices, the novel dramatizes in a most poignant and amusing way the social aspect of the civil rights problem. No great philosopher, Twain was nevertheless a great moralist and storyteller. Like Uncle Remus, he was a great entertainer, a man who looked very sharply at reality and made distinctions between what we said we were—our ideals—and how we acted—our conduct. *Huckleberry Finn* projected the truth about slavery, and it will be many, many years in this country before there will ever again be a novelist so popular, so loved, so understood by people who simply were unable to confront the real moral predicament of their nation in any way other than in the pages of a story.

In the works of all of these men—James, Crane, Twain—the novel was never used merely as a medium of entertainment. These writers suggested possibilities, courses of action, stances against chaos. In their work, as in those who followed them, Hemingway and Fitzgerald, for example, the novel functioned beyond entertainment in helping create the American conception of America.

When Twain wrote *Huckleberry Finn,* some people of my background were already writing, but there were few people indeed who were close to the complexity of this particular aspect of American experience. I don't say this to inflate the experience, but to point to the fact that in this country there is no absolute separation of groups. The American language, this rich, marvelous, relatively unexplored organ, is the creation of many, many people, and it began with the Indians. We walk through the streets of our cities and their names sing in our heads; great poetry has been made of them, but we do not realize that they are Indian names. We forget, conveniently sometimes, that the language which we speak is not English, although it is based on English. We forget that our language is such a flexible instrument because it has had so many dissonances thrown into it—from Africa, from Mexico, from Spain, from, God knows, everywhere. And yet it has been reduced to a working and flexible, highly poetic language. I note this in order to say that what is happening in what you now like to call the ghettos, or what was once called the plantations, didn't just stay there. These milieux influenced how you pronounced your name, how you walked, the things you ate, the tunes you whistled; these things frequently found their way into the larger cultures, something we now call the mainstream. When the immigrants arrived in great waves from Europe and settled on the Lower East Side, as did the Jewish immigrants, cultural variations occurred there but did not remain there. They found their way into other areas. In this sense, our national style is a product of these elusive variations of styles, manners, and customs which emerged from our many subcommunities.

Even today America remains an undiscovered country. Recall, for instance, the shock experienced by the nation when Adam Powell was thrown out of Congress—and people in the Eighteenth District of New York were heard to say: "Put him back, dammit." There is a mystery in this country because we live where we are; we wear the same clothing; we listen to the same television programs; we worship the same God; we read the same textbooks; we have the same heroes in sports, in politics, in music. We are at once very, very unified, and at the same time diversified. On many, many levels we don't know who we are, and there are always moments of confrontation where we meet as absolute strangers. Race is by no means the only thing which divides us in this still-undiscovered country. We're only a partially achieved nation, and I think this is good because it gives the writer of novels a role beyond that of entertainer. The novel's function permits him a maximum freedom to express his own vision of reality. It allows him to write out of his own group background and his own individual background. But the novel also places upon him a responsibility of reporting, imaginatively of course, what is going on in his particular area of the American experience. How does the individual take the strains of his past and use them to illuminate his own sense of life? How are the great American ideals made manifest in his own particular environment? What is his sense of the good life? What is his sense of the high style? What is his sense of the moral dilemma of the nation? These questions and their answers are the novelist's responsibilities. If we do not know so much about ourselves now, if we find that we read sociology and history more than we read novels, then it is not our fault as readers. It is the fault of the novelist, because he has failed his obligation to tell the truth, to describe, with eloquence and imagination, life as it appears from wherever he finds his being. It is easy to say this but it's very difficult to do, because in this country there is a tradition of forgetfulness, a tradition for moving on, of denying the past, of converting the tragic realities of ourselves but most often of others, even if those others are of our own group, into comedy.

Today we are an affluent society and yet we're very unhappy. We no longer know what truth is. We no longer recognize heroism when it's demonstrated to us. We do not understand the nature of forbearance. We do not, far too often, take advantage of the wonderful opportunity which we have to project ourselves into the lives of other people, not to modify those lives but to understand them, to add dimensions to our own sense of wonder, our own sense of the possibility of living in a society like this. We don't know what to do with our money—even poor people. We have no defenses, seemingly, before the great cacophony of styles poured upon us through the marvelous medium of television. Our streets look like circuses. Our sense of taste seems to have been lost. We don't seem to know where we are. Some responsibility for this must rest with our novelists, for once they attain their fame, they begin to forget where they came from; they begin to doubt where they can go.

The state of our novel is not so healthy at the moment. Instead of aspiring to project a vision of the complexity, the diversity of the total experience, the novelist loses faith and falls back upon something which is called "black comedy," which is neither black nor comic. It is a cry of despair. Talent and technique are there; artistic competence is there; but a certain necessary faith in human possibility before the next unknown is not there. I speak from my own sense of the dilemma, and my own sense of what people who work in my form owe to those who would read us, and read us seriously, and who are willing to pay us the respect of lending their imaginations to ours.

The novel was not invented by an American, nor even for Americans; but we are a people who have, perhaps, most need of it—a form which can produce imaginative models of the total society if the individual writer has the imagination, and can endow each character, each scene, each punctuation mark with his own sense of value. If there had been more novelists with the courage of Mark Twain or James or Hemingway, we would not be in the moral confusion in which we find ourselves today. If we do not know good from bad, cowardice from heroism, the marvelous from the mundane and the banal, then we don't know *who* we are. It is a terrible thing to sit in a room with a typewriter and dream, and to tell the truth by telling effective lies; but this seems to be what many novelists opt for. Certainly this society will read books, and we, as writers, have the responsibility of not disappointing it. It's an old cliché that to have great writers, you must have great readers. And yet, I suspect that American readers have been irresponsible, too, because they have not said precisely why they find the works of modern novelists wanting.

—From *Wilson Library Bulletin,* June 1967; based on a lecture, sponsored by the Philadelphia City Institute, delivered March 23, 1967, at the Free Library of Philadelphia

Perspective of Literature

When I was a young boy I often went out to the Oklahoma State Capitol, where I assisted Mr. J. D. Randolph with his duties as custodian of the State Law Library. I was about eleven years old at the time, quite impressionable, and very, very curious about the mysterious legal goings-on of the legislators. All the more so because while I was never able to observe the legislature in session, it was not at all unusual for me to look up from pushing a broom or dusting a desk to see one of the legislators dash into the library to ask Jeff—Mr. Randolph was always addressed by his first name—his opinion regarding some point of law. In fact, I soon came to look forward to such moments because I was amazed by the frequency with which Mr. Randolph managed to come up with satisfactory answers, even without consulting the heavy volumes which ranged the walls.

I wasn't surprised that Mr. Randolph was a janitor instead of a lawyer or legislator; Oklahoma was segregated at the time and Afro-Americans were strictly limited in their freedom to participate in the process of government. We could obey or break laws, but not make or interpret them.

In view of this, I was amazed that Mr. Randolph had come to know so much about the subject. This was a tantalizing mystery, but the fact that white men of power would show no shame in exploiting the knowledge of one far beneath them in status aroused my sense of irony. That "after all" was simply another example of white folks taking advantage of black folks.

I was more impressed with the fact that Mr. Randolph could carry so many of the mysterious details of law and the laws which governed the state of Oklahoma within his own head. Now, I knew he had been one of the first schoolteachers in the city and the state, and that he read and owned a large collection of books. But just how he had come to learn the law was part of an experience about which I was never to hear him talk. I did know, however, that he had never attended college, and I was quite aware that many of our greatest lawyers had acquired their legal knowledge through the process of "reading" law with licensed members of the profession.

I only knew that Mr. Randolph appeared to possess a surer grasp of law than certain of the legislators, and my youthful sense of justice led me to see his exclusion from the profession as an act of injustice. I never heard him complain about the situation, but I felt that there was something shameful, even degrading, about such a state of affairs, and that there was something rotten in the lawyers if not indeed in the law itself.

Nor was it possible for me to ignore the obvious fact that race was a source of that rot, and that even within the mystery of the legal process, the law was colored and rigged against my people.

Later I became aware of the existence of a Negro lawyer, a Mr. Harrison, who was so skilled and eloquent that he got himself chased out of the state. Fortunately, he landed in Chicago, where, in time, he became an Assistant Attorney

General. Following this incident, however, there was much barbershop conversation centered on the Harrison affair, his legal skill, his way with words, and the inability of white lawyers and judges to stomach a Negro more knowledgeable in the law than themselves. Interestingly enough, the men who engaged in these conversations while I shined shoes or swept the floors directed their disapproval not so much against law in general, but against those persons and forces that imposed the law undemocratically.

This was a period during which the struggle to attain an anti-lynching bill was at its height and Mr. Roscoe Dungee, the editor and publisher of our local black newspaper, was writing very eloquent editorials suggesting that the real clue, the real ground for solving the racial predicament, rested in the Constitution. I read his editorials, but I must confess that with my youthful cynicism, I didn't quite believe them. But anyway, the men in the barbershop believed in the spirit of the law, if not in its application.

As for me, I saw no hope in the law. It was to be obeyed in everyday affairs, but in instances of extreme pressure, it was to be defied, even at the cost of one's life.

In our common usage, law was associated more with men than with statutes. Law-enforcement officers in our usage were "Laws," and many were men with reputations for being especially brutal toward Negroes.

If such men were the cutting edge of the racially biased law, those above them were seldom better. "Alfalfa Bill" Murray, who took great pride in his knowledge of Roman constitutions, was the governor of the state and a very loudmouthed white supremacist. And one occupant of the local bench, a certain Judge Estes, was famous for a quip made from the bench, to the effect that a Model T Ford full of Negroes ranging at large on the streets of the city was a more devastating piece of bad luck than having one's path crossed by a squad of thirteen howling jet-black tomcats.

Well, we laughed at it but held it against him. With such opinions issuing from the bench, I felt little inspired to trust the fairness of judges.

During the Depression, which occurred during this period, I noted something else about the relationship between the law and the attitudes of people, in this instance mostly white, who were suffering from the breakdown of economic order. This came in the form of their reaction to "Pretty Boy" Floyd, who at the time was in constant flight and on a rampage of lawbreaking; but he was frequently given sanctuary in Oklahoma City by law-abiding citizens. This was true not only of the city itself, but of towns all around Oklahoma.

Well, it puzzled me.

During June of 1933, I found myself traveling by freight train in an effort to reach Tuskegee Institute in time to take advantage of a scholarship granted me. Having little money and no time left in which to earn the fare for a ticket, I grabbed an armful of freight car, a form of illegal travel quite common during the Great Depression. In fact, so many young men, young women, prostitutes, gamblers, and even some quite respectable but impoverished elderly and middle-aged couples were hoboing that it was quite difficult for the railroad to control such passengers. I justify this out of sheer desperation, college being my one hope of improving my condition.

But I was young and adventurous and regarded hoboing as the next best thing to floating down the Mississippi on a raft. My head was full of readings of the *Rover Boys* and *Huckleberry Finn.* I converted hoboing into a lark, until I found myself in the freight yards of Decatur, Alabama, where two white railroad detectives laying about them with the barrels of long nickel-plated .45 revolvers forced some forty or fifty of us, black and white alike, off the train and ordered us to line up along the tracks. For me, this was a most frightening moment. Not only was I guilty of stealing passage on a freight train, but I realized that I had been caught in the act in the town where, at that very moment, the *Scottsboro* case was being tried. The case and the incident leading to it were widely reported in the black press, and what I had read of the atmosphere of the trial led me to believe that the young men in the case had absolutely no possibility of receiving a just decision. As I saw it, the trial was a macabre circus, a kangaroo proceeding that would be soon followed by an enactment of the gory rite of lynching, that ultimate form of racial victimage.

I had no idea of what the detectives intended to do with me, but given the atmosphere of the town, I feared that it would be most unpleasant and brutal. I, too, might well be a sacrificial scapegoat, simply because I was of the same race as the accused young men then being prepared for death. Therefore, when a group of white boys broke and ran, I plunged into their midst, and running far closer to the ground than I had ever managed to do as a high school football running back, I kept running and moving until I came to a shed with a railroad loading dock, under which I scooted; and there I remained until dawn, when I grabbed the first thing that was smoking and headed south.

A few days later I reached Tuskegee, but that scrape with the law—the fear, the horror and sense of helplessness before legal injustice—was most vivid in my mind, and it has so remained.

Recently a television dramatization of the *Scottsboro* case presented one of the judges that sat on the case as its hero. I was made aware of the snarl of personal and public motives, political and private interests, which had become the focus of the case. I was aware of the many factors locked in contention in the name of the purity of white womanhood, and as a writer I came to ask myself just why was it that American fiction had given so little attention to the law.

Why, I asked myself, has the lawyer or the judge seldom appeared in our literature, serious or popular, in heroic roles?

One answer is that the presentation of the law in an unfavorable light allows for the formal expression and sharing of attitudes which are impious and irreverent, and that given such attitudes, they must be socially controlled, made visible, and socialized; otherwise they might be a force for the destruction of social order.

When one recalls Mark Twain's drawing of the judge in *Adventures of Huckleberry Finn,* the judge comes across as something of a self-serving hypocrite.

Or compare the following incident from *Pudd'nhead Wilson:* Mr. Wilson appears before a reception committee expecting to make a name for himself in the town, but the proceedings are interrupted by the barking of a dog, whereupon Wilson says, "I wish that I owned one half of that dog."

And someone said, "One half of the dog? What would you do with one *half* of the dog?"

He said, "I would kill my half."

Whereupon these legal-minded gentlemen looked at one another and said, "Could he be serious? Doesn't he realize that if he kills his half of the dog, the other owner, the owner of the other half will be upset, will bring litigation against him, and that he will end up in all kinds of trouble?"

Well, for being irreverent on the matter of ownership, poor Wilson was named "Pudd'nhead" and spent most of his life as an alien in the town.

When we recall Melville's *Benito Cerino,* and place it back in its historical perspective, we realize that it was influenced by the *Armistad* case, a case in which a group of Africans were brought to trial at the insistence of Spain because they had revolted against the Spaniards who had sought to enslave them, killed several of the officers, and in attempting to sail the ship back to their homeland, found themselves off the coast of New England. Melville takes the incident and makes of it one of his finest works of fiction.

But what puzzles me a bit, and I know better than to be puzzled about such things, was why he made nothing of the fact that these Africans were freed by having been represented in court by John Quincy Adams. Remember, this was a time of slavery in our own country. Remember that it cost Mr. Adams something just to take that case. But at any rate, Melville did not bother with the lawyer on that occasion.

But in *Bartleby the Scrivener,* we are introduced to the title character by his boss, a Wall Street lawyer who, for all of his goodwill, is as imperceptive in grasping the basic connotation as Captain Delano of *Benito Cerino* is unable to grasp the human complexity of the Africans who believed, like himself, so much in freedom that they were willing to kill for it.

I am not going to burden you with recounting the legal climate of 1894, when Mark Twain published *Pudd'nhead Wilson.* I will just remind you that it was a period of great theft, of much legal skulduggery, and no doubt this had something to do with the presentation. But if we think a little bit about Mark Twain as a humorist, and think about literary form as having a social function, then perhaps Twain was being far more than irreverent when he presented men of the legal profession in a comic light, because by so presenting them he allowed people who were very upset by some of the legal goings-on in the society to reveal their feelings, to laugh at themselves, and most impious of all, to laugh at the courts and perhaps at the Constitution itself.

At some point people, and especially American people, are pushed to recognize that behind the Constitution which we say rests in principles that lie beyond the limits of death and dying, are really man-made, legal fictions. That doesn't stop them from being precious; that doesn't stop them from being sacred. But we can only stand so much of the sacred. We can only stand so much of piety. We must be able to express our dissent, especially when the members of the bench fail to do so for us.

In the reading of *Bartleby the Scrivener,* Melville's story, we encounter a contest of wills between the lawyer, a genteel, learned lawyer who is admired by Mr. John Jacob Astor, a representative of the law and thus of order, a man with what de Tocqueville termed certain aristocratic propensities, and poor Bartleby, who owns hardly anything but the clothing on his back.

Bartleby has been hired to perform the job of copying, transcribing legal documents. The lawyer, as boss, is in the habit of sending his other employees to do various errands. Bartleby replies to each request with a simple phrase "I prefer not to." It is so unusual, this obstinate negativism, that the lawyer doesn't throw him out, but becomes locked in a psychological struggle through which he tries to bring Bartleby to his will. But in the process he reveals how little he understands of certain basic human attitudes which make the law and the order it imposes quite necessary. Bartleby is never forced or persuaded or cajoled to agree.

In the reading of the story, one has a sensation of watching a man walking backward past every boundary of human order and desire, saying, "I prefer not to, I prefer not to," until at last he fades from sight and we are left with but the faint sound of his voice hanging thinly upon the air, still saying No. Bartleby's last remaining force, the force which at the very last he is asked to give up, is the power of the negative, that capability of language which Kenneth Burke has identified as a symbolic agency through which man has separated himself from nature and gone on to establish this complex of human positives which we identify as civilization.

In this view, language is a primary agency of order. Why? Because it is the identifying characteristic of a symbol-using, symbol-misusing animal. It is through language that man has separated himself from his natural biologic condition as an animal, but it is through the symbolic action, the symbolic capabilities of language, that we seek simultaneously to maintain and evade our commitments as social beings. Human society in this regard is fictitious, and it might well be that at this point the legal fictions through which we seek to impose order upon society meet with, coincide with, the fictions of literature. Perhaps law and literature operate or cooperate, if the term is suitable for an interaction which is far less than implicit; in their respective ways these two systems, these two symbolic systems, work in the interests of social order. The one for stability —that is, the law is the law—the other striving to socialize those emotions and interests held in check by manners, conventions, and again, by law.

"Does not law, like art," writes Professor Paul Freund, "seek change within the framework of continuity, to bring heresy and heritage into fruitful tension? They are not dissimilar, and in their resolution, the resolution of passion and pattern, of frenzy and form, of contention and revolt, of order and spontaneity lies the clue to the creativity that will endure."

Given the bits of personal experience which I outlined at the start of this paper, I must both agree and disagree with the professor. He states the ideal as a writer; with my background, I must state something of the exception. By the way, I always found Justice Holmes and Justice Frankfurter a bit less attractive as human beings than I did as men of scholarly excellence. But then, I was always a bit impatient and something of the cat who was fated to stare at the kings.

I would also remind you, as one who somehow fits into the profession of Mark Twain, Emerson, and Thoreau, that it is the writer's function precisely to yell "Fire" in crowded theaters, and we do so, of course, through the form in which we work, and the forms of literature are social forms. We don't always take them seriously, but they are the start of seriousness, and an irreplaceable part of social order.

But if there is one Freund statement with which I could agree wholeheartedly, it is this: "I have likened the Constitution to a work of art in its capacity to respond through interpretation to changing needs, concerns and aspirations." For I look upon the Constitution as the still-vital convenant by which Americans of diverse backgrounds, religions, races, and interests are bound. They are bound by the principles with which it inspirits us no less than by the legal apparatus that identifies us as a single American people. The Constitution is a script by which we seek to act out the drama of democracy and the stage upon which we enact our roles.

Viewed "dramatistically," which is Kenneth Burke's term, we can even suggest that the Declaration of Independence marked the verbalization of our colonial forefathers' intentions of disposing of the king's authority. The Revolutionary War marked the agonistic contest of wills through which the opposing forces were overthrown. The Constitution marked the gloriously optimistic assertion and legitimization of a new form of authority and the proclaiming of a new set of purposes and promises. Upon these principles, which would be made manifest through the enactment of a new set of democratic hierarchal roles (or identities), the young nation would act. And through the dramatic conflict of democratic society, it would seek to fulfill its revolutionary assertions.

But then came a swift change of direction in which the young nation was forced to recognize that the mere assertion of revolutionary will was not enough to lead immediately to domestic tranquillity. It brought upon the stage a new alignment of political forces in which the collectivity that had made the Revolution became fragmented. Under the new dispensation the rights of individuals and minorities required protection from the will of the majority. As a new hierarchy began to function, those at its top were in better position to take advantage of the new-found benefits, while those at the bottom were hardly better off than they had been under the Crown.

Ironically, the nation's recognition of the new problems of its hierarchy was coeval with its increasing concern with its language, with its linguistic style, which reminds us of the paradox that the revolutionary documents which formed the constitutional grounds of our new system of justice and which set the stage for the enactment of a new democratic drama of human rights—these documents were written in the language of the very hierarchy which they had overthrown. And indeed, the new conflict of interest was foreshadowed in the very process of drawing up the new ground for action out of the English language. Even as the democratic documents of state announced a new corporate purpose, proclaimed a new identity, assigned new roles, and aroused new expectations for a redistribution of material resources and authority, a conflict arose between the terms in which revolutionary action had been taken and those in which it would be fulfilled.

In drafting the Declaration of Independence, Thomas Jefferson had changed the old emotion-charged revolutionary slogan of equality, liberty, and property to equality, liberty, and the pursuit of happiness. And his demands for eternal separation from England and its people were deleted. Also rejected was Jefferson's indictment of slavery in which he overloaded the scapegoat, King George III, with a malignancy that was all too obviously shared by Americans. There was mystification here, if not blatant hypocrisy, because as Katherine Drinker Bowen observed of Jefferson's discarded first draft, "in Jefferson's indictment of the King he nowhere states that slavery is a disgrace to America, and should be abolished root and branch by Americans. Instead, he turns his anger on the wrong culprit, twists a shameful fact of American life into an instrument of propaganda against George III, condemns the slave trade, then draws the sting by putting the blame and responsibility on the King of England."

Ironically, by his extreme eloquence, Jefferson provided his pro-slavery colleagues an escape from having to undergo the rigors of economic and perhaps spiritual mortification that would have given full credibility to their proclaimed principles of freedom and equality.

Thus the new edenic political scene incorporated a flaw similar to the crack that appeared in the Liberty Bell and embodied a serpentlike malignancy that would tempt government and individual alike to a constantly recurring fall from democratic innocence. With one of its cardinal principles violated, the drama of democratic equality began with its main actors revealing in their noblest gestures "mots vagues" that were at odds with their spoken lines. Indeed, more often than not they ignored the acting script, and being good Americans, they improvised. Portentously, the Founding Fathers' refusal to cleanse themselves was motivated by hierarchical status and economic interests. It was rationalized by the code of social manners that went with their inherited form and manner of speech, their linguistic style. Revolutionary fervor notwithstanding, they were gentlemen, and Jefferson's indictment provided these men the convenient excuse for not violating their private interests and their standards of good taste. Thus the glaring transparencies of Jefferson's rhetoric afforded them a purely formal escape from the immediate dilemma posed by the conflict between freedom and slavery, and allowed them to use social tact as a tactic of moral evasion.

One result of this evasion was to prove of far-reaching consequence, in that the principles of equality and freedom were splintered into warring entities, thus making for the unheralded emergence of a new principle or motive in the drama of American democracy. That motive or principle—and principles are motives, I will remind you—was race, a motive that would become a source of vast political power and authority and a major theme in American literature. And though not committed to sacred print, it was to radiate a qualifying influence upon all of the nation's principles and become the source of a war of words that has continued unto this day.

Men like John Adams fought against it, as did Jefferson, who himself owned slaves. But because this principle operated in the ethical sphere no less than in the material world—the principle of equality being a command that all men be treated as equals, while some were very obviously being designated unequal on the basis of color and race—it made for a split in America's moral identity that would infuse all of its acts and institutions with a quality of hypocrisy. Worse, it would fog the American's perception of himself, distort his national image, and blind him to the true nature of his cultural complexity.

Later, behind the guise of States' rights, it would explode the issue which led to the Civil War. So even as the English supports of the old hierarchical psychosis collapsed, it quickly reasserted itself in the immature and unfinished psyche of the new political order. That absentee authority and privilege once vested in kingship now reappeared as the all-too-present authoritarian privilege of those possessing property and high social position. Social order is arduous and power filters down to the lower levels of society only under constant pressure. Thus new tensions arose, and while the Bill of Rights was enacted to relieve the new imbalance, the manifestations of those rights in the lives of those low in the order of social hierarchy would require time, contention, and endless improvisation and many lawyers. As this process ensued, not even the most optimistic citizens found an adequate fulfillment of revolutionary expectations. Indeed, these expectations seemed for some to recede before the anguishing complexity of the new social reality.

Instead of domestic tranquillity, the Americans discovered that what their bloodshed and sacrifice had actually purchased them was not social perfection, but at best a firm new ground of hope. This was a great deal, but democratic equality remained the promise that would have to be achieved in the vividly imagined but illusory future.

At Philadelphia, the Founding Fathers were presented the fleeting opportunity of mounting to the very peak of social possibility afforded by democracy. But after ascending to within a few yards of the summit they paused, finding the view to be one combining splendor with terror. From this height of human aspiration the ethical implications of democratic equality were revealed as tragic, for if there was radiance and glory in the future that stretched so grandly before them, there was also mystery and turbulence and darkness astir in its depths. Therefore, the final climb would require not only courage, but an acceptance of the tragic nature of their enterprise, and the adoption of a tragic attitude that was rendered unacceptable by the optimism developed in revolutionary struggle, no less than by the tempting and virginal richness of the land which was now rendered accessible.

So having climbed so heroically, they descended and laid a foundation for democracy at a less breathtaking altitude, and in justification of their failure of nerve before the challenge of the summit, the Founding Fathers committed the sin of American racial pride. They designated one section of the American people to be the sacrificial victims for the benefit of the rest. And in failing their testing by what was later to be termed the American dilemma, they prepared the way for the evils that Jefferson had hoped to pile upon the royal head of England's king, and loaded them upon the black backs of anonymous American slaves. Worse, these Americans were designated as perfect victims for sacrifice and were placed beyond any possibility of democratic redemption, not because of any overt act of social guilt, but simply by virtue of their position in the social hierarchy. Indeed, they were thrust beneath the threshold of social hierarchy and expected to stay there.

To further justify this act of pride and failure of nerve, myths of racial superiority and inferiority were evoked, and endless sacrificial rights of moral evasion were set in motion. These appeared in folktales, jokes, and then popular stories; indeed, in some unpopular but quite serious works. Ironically, however, this initial act of pride was to give the Afro-American an inadvertent and unrecognized but crucial role in the nation's drama of conscience. Racism took on the symbolic force of an American form of original sin, and as a man chosen to suffer to advance the nation's spiritual and material well-being, the black American was endowed linguistically with an ambivalent power, like that vested in Elizabethan clowns, Christian martyrs, and tragic heroes. This is important if we are to understand the prevalence of black figures in our literature.

As a symbol of guilt and redemption, the Negro entered the deepest recesses of the American psyche and became crucially involved in its consciousness, subconsciousness, and conscience. He became keeper of the nation's sense of democratic achievement, and the human scale by which would be measured its painfully slow advance toward true equality. Regardless of the white American's feelings about the economic, psychological, and social conditions summed up in the term and symbol "Negro," that term and symbol was now firmly embedded in the operation of the American language. Despite their social powerlessness, Negro Americans were all unwittingly endowed with the vast powers of the linguistic negative, and would now be intricately involved in the use and misuse of a specific American form of symbolic action, the terminology of democracy. Not only in language, but through language into law and social arrangements, social ethics and manners, into sexuality and city planning (or no planning), or nonplanning, and into art, religion, and literature.

In brief, race became a major cause, form, and symbol of the American hierarchical psychosis. As the unwilling and unjust personification of that psychosis and its major victim, the Afro-American took on the complex symbolism of social health and social sickness. He became the raw labor force, the victim of social degradation, and symbolic of America's hope for future perfection. He was to be viewed, at least by many whites, as both cause and cure of our social malaise.

This development, of course, contained a lot of mystification, for if there was hope for a cure to our condition, it lay in the direction of both white and black men undergoing that agonistic effort necessary to the fulfillment of the nation's commitment to those ethical principles compromised by the Founding Fathers. Until the time that this should come about, race would assert a malignant effect in areas of national life that were far removed from that of civil rights for black Americans.

It would function as a motive in Melville's *Moby-Dick;* and far beneath the fine prose of Henry James, it would goad the consciousness of his characters. It would form the moral core of Mark Twain's *Huckleberry Finn,* dominate the world of William Faulkner's fiction, and it would influence the attitudes of individual "secessionism" displayed by the heroes of Ernest Hemingway. Further, the contentions it inspired would hinder the establishment of a National Drama, a theater, and account for the dismal stereotypes of popular literature, plays, motion pictures, and television dramas, and for their triviality and lack of moral seriousness. What is more, it would lead to the moral negations of the current crop of black films and to much of what we dislike in rock music.

But here we should pause. Here we will not recapitulate the Civil War. We know to what extent it was a war of words as well as of arms. We know to what extent the black American was involved. Very often, however, the issues of the Civil War and even the blacks appear in novels and other works of literature by other names. For instance, Crane's *The Red Badge of Courage* is about the Civil War, but only one black person appears, and then very briefly. It is concerned with the invasion of the private life by warfare, by the army, and by large impersonal social processes, a fact of American democratic life which was becoming a matter of consciousness some thirty years after the Civil War.

We are in a period today when many of the men of my profession complain that American life has gotten out of hand, that it is too much for the methods and modes of fiction. They say that it is too dramatic, that it overwhelms the fictional imagination. I am not so sure about that. I think that the resources are there, we have only to seek to use them. But I think something else should be said, since much of the atmosphere of our time is created by major transformations in our way of looking at the law and looking at the racial aspects of the law, going back to 1954 and coming through the measures passed during the sixties.

We went about that with a feeling of good intentions, we sacrificed. We did much to rectify past injustices. But then, with our usual American innocence, we failed to grasp that it was going to cost us something. It would cost us something in terms of personal sacrifices, it would cost us something in the rearrangement of the cities and the suburbs. It would cost us something in terms of the sheer acceleration of turmoil and conflict. And so, we became and have become a bit tired of this old business.

I, as a writer, would remind you, however, that when the Afro-American became symbolic of so many other issues in American life, his increase in freedom acted on the youth at least as a sort of sudden release for which they were unprepared. It was as though the word had gone out that the outsider, the unacceptable, was now acceptable, and they translated it to mean that all of the repressed psychological drives, all of the discipline of the instincts were now fair game. "Let it all hang out," they said. "We have all become black men and women."

This projection, this identification of the socially unacceptable with the blacks, must be raised to consciousness. We must be aware of what is going on, because only through this will we be able to reassume that optimism so necessary for living and dealing with the many problems of this diverse pluralistic society. Democracy is a collectivity of individuals.

The great writers of the nineteenth century and the best of the twentieth have always reminded us that the business of being an American is an arduous task, as Henry James said, and it requires constant attention to our consciousness and to our conscientiousness. The law ensures the conditions, the stage upon which we act; the rest of it is up to the individual.

—From *American Law: The Third Century,*
Fred B. Rothman & Co., 1976

ABOUT THE AUTHOR

RALPH ELLISON was born in Oklahoma and trained as a musician at Tuskegee Institute from 1933 to 1936, at which time a visit to New York and a meeting with Richard Wright led to his first attempts at fiction. Since then, his reviews, short stories, articles and criticism have appeared in many national magazines and anthologies. *Invisible Man* won the National Book Award and the Russwurm Award. From 1955 to 1957 he was a fellow of the American Academy in Rome. He taught at Bard College and in 1961 served as an Alexander White Visiting Professor at the University of Chicago. From 1962 to 1964 he was Visiting Professor of Writing at Rutgers University. During 1964 he delivered the Gertrude Clark Whittall Lecture at the Library of Congress and the Ewing Lectures at the University of California. He was appointed to the American Academy of Arts and Letters in 1964. In 1969 he was awarded the Medal of Freedom; in 1970, the *Chevalier de l'Ordre des Artes et Lettres;* and in 1985, the National Medal of Arts. From 1970 to 1980 he was Albert Schweitzer Professor of Humanities at New York University. He was a charter member of the National Council on the Arts and Humanities and a member of the Carnegie Commission on Public Television; a trustee of the John F. Kennedy Center for the Performing Arts from 1967 to 1977 and a trustee of the Colonial Williamsburg Foundation from 1971 to 1984.